I0257898

2nd EDITION
THE RELIVING
A True Story

An Interactive Paranormal Experience
Written & Designed by
JUNE MATTHEWS

2ND EDITION
THE RELIVING
A True Story

June Matthews

Originally a book and companion DVD, today the format has changed. Now we are using QR Codes.

Grab your Phone or Pad.
As you read the book, some chapters will have a QR Code.

1st Scan QR Code in the book – to open a web page
2nd Find the matching name from the book on the web pages link menu

3rd Watch the Corresponding Chapter Video

Copyright © 2022 June Matthews

All rights reserved. The Matthews Family

All photos, videos, and audio files are the sole property of
The Matthews Family

ISBN: 979-8986058313

DEDICATION

For my husband,
You are the most amazing man I have ever known. You teach me to love myself every day, just as I am. You love me unconditionally, body, mind, and spirit. It is an honor to be your wife.
I love you.

CONTENTS

	EDITORIAL REVIEW		ix
	INTRODUCTION	Page	01
Chapter 01	THE COMMENCING	Page	09
Chapter 02	RELIVING THE PAST	Page	15
Chapter 03	FINDING THE HOUSE *	Page	23
Chapter 04	SAYING GOODBYE	Page	41
Chapter 05	DRIVING AWAY	Page	51
Chapter 06	MOVING IN	Page	59
Chapter 07	ALONE IN THE HOUSE- Day 1 *	Page	71
Chapter 08	ALONE IN THE HOUSE- Day 2 *	Page	85
Chapter 09	INTRUDER INSIDE *	Page	107
Chapter 10	UNEXPLAINED	Page	125
Chapter 11	REDUPDIATION	Page	137
Chapter 12	INTO THE PARANORMAL	Page	153
Chapter 13	THERE ARE NO GHOSTS	Page	169
Chapter 14	VALIDATION	Page	181

Chapter 15	NOT ALONE	Page	191
Chapter 16	SIGNS OF A HAUNTING *	Page	201
Chapter 17	MOVING OBJECTS	Page	217
Chapter 18	THE FIRST RECORDING	Page	229
Chapter 19	SOMETHING IS HERE *	Page	247
Chapter 20	ORBS *	Page	261
Chapter 21	NEW FRIENDS	Page	271
Chapter 22	IT CAN TOUCH US *	Page	281
Chapter 23	ANIMALS REACT TO IT *	Page	291
Chapter 24	A RELIVING	Page	301
Chapter 25	SEARCHING FOR ANSWERS *	Page	309
Chapter 26	THE PAST EXPLAINED	Page	321
Chapter 27	THE SéANCE *	Page	331
Chapter 28	IT'S TIME TO WAKE UP *	Page	343
Chapter 29	MORE VISITORS *	Page	357
Chapter 30	HALLOWEEN *	Page	383
Chapter 31	THE BOARD *	Page	391
Chapter 32	EMBRACED FROM BEYOND *	Page	403
Chapter 33	THEIR MEETING PLACE *	Page	409
Chapter 34	TESTIMONIALS	Page	417
Chapter 35	ABOUT C-PTSD	Page	433
Chapter 36	C-PTSD & THE PARANORMAL	Page	435

Chapter 37	TRAUMA & THE PARANORMAL	Page	439
Chapter 38	ABOUT THE AUTHOR	Page	441
Chapter 39	GLOSSARY	Page	457

EDITORIAL REVIEW

In The Reliving, author June Matthews explores the link between paranormal events and a form of PTSD called Complex Post Traumatic Stress Disorder, a condition that re-plays past trauma over and over again. What some doctors refer to as "A Reliving."

In 2010, career changes led June and her husband to pack up their life in California and move into their dream house in an idyllic rural town just north of Spokane, Washington. Alone in their new home, unexplained events began to happen while he traveled for work. Items would disappear and even move on their own; appliances turned on and off, lights flickered, doors opened and closed. Never believing in the paranormal, the unexplained crashing, banging, and talking led her to believe someone was hiding in the house. The activity also coincided with a terrifying resurfacing memory from her childhood; she threw herself into researching and documenting the events. She recorded the chilling voices she heard and videotaped many unexplained happenings.

She complied those first few terrifying years in the house into THE RELIVING DVD as a companion for the book of the same name.

In 2022, This 2nd Edition includes all of the original DVD contents accessible to the reader.
With the sequel to The Reliving: THEIR MEETING PLACE released, the author wanted everyone to see the original captured evidence and its connection to the sequel.

Author June Matthews re-wrote the book. Additional content and photos that did not make it into the 1st Edition and fixed errors in the 1st Edition version that had gone overlooked.

In THE RELIVING 2nd EDITION, Matthews includes testimony from various people who experienced paranormal activity while inside the house. She uses these different perspectives to provide a comprehensive view of the phenomena. Many photos taken by automatic cameras have captured images that defy logic and explanation. Audio recordings are the actual EVPs recorded from the house, and videos of paranormal and psychokinetic occurrences are the actual events as they happened. Photos, Audio Recordings, and Videos are real and unedited.

    Experience the Paranormal as it happens in the book

INTRODUCTION

When you tell someone you live in a haunted house, you will find out a lot about the people in your life. Most people close their minds to the possibility of anything they have not directly experienced themselves. Ridicule soon comes from the most unexpected friends and family in the form of quiet pauses or offensive statements. You learn a lot about the individuals you thought were there to support and love you. Then you will learn a lot about yourself. Your world will change.

Since moving into the house, I have watched numerous television programs on haunted houses, desperately trying to find similarities in our homes. I discovered most of the shows focus on the negative impacts of the paranormal, and I have seen both negative and positive outcomes of living in an unnatural house. The occurrences here are far different from the demonic tellings and dramatic stories of evil on television or in movies. I had always enjoyed ghost stories or haunted house movies, and, as a non-believer, I could be scared while watching the movie, remaining unaffected once I left the theatre. I never believed any of it was possible.

Three days after we moved into the house, unexplainable things began to happen. The atmosphere was ominous, and I was petrified and confused. I cannot even say which was terrifying, someone hiding inside our house or the possible onset of insanity. At times, I convinced myself I was losing my mind. I could find no explanation for the things happening to me and around me. They were not possible! I had never believed in the paranormal. I am shocked and amazed by the things I hear and see inside our home, quiet voices, walking, things unexplainably moving, running, and crashing sounds like the walls themselves are coming down.

This kind of fear changed my entire belief system. I learned to trust my instincts and feelings in a new way. I believe a paranormal experience is unique for each person. How long does someone rationalize what they can not explain, and how long until you accept what is happening? For me, it took three years.

It did not take long for me to discover the normal sounds here; all homes have them. Noises sounded like someone was breaking in or even kicking down the front (we have two) doors. I would pick up my gun and check the house every night. Terrified of whom I would find, confident I would kill any intruder with no questions asked. I know some people find this reaction paranoid and even violent. I recently spoke with a friend who has also had this argument with someone who believes you should try to talk to him first if you have an intruder in your home. I value human life above all, but I also know how evil human beings can be. I will die, kill, or both before I am a victim of another person again.

To those who have visited the house and felt compelled to let us know, "Oh, it's just you're house settling, that's all." You are highly insulting.
I have never been a person who pushes their beliefs on someone. I questioned what was happening. I was only looking for comfort from a fear I could not understand. I feel for anyone else who has experienced this from family and friends. It is heartbreaking when those who claim to love you quickly judge and dismiss your feelings. I can only attribute these reactions from people as fear;

this great need to explain they know what it is. Those condescending rationalizations some people are hell-bent on explicating, even if their explanation creates a barricade in our relationship or ends it altogether.

One experience was a utility room door constantly opening. Being the only one in the house to witness what was happening, I would take notes when I closed the door and when I found it open again. I needed confirmation; this was not my imagination. I was not crazy or losing my mind. The more fear I underwent, the more I wrote. Writing was the only way to make myself feel better and escape anxiety. I found the only time I could write was when I was in fear, as if this excess energy channeled into my computer, until one day, I had written a book.

I felt everything was all in my head for a long time due to post-traumatic events from my earlier life. Memories from my past also seemed to coincide with moving into this house. For a long time, my number one question was, "is the house haunted, or am I?" I had a challenging and traumatic childhood. One of my earliest memories was throwing myself down the stairs at age six. I consider it a suicide attempt, a desperate act to get away from my mother. Soon after, I had taken to drinking the remnants from cocktail glasses left on the tables after my mother's many parties. I clearly remember the liquid warming my throat and body like a loving hug I desperately needed. By the time I was 13, people had become my only fear. After years of abuse and exposure to things no child should see or know about, I feared all humans. Drugs and alcohol became a constant in my life. As weird as it sounds, I am grateful the drugs were there when I needed them. I am thankful for sobriety in my life today, and I am thankful God created human beings with the unique gift of being able to forget things too terrible to remember. Later in my life, I went to treatment and learned how to "live in my skin" clean and sober. While in treatment, I addressed many issues with my past, and my life finally became one worth living. I believed I had processed all of my memories of past trauma, and the ones I could not remember, I thought would stay buried. I was wrong.

Strange as it sounds, people change here. Some visitors are no longer able to hide their genuine opinions and feelings. After only a few days in our home, some people seemed compelled to vomit out their secret thoughts and feelings. I stood in shock as I listened to a friend I had known since I was twelve years old say the most hurtful and derogatory things to my face. I do not think she even remembers the heinous words she said. I remained calm for the rest of the visit, knowing I would end this friendship forever. While the people who love us just become closer and more loving after visiting the house. Unhealthy people seem to get sicker. This house is almost a guide for me, exposing who I should omit from my life. I see people's true character far better now than I ever had before. This book is a true story, although I have excluded some people or changed names in situations for the safety of my family. The people who genuinely love us and have our best interest at heart have a wonderful experience here. The people I should have removed from my life years ago; leave terrified. I think that's interesting.

I am very blessed to have my husband. He is the most amazing man I have ever known. He is always supporting me and believing in me. Even before he had any experiences here, he listened intently and never questioned anything I said. Some of his explanations for the phenomena in the house frustrated the hell out of me; eventually, I realized there was nothing else he could do. He travels for work and cannot be home most of the time. He could not be the person who heads out the door saying, "Yes, I think the house is haunted; see you next week." It was a relief to me when he began openly talking about the strange occurrences in our home. Our marriage, which was already great, became even better.

Our children have also believed from the beginning and later had their own experiences here. I have friends who visit the house, and I credit this house for strengthening our friendships. A miraculous or paranormal event forms a different type of bond when two people experience it together, full of trust and love.

You may or may not be a believer in the paranormal. I used to be a skeptic. I have told many people there may be logical reasons for some of what is happening here, and I am open-minded to other possibilities and not one who believes everything is paranormal. Many people have (with certainty) proclaimed its all demons, geological, or even water are under the house. No one knows, and I think we know very little about this world.

When asked why I wanted to write the book, I had many answers;

1st: I hope to remind people that what we see in the media is a dramatic exaggeration of what may have initially been an authentic experience. So many people who have visited our home expect to see those theatrical events; they do not exist here, and our walls do not drip blood.

2nd: To open the minds of those who believe anything paranormal is evil, demic, and something to fear and ignore. God is stronger than that which you fear. Many even balk at the word paranormal, though the definition is: 'Out of the realm of ordinary experiences.' That describes our home.

3rd: To survivors of sexual, mental, and physical abuse: The traumatic events connected to Complex PTSD are long-lasting and generally involve some form of physical or emotional captivity. In these types of events, a victim is under the control of another person, usually in captivity, with no ability to escape. Those memories do not just disappear; they never leave altogether, and they can resurface just when you least expect it; I now believe this is when we are ready to deal with them; We were strong enough to survive, then we are all strong enough to start healing. I know we do not fully recover, but we can learn ways to manage; The Murder of our Soul. What I experienced in this house feels like the spiritual world wants to help us heal.

From the Diagnostic and Statistical Manual of Psychiatric Disorders (DSM-IV). Sexual abuse is considered "soul murder."

Lastly, I hope the closed minds of this world would understand, "When you already know everything, you learn nothing." I have learned the more open-minded I try to be, the more God (my higher power) changes me, and the less I have to fear, whether it's living with my haunted memories or living in a
HAUNTED HOUSE.

CHAPTER ONE
THE COMMENCING

I wiped the tears from my eyes, hating the fact it still had power over me after all this time. It happened so long ago. I had not thought about this part for years. Why now, why suddenly now, would I hear the man's voice in my head. I was making dinner, waiting for my husband; everything was normal. Like a locked door opening after so many years, the deep and raspy voice was free, bursting back into my life as his words rang through my head.

"Why the fuck do they always cry?"

I could feel the terror rise inside of me just as I had that night. I realized I was only one of many young girls those two men had brought out to the desert that horrible night.

I dropped to the kitchen floor, squirming in an attempt to stop the pain, drawing my legs up to my chest, and wailed. It is difficult to explain how this felt, and my best attempt to describe it is; I was feeling the pain and degradation as if I had experienced a rape just minutes before.

I never remembered much about this traumatic night; the details seemed lost as soon as they happened. Even how I escaped remained a mystery; for all of these years, those deep, ugly voices discussing how I would die that night remained locked away, somewhere, Just an insignificant memory no more important than a trip to the grocery store. I knew it happened, but it felt as if I flipped a switch and turned myself off before this day. Much of my early life was full of memories like this. My existence felt like a puzzle missing many of its pieces. Therapists and doctors I had seen in the past all agreed on the exact diagnosis: Complex Post-Traumatic Stress Disorder (CPTSD).

It took less than forty-five minutes for me to pull myself together, but it felt like hours. I felt confused, scared, and shocked. I would never let a human hurt me in that way again. I was a different person now, no longer a lost and frightened child. I was always astonished that my memories could affect me with physiological pain.

I wiped the tears back and pulled the oven door open to check the roast, watching my hand shaking inside the oven mitt as I reached for the pan. "You're okay; no one will ever be able to hurt you like that again. Okay, get ahold of yourself. Just forget it." I said aloud, swallowing hard.
My best plan of attack for anything reminding me of the most horrifying times in my life was, forget it, and it will go away.

Years before, I had emerged from a sea of drug addiction, which almost everyone said was understandable. My sponsor had once said, "Thank god you had the drugs; how else would you have made it through?" Now clean and sober, I had a dream life and marriage. My husband Jim and three beautiful kids I thank God for every morning. Jim has always been supportive and understanding of my fears and difficulties with my past, and he is still the only man I have ever trusted.

Jim had called earlier to tell me he had important news and wanted to talk before dinner. I knew what it was. Several companies had recently approached him with job offers, and he was anxious to move on. I smiled as soon as I heard the front door open. He walked into the kitchen full of energy and eagerness. I had not seen him this happy on a weekday in years. I wrapped my arms around his waist and held on tight, squeezing my eyes shut to ensure I would not cry. As much as I wanted to talk to him about what had just happened, I chose to stay silent. He is my best friend and knows everything about me, including the traumas I experienced when I was younger. I could talk to him about anything. Even so, I could not shake the feeling that talking about my past life would allow it to infiltrate my current life.

"So, what's the news?" I asked.

We sat down, and he began cautiously explaining the new job offer.
Smiling as he talked, "It is the kind of job I have always wanted, the pay is better, and so are the hours. The downside is the travel: I would be gone a few days out of every month, but I would also work from home much of the time." He took a deep breath and clasped his hand around mine.
"It means moving to Spokane, Washington."

"Washington!" I shouted.

He continued to explain the details. The new company offered to fly us out for four days. We were to tour Spokane and its nearby towns to see if this might be suitable for us to live.

"They need me to decide right away, so they arranged for us to fly out next week," he said.

The thought of leaving California did not bother me at first. I lived in a small village near Lake Tahoe when I was very young. I have been fascinated with this part of the country my entire life. The forest has always given me comfort. There are only a few good memories of my childhood, hiding from my biological mother in the woods behind our house and later when I was away from my family at summer camp. At every opportunity, we spent vacations and weekend getaways in the mountains. Even our honeymoon took place in a mountain resort. Living in this setting had only been a retirement dream we shared. Jim never planned to leave his job until the kids were grown-up and on their own. Now all three kids were adults with their own lives.

Excitedly, he talked about the possibilities of owning acreage property, something we would most likely never have in California. Much of his enthusiasm centered on outdoor activities; my husband relishes fishing, hunting, hiking, and gun collecting. He talked about the gun laws and wildlife in Washington State. With eagerness, he explained in the rural communities just outside of Spokane, it was legal to shoot guns right in your backyard.

I smiled as he talked. I could no longer hear him speaking; I could only focus on the light in his eyes and excitement on his face, neither of which I had seen in some time. Without question, he deserves this, and he deserves to have a job he can feel happy doing.

Jim jumped up from the sofa. "Hey, if we decide we don't like it, it's a free vacation. Can't beat that."

I laughed and got up to finish preparing dinner. I have been continuously amazed at the impact my husband has on me. Being in the same room with him makes me feel safe and happy. I let out a sigh of relief, forgetting my tortured feelings from earlier, as I watched my now still hand cutting the roast.

After dinner, I lay in bed, unable to sleep. The idea of picking up and leaving family and friends gave me agonizing guilt. Separation from the children, although grown adults now, seemed unbearable. Laurel, our oldest, is definitively a "Daddy's Girl" with a bubbly personality and what everyone described as a contagious giggle. Our oldest son has an excellent prankster-type sense of humor and is an outstanding artist. Our youngest son, Joshua, takes life very seriously. Joshua is always ready to give the shirt off his back to anyone who needs it. All three have grown into remarkable adults. There is no need to worry. Still, my irrational motherly concerns began whirling in my head- Emergencies, accidents, someone getting sick, and we would not be there. It always remains a struggle to think of them as adults. Whenever I think of them, they still wear the small innocent faces of early childhood. It was hours until I fell asleep.

CHAPTER 2
RELIVING THE PAST

It opened the door and sat on the front steps of our suburban home, tightly clasping my cup of morning coffee; I looked out at the front of the house. There were the flowers we planted on each side of the steps, the landscaping we both worked so hard on, and the perfect table and chairs for the front porch. Memories began flooding over me. This house was our home; how could we pick up and leave? I could feel my heart start to beat faster and water beginning to form in my eyes.

"Why the fuck do they always cry?" roared back into my head.

I felt cold washing over me, a sharp feeling in my lower back, and my entire body shook. The temperature outside was already eighty degrees, but it felt like my body was ice. My arms and legs began to throb.

I jumped up quickly, breaking the coffee cup against the concrete step. I looked down at the brown liquid and dots of blood dripping from my hand and ran inside to find the phone.

"Serena, it's June. Did you have time to see me," I asked, choking back my tears?

"I have an opening for the next few hours; can you come in now?" Serena inquired.

"I'll be right there. Thank you."

Serena is a beautiful woman with dark brown eyes. She is a licensed therapist who specializes in drug and alcohol recovery and incorporates alternative methods of pain management and meditation techniques in her treatment. I had sought her help in dealing with anxiety and drug-free ways to control my back pain. Serena teaches many optional approaches to deal with severe pain and assists her clients in remaining drug-free whenever possible. I was surprised when six months earlier, she began to focus more on my past than the pain in my back; always driving home the point about dealing with my past would certainly not cure me but could help to minimize the pain. One afternoon, Serena revealed her notes about my back pain; when it was more severe, she had been asking me to talk about my teenage years.

Sitting in Serena's sterile and yet comforting office, I nervously began to explain the memory of the man and how angry I was about having his deep, ugly voice stuck in my head. I revealed how shocked I was that this part of my life was rearing its ugly head. I hesitated for a moment and proceeded to tell her what I was feeling. I explained the pain in my entire body and the repulsive sensations crawling over my skin after a rape. Intimate parts of my body throbbed in pain as if their disgusting hands were still on me.

"I know you believe you have dealt with the vast trauma you have experienced. The night of your abduction was just one of many terrible things to happen to you. I know it feels terrible, but this is normal and healthy. It only means you are ready to deal with these feelings. The horrific events from your past have created who you are today. Traumatic experiences will not go away; they surface throughout your life. No matter how much you may struggle to keep something inside, it will always find a way to come out, whether if it's by a sudden memory or even pain in your back." relayed Serena while she lifted her eyebrows.

"Why do you think I feel so scared? I know I have nothing to fear now. The minute I heard his voice, I felt overcome with fear, as if he was right in front of me."

"Your memories can trigger the same Fight or Flight response you had back then. It is unsurprising you would feel frightened, you were frightened then, and now you remember it as it was for you during the experience. Do you remember anything else?" Serena asked.

"No. Just…It feels disgusting; I feel disgusting." Tears streamed down my face. "It's making me feel crazy. It has been so long; I don't understand why it's bothering me now."

Serena leaned in closer with her ever-compassionate tone in her voice and asked, "What are you feeling now?"

"Angry! I feel angry those men affect me after all this time. I feel like it just happened, and I want to rip my skin off!" I exploded with a deepening rage.

"These are feelings and events too horrible for you to acknowledge at the time. As bad as this feels, I believe it means you are ready to process these feelings now. Go home, talk to Jim about it, and...."

"He already knows what happened!" I interrupted.

"No, dear, he knows the event happened. He does not know how it makes you feel. It is important to tell him. You are not just having a memory of what happened; you are reliving what happened. These are the feelings and emotions behind the facts he does not know. The feelings from your trauma are affecting you now, in the present. Talk about it with Jim. Call your sponsor and tell her, as well. Where are you at now?" now back in Serena's utmost professional tone.

I wiped my face and forced a smile. I felt safe with Serena but always left her office feeling a little stupid. The answers were still so logical and straightforward.

I stirred nervously in my poorly cushioned office chair, and with as much confidence as I could make myself, I muttered, "Better, I will talk about it with Jim."

We talked for another few minutes about the trip to Spokane and the new future it could offer. We both stood up to go, and as Serena walked me to my car, she cheerfully quipped, "Okay, we will cancel your appointment for next week. Have fun and feel free to call me if you need me; I am always here for you."

I slipped into the driver's seat and turned on the sporty silver sedan. Backing out of the parking space, I glanced through the rearview mirror and caught a glimpse of Serena waving goodbye as her long dark hair blew effortlessly in the wind. I thought to myself, how blessed I am to have met such a wonderful friend. Of course, we were not friends. Serena never crossed the professional line, but I trusted her like one; I trusted her more than family. Years later, when she was no longer my therapist, she became my trusted friend.

I sifted through a pile of post-it notes at home on my desk until I found the scribbled note I made earlier: JOANNE MILLS- Spokane Real Estate Agent.
I reached for a cigarette and made the call.

We spoke for almost an hour as I explained what we were looking for a rural property not too far from town and large enough to accommodate our family during holidays and visits.

After chatting with Joanne, the agent told me all I might love about living in Washington and directed me to the most impressive listings on her website. Joanne, a very nice older woman, had lived in Spokane her whole life and sang nothing but praises for her city and the surrounding areas. Joanne was amiable and with a dynamic and chipper personality, more than just a sales presentation or the typically overly sugared response of a salesperson who wants to force you into liking them. She seemed very sincere as well as professional. I knew we had stumbled upon the right person and had a good feeling about the possible move.

"Oh, it's the most beautiful place ever; you are going to love it here. By the way, I have about fourteen listings for us to look at in your price range, and some of the properties have even more land than you asked for, up to forty acres! I know your husband will like that, and I will set up all the appointments and take care of everything on this end." Joanne prattled on in her now typical down-to-earth charm.

Every night during the week, when Jim came home from work, we spent hours talking about the listings Joanne emailed throughout the day. We talked about how fun it would be to finally own a large piece of land and a home in the woods away from the constant noise, pollution, and general overcrowding we have in Los Angeles. We daydreamed together about quiet hikes and sipping coffee, looking out onto pine trees, and enjoying wildlife roaming our land. Maybe we were dreaming too much, but it was a pleasant distraction from the tense feelings and the fear of leaving our children and friends behind.

I had still not mentioned the voice to Jim or the violating feelings I had. Reliving the night was scary, confusing, and disgusting, and I was afraid that talking about it might make it start all over again. I felt crazy, stupid, and scared. I would have cut my fingers off if it meant I never had to experience those repulsive memories again. The week raced by, and we were off to Spokane, Washington.

CHAPTER: 3

CHAPTER 3
FINDING THE HOUSE

I watched as Jim pulled the curtain open in the hotel and stood in awe, gazing out the window. The sky was full of brilliant colors behind a row of white clouds. Large pine trees coved the landscape while the purple, pink, and orange hues sparkled in the river below. I was not sure what I was feeling, excited at the opportunity to live in this fantastic place or anxious our entire lives could change in this next month.

Downtown Spokane Wa.

I winced from the pain in my back.

"You okay, honey?" Jim asked.

"Sure." I lied.

"Okay, you relax, maybe start a nice hot bubble bath, and I am going to grab us a few burgers and fries."

"Oh, that would be great, thanks," I said.

"Back soon," Echoed in the hallway as the door shut behind him.

I sat on the edge of the hotel bed and took a deep, exasperated breath. The pain in my spine was a constant aching and throbbing. The aggravation was how the pain worsened just when I started to have fun. The doctors had diagnosed me with a degenerative spinal condition: though typically a disease for much older women, they had attributed this illness at such a young age to the unfortunate ordeal I had experienced as a teenager. Sometimes soaking in hot water would help. The doctors always tried to find alternative ways to manage the pain, acupuncture, patches, electro-therapy, and non-narcotic muscle relaxers. I went into the bathroom and pulled the tub's hot water lever. Even with the pain in my back, I was excited. I limped back to the hotel window, looking out into the skyline. It is so beautiful here.

We spent the next three days doing the same routine: the cheery woman would pick us up by 8:00 a.m. and drop us back at the hotel by 7:00 p.m. The agent had us view as many homes as possible each day. At least twenty-two houses had been in our price range, but most of the homes only met our requirements on paper. It was overwhelming to see the amount of work needed. This area had very reasonable home prices. We could have afforded a brand-new home in the city similar to what we had in California, but there would have to be a tradeoff to get the land we wanted. A new house, with neighbors packed in like sardines or twenty beautiful acres of untouched forest surrounding an older house that needs repairs. We had seen one home with possibilities. Jim liked the property surrounding the house, a magnificent piece of land, I agreed, but the house itself had a seventies atmosphere, making me feel uncomfortable. We both decided to keep looking. Every day felt more discouraging than the next: too small, too old, too rundown, not enough land, and so on. I hoped for the feeling from when we walked into our house in California for the first time, the sense of this is it, you are home.

On day four, Joanne picked us up by eight o'clock in the morning in front of the hotel with hot caramel coffees in her hands and a big smile on her face. "Let's go; we have quite a few houses to see today, but the best one I am gonna show you first! It's also the closest, so I thought it would be best to start there."

We sat in the agent's big silver Mercedes and began driving out of town. We drove for what seemed like forever down a small but scenic highway.

"It's not as far from town as it seems, folks, just very far from the hotel. The shopping center we passed back there has the closest grocery store, and there is a lot of other shopping there also."

Within minutes, civilization seemed to vanish, no business, house, or even a car in sight; only the giant pine trees stood witness to our presence. So amazingly tall, I could not see the tops of the trees from the car window. The thick forest on each side of the highway seemed unscathed by people, and only a wire property fence confirmed humans even inhabited this area. Rolling down the window, I instantly recognized the familiar smell of Christmas trees.

"Wow, it is really beautiful here," I murmured.

The agent proceeded to make a quick right turn onto a small street and continued down a picturesque curvy road stopping the car in front of a steep driveway entrance.

"This is it; they must have forgotten to open the gates. I'll be back."

She got out of the car, walked up the hill, and pushed the metal gates open. I strained to see any part of the house from the car, but the immense variety of pine trees blocked any view of the property.

"Okay, here we go." the real estate agent jumped back into the car and proceeded up the long and steep driveway.

Joanne stopped the car and parked in front of a massive garage. The agent noticed my reaction and responded: "Oh, many people out in these parts have a home business, and they all have one of these; they call them Out Buildings or Shops, this one is pretty big, but the house is still up there." She pointed up and drew my attention to the massive two-story dwelling.

Jim noticed a delicate wooden bridge halfway up the steps granting access across the small creek. "Hey, there's a secret garden in here; you have got to see this!"

Steps up to the downstairs front door

I walked over the rustic bridge, seemingly made of the trees themselves. Stepping through an arch-shaped clearing in the trees someone had intentionally cut out, I saw a sizeable garden opened up: overgrown now, but the possibilities were endless.

"We could do all kinds of things with this space," I squealed.

"I could build my barbeque and smoker right over here," Jim said as he hurried over to me and took my hand. "Careful of your back; this bridge is not sturdy."

We crossed the bridge again with smiles on both our faces and headed up the remaining steps hand in hand. To the left of the staircase sat a steep hill with plants and flowers of so many colors, you could not count them all. Scattered dwarf pine trees looked like the small Christmas trees I bought at the grocery store every December. The creek on the right continued until finally at the top, revealing a small pond. The trickling water sounded soothing and comforting as we continued to the top. A large grassy area and stepping stones shaped the space into a courtyard at the peak of the steps. An old outdoor fireplace, a wrought iron bench, and a large hot tub occupied the patio. The front walkway looked more senior than the rest of the house, covered in gray cobblestones, and a square inlay of terra cotta tiles simulated a stone doormat. Porch lights on each side of the door looked like reproduction gas lamps from another era.

I could feel my anticipation fizzing up inside me. I cannot wait to see inside, I thought.

The agent fished in her handbag to find the key. "Ah, hah, here it is!" She unsuccessfully tried to push the key into the lock, "Maybe this key only opens the top entrance; okay, guess we have to hike up to the next level, sorry folks."
Around the corner, to the right of the house, another staircase led to the home's top floor.

"The other door is just up here," she continued as she led us up the steps.

Reaching the top floor entrance showed the wooden deck from below wrapping around this entire side of the house as if a sizeable protective arm were cradling the house and keeping it safe from outsiders. The decking extended past the front door like a large custom front porch. As we drew near the front door, we noticed a visible back section. Amidst the natural setting, the homeowners set up various shooting targets in the backyard, making Jim grin. I could easily imagine my husband standing in the yard with his guns and smiling wide.

The agent approached the door; this time, the key worked, the door opened with ease as if the residents were inviting us to come in.

WATCH: Chapter 3: FINDING THE HOUSE
SCAN QR Code

Stepping into the house revealed an interior distinctly different from the homes we had seen over the last few days. A long stone hallway led to an open-style formal living room on the left. A vast array of artistic embellishments and details typically found in a hundred-year-old home graced the living space. The room had three windows, two of which revealed just a section of the secret garden below. An antique light hung in the far corner. The room's recently refinished wooden floor sparkled from the sunlight. The tray ceiling with sculptured crown molding held wooden rosettes in each corner, appearing to be much older than the home itself.

"When was the house built?" I asked the realtor.

"Let me see." Joanne shuffled through the stack of papers she had been carrying. "Looks like 2005, so only five years old! Now, this is your formal living room or sitting room."

The wall separating the living room from the staircase caught my eye. At first glance, it held two large vaulted cutouts appearing to be windows until I saw they had no glass.

The agent guided us into the next room. "Now, this is your dining room."

I followed her through an arched doorway on the right. I smiled as I stepped into the oddly shaped dining room: wooden floors, large windows, and an impressive built-in buffet table with a striking black granite top. Above the buffet, another arch-shaped cutout in the wall served as a "pass-through" into the kitchen, with the same granite counters flowing seamlessly.

We followed the agent into the next room, "And this is your kitchen!" she announced.

It was huge, not what I had expected at all. I had only seen a kitchen like this in decorating magazines or model homes typically way over our price range.
"Yeah, maybe a bit big for the two of you, but you can make it work, and you have all these cabinets; you can never have enough of them," Joanne proclaimed.

The same black granite as in the dining room flowed throughout the kitchen. Traces of dark green intermittently glistened in the stone from the overhead lights. The pine cabinetry, obviously new, had an inlay of the same arch-like design found throughout the property. Two large glass front cabinets in each corner were performing as china displays. The lower cabinets had more drawers and storage than we would ever need. A commanding granite top island sat in the center of the room, with additional cupboards and drawers on both sides. The kitchen went all the way to the back of the house. A window over the sink overlooking the large backyard seemed to frame the forest outside like a painting.

The opposite side of the kitchen had an extended and open-style seating area capable of fitting another two dining room tables. A half-wall enabled you to sit at the table and pear down to the black slate foyer below.
The amount of space here is astonishing. I thought.

I stood breathless, gazing out the three massive arch-shaped windows. Towering mountains stood tall in the background with towering pine trees emanating downward to a stunning river winding around an entire untouched field. I could see no houses, no cars, or people, only the spectacular landscape and assorted birds flying above the waterway.

The real estate agent looked up from her paperwork. "The tallest mountain is Mt Spokane, and down over there is the Little Spokane River."

Jim opened one of the doors in the hallway, clicked on the light, and examined the inside.
"It's amazing, the workmanship and thought put into this simple coat closet."

 I turned to see a custom-made shelf for gloves and hats, an expensive wooden floor, and a varnished wooden frame for shoes. Even the light fixture was something you would typically see as a bathroom centerpiece, with its antique-looking spirals and glass lampshades. Not a light one would generally hide in a coat closet.

Jim walked up behind me and put his arm around my shoulder. "This is pretty nice. What do you think?"

"It's stunning!"

"How are you doing? Is your back hurting? If we need to stop, just say the word."

"No, surprisingly, it's not hurting much," I said, leaning in to get closer to him. "The view is remarkable; Joanne could have shown us this one first and saved a lot of time."

Jim laughed. "Oh really, this is it, Hugh?"

Our attention now shook away from the striking view as the realtor chimed, "Come and see the primary bedroom. We can't stay long; we have an appointment to see another house in 45 minutes, and it's a long drive from here."

We hurried to follow the voice through the only open door. The primary bedroom was a large size. I was excited to see a set of French doors opening onto the deck, and two of the windows in the room had etched glass scenes of mountain landscapes.
The closet off the bedroom offered very small his and hers walk-ins on each side of a hallway leading the way into an enormous main bathroom.

Jim stepped into one section of the closet. "There is not much room in here. Is this going to be okay? It's kind of small."

"Okay, I want to live here!" I squealed.

I stood in the main bathroom. The sinks in the bathroom looked like carved furniture with granite countertops and dark bronze-colored faucets. The floors were all brown, beige, and terracotta-colored tiles. They formed a peculiar rectangular pattern, seemingly un-centered and out of place as if this room had once been something else.

"This bathroom is huge! It looks like they designed this room for someone in a wheelchair, it's so big, and there is so much unused space." Jim said.

"Not sure why it's so big, but any girl would be happy to have such a big bathroom; also, there is a laundry room access over here, washer and dryer included," the agent answered.

A small clawfoot bathtub off to the left side of the room looked like a miniature version of any tub we could ever really use. My husband is six feet four inches tall and has trouble with showers being too short. Baths had always been a problem; he rarely even tried to use a bathtub with no room for him to stretch out. "Everything was pretty good until…," Jim said, pointing to the tiny tub.
"We will have to replace the tub, and I don't like this bathroom at all; we would have to remodel this." He looked over at me and saw the sad expression on my face. "But if that's all that's wrong, it will be okay; it's fixable," Jim said.

"Okay, folk's, let's get downstairs; we are running out of time," Joanne announced.

I stopped to survey the lack of space, much smaller than the walk-in closet we shared at home. Walking into one side, trying to decide how my clothes would fit, I scanned the top shelves, wondering how to make this work. I looked up at the attic entrance when a cold breeze that seemed to come from nowhere startled me. The rush of cold air lightly brushed my cheek like a gentle slap in the face. Instantly I felt an unsettling impression someone was standing behind me. Swinging around, I expected to see the agent or my husband, but there was no one. I giggled to myself at how silly I was. "Guess we have to fix that too," I mumbled at the attic door, quickly walking out to join the conversation I could hear in the hallway.

"The stairs have hand-carved pillars on the base of each post, see there?" The agent pointed to the bottom of the staircase posts.

The staircase, custom-made by the previous owner, proudly displayed its carved wooden newel posts. Wrought iron spindles cascaded down the handrail, and the smaller carved pillars the agent spoke about stood brandished at the base of each post.

I stood at the top of the large staircase, staring down. Right away, the agent noticed my look of concern. "Are you okay, dear?"

"I have a bad back, and when it acts up, stairs can make it worse, doesn't hurt now but-"

The agent interrupted.
"Ya know, it's like this house was made for you, sweetie. When your back hurts too much, there may be no need to go downstairs. The house has been designed, so all you need is already upstairs, kitchen, formal living room, dining room, closets, and extra storage, your laundry room, main bedroom, bathroom, access to the outdoor deck, all upstairs!"

I looked around for Jim, who had seemed to vanish right before my eyes. The agent saw me looking around, "Oh, he seems pretty excited; I think he went outside to check out the grounds. Come on, let's show ya the rest of this house."

The agent took my hand and led me down the wooden steps. It was interesting to see the design in the staircase balusters matched the tall black iron candleholders we had at home. I was speechless as I looked around the house and saw the changes I had wanted to make in our place in California were already here. The handrail and staircase spindles were the black wrought iron I had wanted, French doors in our bedroom leading to a second-floor deck. Even the kitchen countertops were already the granite I had priced a year before.

The cost of remodeling our current home to the condition I wanted would have been too expensive, and our homeowner's association would have never permitted the building of a deck. I was excited to see this home had these changes in place, and what I did want to change would be in our budget.

The stairs ended in a large and impressive entrance hall covered in black slate tiles. The baseboards were thick wood with pillar-like sculptured blocks in every corner matching the staircase posts. This house had two entrances, the downstairs front door had long arched windows on each side, and a stained glass arch window sat proudly in the center of the large wooden door.

The fireplace itself was of medium size, but the vast rock wall made it the centerpiece of this house and even made it appear oversized. Each side of the fireplace had built-in wood storage boxes with wood stacked up neatly inside.

"Makes you feel like you want to curl up with a good book and sit by the fire, don't it?" the agent said.

The rock wall went all the way to the second floor to meet a stunning wooden ceiling. The slate vestibule streamed into the family room, and as we walked in, I observed the only windows were in the foyer, but there were none in the family room.

"This is really the basement; it's called an open basement, the front half is open with windows and the back half is basement, don't worry, all the bedrooms and office all have windows," Joanne assured me.

The room gave me an eerie feeling I could not identify; perhaps the lack of windows or the wood covering the back wall made the room feel ominous. The family room was much bigger than our family room at home. Separated into two sections, one-half of the space acted as a theatre and the other half as a game room. This room would be so much fun when the kids visit. I thought.

Even with the creepy feeling the place gave me, I knew I could change into something perfect for our family. I had always had a gift for visualization before I left the room, and I knew what colors I wanted to paint the walls and where I would place the furniture.

Off the family room was an oversized guest room, with deep-set windows peering out to the lush downstairs courtyard. Another window offered a view of a rickety woodshed as if someone had quickly built it out of scrap wood, and I saw two axes leaning on the stacks of wood inside.

"That looks like something out of a horror movie set," I said.

Ignoring my comment, the agent opened up a sliding door. "There is lots of closet space in all the rooms."

I looked over to see the entire wall of sliding doors contained a surprisingly deep closet, necessitating you to walk into a dark cavern to hang your clothes.
"Okay, let's move on, more to see." The agent quickly walked me through the remaining rooms downstairs.

The guest bathroom, in need of new floors and paint, still impressed me due to its large size. A smaller bedroom was displaying the same designs as the sizeable guest room was unexpected, and a large storage closet next to it.

I walked over to another door. "What's in here?"
I turned the knob on the big wooden door of the room that the real estate agent called the Water Room.

"The water room contains everything to run the house, electrical panels, water softener, water heater, a wash sink, and your alarm boxes."

I felt the eerie feeling come over me again and slowly backed out of the oversized room. I gently shut the door as if I might awaken some creepy thing living inside.

"The office, gym, and more storage are over here. The last rooms are unfinished, and the gym and storage room both need finished drywall, floors, and baseboards."

"This house is beautiful; it should be priced much higher. They must really want to sell,"

"Don't know anything about that," the agent muttered.

The previous houses needed more work than I could manage on my own while Jim would be at work full time. Here was the only property with the lot size we wanted, and inside, more footage than we thought we needed.
Joanne motioned me out the front door, "So what do you think, dear?"

"This place needs some work, painting, some new floors, but it's nothing we have not done before. This one is perfect," I said, smiling as I watched Jim running to meet us.

"We have three more appointments, and we are already running behind schedule; we better go," Joanne said.

I took one last look at the striking manor house and whispered to Jim
"We have to have this house; this is the one."

My husband smiled and took my hand to walk me down the steep steps.

We toured the following few homes on the agent's list, but each house fell short of the picturesque hilltop home. The energetic woman who had been showing us her beloved city and surrounding towns all day continued to be as lively at sunset as she was in the morning. She parked in the driveway of the last home, grabbed her stack of listings, and dumped them into her lap.

"Well, what do we think? Do you have any favorites you want to see again before you go back to California?" she asked.

"My wife and I are going to have a nice dinner tonight and talk it over, but there are a few houses with promise; we can call you in the morning," Jim said

"Great, let me give you the copies of the listings; you take a look later; all the information on each home is in each packet," she said, leaning back and handing the heap of papers to Jim.

I did not comment. Hungry and tired with my back hurting, I just sat back in the seat and closed my eyes.

What other houses, There is only one house! When we could live in a place so truly amazing, why in the world would we even consider any of the others?

The agent leaned over to me and whispered, "You'll need to hold onto this one, dear."
Handing me a stack of papers stapled together, I smiled at the large photo of the house on the hill.

"I know Hill House was your favorite." The agent said.

"You say that like it's the name of the house," I said.

"Yeah, look right there on the listing," Joanne said.

The agent pointed to the underlined bold font affirming the home's name as
HILL HOUSE ESTATE.

"Wow, so cool, the house has a name!" I said, gleaming.

I smiled. *We have to get this place; this is the house.*

CHAPTER 4
SAYING GOODBYE

After walking through the airport, I felt drained, crammed with people, and sitting in an uncomfortable plane seat. My back ached more than usual, and I could not wait to get home. As we crept along the packed California freeway, I thought how ugly everything looked. Litter and trash bags stacking up on the side of the divided highway, the sky with its brownish tint, and the graffiti on every overpass.

"I don't' remember seeing any graffiti out there, did you?" I asked.

"No, I didn't see any either," he said, reaching over and placing his hand on mine.

"Are you sure you are going to be all right with this? If not, it is okay, this is a big change, and I will understand if you just can't do it."

I smiled. "I feel much better about it now; let's do it."
"So we will make an offer on the Hill House tonight! We should be home soon. I love you," he said.

Once we were home, Jim went straight to the office to call Joanne while I went to our bedroom to lie down and rest my back.
I closed my eyes, and in only minutes, I was back in the real estate agent's car, parked in front of a large house.

I opened the car door and carefully walked toward the house. Looking over my shoulder, I saw the agent waving from her car. I stopped at the front door. I took a second look back, but the car was no longer there.

Wait, she has gone! I did not even hear her leave. Why would she leave me?
I pushed open the big heavy door.

Stepping into a large stone hallway, I see I am on the top floor.
I felt a cold blast of air blow across my body as the room darkened.
I searched for a light switch. "It's so cold in here. Why is there no light switch? Where the hell is the light switch?"

A chill in the air makes my whole body shiver in the dark entryway. At the staircase in the center of the house, I can hear a man quietly talking, but I cannot make out what he is saying. A dim light is coming from one of the rooms downstairs.

"Hello? Hello, who's there?" No one answers.
"I'm here about the house?" A door slams, then another.
My heart beats fast with fear, and my whole body begins to shiver. I can hear the man still talking but cannot make out the words.

"Hello, where are you? I can't hear what you are saying."

Without warning, the faint light from below disappears and engulfs me in darkness. Frantically I try to find the door to get out, but in the blackness of the room, I can see nothing.

Terror fills my entire body.

"I can't find the door; I have to get out of here! Oh, God!"

Footsteps come from somewhere behind me. The room is in total darkness. The house is getting colder, the footsteps louder, something grabs my arm.

"Honey, are you all right? You were screaming in your sleep."

"Just a dream; sorry I woke you,"

Over the next three weeks, there were countless calls to the real estate agent and endless amounts of paperwork. Purchasing a home from out of state stood to be more complicated than I had ever anticipated. The task lists were starting to seem endless and impossible to complete.
Leaving our kids and moving so far away created sadness; I did not have time to feel. Emotions would rise, then quickly banished by waves of frantic phone calls, rushed paperwork, and the hurry of packing a three-bedroom home in one month. The last week before we were to leave was full of sad goodbye dinners, lunches with friends and family, last-minute phone calls, and packing.
I was going to miss everyone so much. Especially Sandy, she is the most amazing friend. She helped me through many difficult times when the kids were younger, and she was always there.

"Oh, Sandy, I am going to miss you so much," I said.

"I'm always a phone call away, drama queen. You are going to love it up there! And I expect to be invited as soon as the house is ready." Sandy laughed as I hugged her hard.

"I love you. Talk to you soon." I cried

The night before we left California, all the kids had come over to say their farewells, and I felt emotionally drained from the tearful goodbyes.
I hugged our daughter as hard as I could.
"I am going to miss you so much, sweetheart," I whispered to her.

"I know, Mom, I will miss you too, but we will talk every day, and as soon as my lease is up, I will be living in Spokane!"

Laurel had taken our move much harder than her brother's, and she decided she had nothing to keep her in California. After researching the internet, she found jobs she qualified for and apartments she could afford. So moving was a natural choice for her.

I cried in my sons' arms. Now, grown men, it was still hard to leave them.
"Don't cry, Mom; we are going to come and visit; we both talked about it, and we are going to spend all our vacation time in Washington with you and Dad. Try to have fun and fix up the guest room for us!"

"Mom, we all might move up there someday, and I will not raise my kids in California."
"Kids?" I shrieked.

"Someday, Mom, when I have a wife and kids, we will all move close," Joshua said.

"I love you. I will call you guys every day!"

I felt relieved when the car drove away. Another few minutes, and I would have gone into hysterics. Oh my god, how can we leave them? I thought.

Jim wrapped his arms around me. "They are going to be fine, sweetheart. I will make sure we always have emergency plane tickets. If anything happens, we can fly them out or fly back at a moment's notice. I love you."

"I love you too," I said as we both waved goodbye.

An unexpected rainstorm prevented us from packing the cars the night before. With the rain pounding on the windows and guilt over leaving the kids, I laid awake much of the night.

The movers arrived in the morning, stacking the furniture, mirrors, paintings, and over a hundred boxes into the moving truck. I rushed around the quickly emptying house, taking last-minute surveys of anything left behind. The movers would take all the large furniture and boxes, but the truck would get there long after arriving at the new house. We hurried to pack our cars as tight as possible with all the supplies we would need for the pets and us. All four of our pets are rescues. Jim has always been a sucker for any animal in trouble. The dogs, one male and one female were both a Min-Pin Chihuahua mix. The female I named Briquette. A small 4 pound, dainty dog with a pronounced Chihuahua head and face sporting a prissy attitude. The kind of dog you have to pick up if there is a puddle of water in front of her on the sidewalk, the type of dog who would stop in her tracks and look at you as if to say, '*Are you crazy? I will not allow my delicate paws to get wet; I demand you pick me up!*'

Jim had named the male dog Barkley after Charles Barkley. More Miniature-Pincher than Chihuahua, Barkley resembled a tiny stuffed toy version of a Doberman pinscher. Barkley was always happiest rolling around in the mud and chasing birds in the yard.

The cats, also male and female, were handicapped rescues. The female cat came first, and I named Trinity. The three-legged cat limped along, terrified of everyone but me. I nursed her back to health after the surgery to remove the last part of her leg damaged at birth, creating a weird bond she did not seem to have with anyone else.
My husband Jim named the male cat Blinky because it had been born with only one eye. Blinky was undoubtedly my husband's pet; he could pick him up and cradle him like a baby. If I simply pet Blinky, he would launch into a frenzy, biting, and clawing at me; so he was ultimately Jim's cat.

With the cats in their carriers and the dog seats placed in my car, I took one last look around. Everywhere I looked were memories of our happy life in this home. I was overwhelmed with sadness as tears began uncontrollably running down my face. I ran into the bathroom and closed the door. Grateful Jim was still upstairs, making a last-minute run through the house, and could not see me crying. I splashed cold water on my face trying to settle myself down.

I am going to miss this house so much. I let out a long sigh and opened the door to see Jim holding Barkley with a big smile on his face.

"Okay, let's blow this place!" he said.

I scooped up Briquette in my arms and walked out the front door. Taking one last glance over my shoulder as the door shut behind me, I wiped the small tear from my cheek as the sadistic voice rang back into my head.

"Why the fuck do they always cry!"

CHAPTER 5
DRIVING AWAY

Arriving out of the community gates, I hoped Jim could not see me crying in his rearview mirror. Now struck with the finality of the whole situation, I could not calm myself down. The vivid memory of the repulsive man's raspy voice made me feel sick, and leaving the house I loved, moving so far away from the kids, inundated me with grief and sadness.

I tried to focus on my last visit with Serena. Replaying the words in my head, "You are going back to where you came from, the forest, the place you loved as a child—that place where you felt safe. You are going to have an amazing time, and it's a new chapter in your life...."

I forced a smile and followed closely behind Jim's truck as we approached the freeway foraging the pathway for us out of California and on to a new and exciting new life.

The drive to Spokane would take two days. We would follow the route we mapped out and timed weeks before. I had no idea how hard this would be on me physically. By the time we reached Oregon, I was unsure if the stress of leaving or merely sitting in the same position for so long caused my back to throb in more pain than usual.

Now at almost ten o'clock at night, I felt liberated when we pulled into the Oregon hotel and parked the cars. Grabbing my overnight bag, I led Barkley and Briquette out of the vehicle.

"Let's take the animals up to the room, feed them, and we can have dinner in the restaurant over there. " my husband said, pointing to the cabin-like building.
"Yes, please, I am starving, " I said.

Jim went to check in, and I wiped the tears uncontrollably streaming down my face the moment he turned his back. As soon as I saw him emerge from the lobby door, I wiped my face and strained to smile.

"The room is just up there, " he said as he pointed up to the second floor.

I grabbed the overnight bags, tightened dog leashes, and walked toward the staircase. Jim, loaded with the large carrier, cat box, litter, and bags of food, followed close behind.

As soon as we settled the animals, we walked over to the small diner. I smiled as we walked inside. The woodland-style decorations and carved bears on every table reminded me of my childhood. I'm not sure why, but this style of décor always made me feel the escape from reality I needed so much as a child. Being in the forest, hiding in the trees, and camouflaging myself from my abusive biological mother was sadly one of my happy childhood memories.

We ate a quick dinner and went back to the room.

We had not snuck the animals into the room; this crappy motel allowed pets. Which also meant the sounds of dogs barking or whining echoed from every wall. Sleep was impossible; just as we would start to fall asleep, a dog in the next room would begin to howl or bark. At three in the morning,
Jim began to laugh aloud, "This is ridiculous; we're not going to get any sleep. Are you up for just driving on? " he asked.

"Sure, let's get some coffee first? " I asked.

With the bags and pets back into the car, Jim walked over and hugged me as hard as he could.

"Turn on your "walkie-talkie" so we can talk the rest of the way up, " he said.

"Good idea; it will help us stay awake. "

"I love you. "

"Love you too, coffee? " I asked again.

"Okay, follow me. "

We watched the stunning sunrise through the tall trees while driving down the Oregon highway.

"Hello, breaker-breaker, this is big hubby calling wifey pants; come in. "

"Hi Honey, I'm here; everything okay? " I asked.

"Just checking on you, it's been a long drive, and it's dark; you okay? "

"I'm good; coffee helps, might need some more soon." I giggled.

"Okay next stop, more coffee for wifey pants and a bathroom break for me."

My husband's optimistic attitude made the long trip bearable; the drive seemed to go on forever as if we were driving in circles, never making any real progress.
By 2:00 p.m, I was so frustrated I began to cry. For the first time in three weeks, my tears were not about leaving the kids, our home, or the men in the truck, just the intense pain.

Jim called my cell phone an hour later to let me in on the news. Joanne, the real estate agent who had shown us the house, had taken ill and was in a hospital in Texas. Her assistant informed Jim we would need to meet at the office to pick up the house keys.

"What happened to her?" I asked.

"Her office said she collapsed, they took her to the hospital, and she was diagnosed with cancer," Jim stated with disbelief.

"Oh, no, is she going to be okay?"

"No honey, they said it was bad; it's all over her body."

The horrible reality of the news finally sunk in, "Oh my god!"

Thoughts raced through my head; Joanne was so active and lively. She seemed to be in much better shape than I am. I cannot believe she is so sick in just a month.
I fought to push the selfish thoughts I was having from my mind. Disappointment over the plans we had to meet for coffee, now canceled, and the sadness now subduing me; I would not know anyone in this new town.

I followed Jim's truck into the narrow driveway and shut off the car.

Leaning into my window, he gave me a big smile. "I know you're tired; wait here and take a break; I will be right back with the keys. It won't be long now!"

I opened the car door and attached leashes on the small dogs. "Come on, puppies, go potty."
My back was now burning in pain; I still could not stop thinking about Joanne. She seemed so healthy had more energy than anyone I had ever met. I just talked to her last week, and she was fine. We made plans, and she never said anything. Watching my husband appear from around the building dancing and dangling the house keys wiped away my sad thoughts. I laughed for the first time since we had decided to move.

HILL HOUSE ESTATE

CHAPTER 6
MOVING IN

The drive to the house remained as stunning as I had remembered. I tried hard to appreciate the beauty all around me, but the pain in my back just made me want to cry. We pulled up the long and steep driveway, going all the way to the top entrance, and parked. I opened the car door, and the little dogs spilled out onto the driveway, wagging their tails and barking.

Upstairs top of the driveway

Jim unlocked the house's front door and pushed it open for me to enter first, as he always did, one of the many things I love about him. Even though I felt exhausted and in pain, my enthusiasm instantly returned. We were about to cross the threshold into our new house. I smiled up at him and stepped into the massive tiled entryway into our home.

An immediate overpowering smell made us both back up. As we walked in further, the air seemed to get thicker, making it increasingly difficult to breathe.

"Holy shit, I'll open the windows!" Jim yelled.

Walking past the formal living room revealed the appalling condition of the house, with handprints and fingerprints spattered on the walls and ceilings. What looked like a copious finish of mud and dust was covering every fixture and surface in the house. Light switches, once white, were now brown and covered in a muddy-type substance, making my skin crawl.

This house did not look anything like this when we saw it just thirty-two days ago. The further we walked in, the worse it became. Mud and fingerprints seemed to be everywhere.
Once sparkling so brilliantly, the granite countertops were now hazy and dull in the kitchen.
The refrigerator looked like someone had smeared mud on the doors and handles, and I was shocked to open it and find the same muddy substance smeared inside.
Everything about this house now seemed dark and unpleasant.

Downstairs front door & Foyer

"My God, what happened here?" I whispered.

A powerful sense of dread surged over me suddenly. I quickly turned to look out the kitchen window, so Jim could not see me, and in silence, tears began to stream down my face.

"Okay, we need to find the grocery store and buy cleaning supplies." He put his hand on the small of my back and guided me away towards the front door.
"It's going to be okay, honey, don't cry." Jim wrapped his arms around me.
"I know this has been a horrible few days. We can pick up some food and cleaning supplies when we get back; you can get some rest. Well, this is disappointing, but it will all get cleaned up."

Jim opened his truck door and helped me in.

"Joanne showed us the grocery store just down the road. It is only about 30 minutes away, and I also saw some fast-food places there. What do you feel like eating?" He asked.

"Eating, are you kidding?" I exclaimed.

Jim laughed, "We will stop and eat at a restaurant. You have to eat something."

"Okay, can we stop and get coffee?" I asked.
"Of course, right now, I am willing to get you anything you want. I just don't understand leaving the house so dirty; what in the hell is wrong with people?

It took three hours to get supplies and eat a quick dinner. We returned to a dark and cold house.

At the front door, while Jim looked in his pocket for the key, I could hear the puppies crying and whining inside. 'Puppies' is my nickname for the two small dogs. Even though they were fully grown, it never made sense to call them anything else. Both dogs put together did not weigh more than ten pounds.

"Oh my god, honey, can you hear them?"

"Yeah, they probably just need to go out," Jim said.

"I never heard them cry like that," I said.

I set a grocery bag on the counter and strained to bend down and check on the dogs.
"I wonder where the cats are," I said.

"Hiding in here somewhere, I'm going to go blow up the air mattress so you can lie down; you'll be all right for a few minutes?" He asked.

"Yes, I'll take the dogs out. Don't cry, puppies; you're okay."

I walked the dogs outside and felt relieved that the automated lamps flooded this yard with light. I stood on the deck, waiting for the puppies to find just the right place. This sprawling estate was now ours, these were our trees, our land, and we could do anything we wanted with this property.

Backyard -left

It was all supposed to be an exciting and fun time. When we moved into the new house in California, the first day gave me such an exhilarated sensation. It was such a happy day full of hopes and dreams.

Today we were moving into our dream house in the forest. I never expected to feel his kind of apprehension and such intense sadness.

I followed the scampering puppies back into the house and straight to the bedroom.
Grabbing my small suitcase, I crept into the bathroom to change clothes. This same space initially had impressed me weeks ago now felt threatening. I glanced over to the window, double-checking the curtains were closed, assuming the overpowering feeling of exposure was due to the curtains being left open. The thick velvet curtain should have assured me, but the feeling of being watched did not go. I changed fast and left the room like a child afraid of the boogeyman.

I was exhausted and struggled to get down to the floor onto the air mattress. I looked around as I crawled into the blankets, and my stomach felt sick.
With the bedroom door open, I could see part of the kitchen and hallway. This house was nothing like what it had been. Everything was darker and dirty; it was hard to shake the feeling we were in someone else's house, trespassing. I struggled to close my eyes. Even on an air mattress and with the puppies lying on my feet, I fell asleep immediately.

Upstairs Eat-In Kitchen area

We constantly cleaned for the next few days; every room was filthy. I spent two days cleaning the kitchen, scrubbing down the refrigerator and cabinets, and trying to polish the countertops back to their original state. Jim scoured the downstairs bathroom. The bathtub looked as if no one had ever cleaned it, the mud stuck to the surface like cement, and yet we both remembered it sparkling white a month ago.

At the end of each day, Jim would unfold the green fabric camping chairs, and we would spend the evenings sitting on the deck, admiring the spectacular view. We watched the deer leaping across the river, the ducks flying above, and listened to the sounds of our new surroundings. The occasional mooing sounds from the farm down the road always made us laugh. I felt better about this move until he started packing for his first trip.

I swallowed hard. *Do not cry; do not cry!* I silently screamed at myself.

"I can't believe you have to go on a trip already; I am going to miss you so much."

"I will be back before you know it," Jim said.

This trip meant I would spend the next three nights alone. Usually, I did not mind the idea of being alone, I enjoy alone time, but now there was this overwhelmingly empty and sad feeling. No, I will be so busy I will not have time to feel sad; there is so much work to do in this house, I thought to myself as I stroked Barkley's head. We purchased paint for a few rooms and ten different paint samples to test colors. I will be swamped painting and cleaning.

He had to take many business trips with his job in California, so this was nothing new for me, but watching him pack his suitcase, buried me in anxiety.
Maybe it's just being alone in a new place. I thought.

"Sure, you're going to be okay, honey?" Jim asked.

"Yes, I need to call Sandy and the kids, and I can finally unpack all those boxes now the kitchen is clean. I will be okay; you excited about your new job?" I asked

"Yeah, I'm going to miss you, though. I wish I could stay and help you more. Don't do too much work. I will be back on Friday to help you."

"Everything will be fine," I said nervously.

I looked off into the other room. Maybe it was the fact the house just looked different, vacant and hollow, no longer staged with furniture. It was dark, dirty, and creepy now. As I stared into the hallway and kitchen, my stomach turned with a fear something terrible was about to happen.

Downstairs Foyer & Front Door

I always dreamed of what it would be like to move to a place like this, and I never imagined I would feel what I was feeling right now. RUN!

CHAPTER 7

CHAPTER 7
ALONE IN THE HOUSE
DAY ONE

I walked my husband to the door and gave him a big hug and a kiss goodbye.
"I love you. I'm going to miss you." I said softly.

"I'll call you as often as I can from the road and for sure every night. I love you too."

I stood at the living room window to watch him go down the long driveway until the last of his brake lights were gone.
"Bye. I love you." I whispered

Now alone in the house for the first time, I could slowly organize the kitchen cabinets and start unpacking the thirty or so boxes we had brought with us. I wandered into the kitchen, picked up a small paring knife from the counter, and sliced open the box I had boldly marked dishes. I pulled open the flaps, retrieved one newspaper-wrapped bundle after another, and placed them carefully on the black granite countertop.

Flipping the faucet to the hot position, I ran my hand back and forth, waiting for the water to heat up. *It will be nice to use real dishes again. When Jim gets home, I can make a real dinner on a real plate, no more paper plates, and plastic forks.*

Motionless, except for my hand still moving side-to-side under the water flow, I stood gazing out the window into the large piece of land, now our backyard. I started to smile, then a distressed and lonely feeling poured over me.
I miss everyone; I cannot believe we are so far away from the kids. I cannot believe I am here. I want to go home. I do not want to be here!

A familiar lump began to settle in my throat, and the indicative burning in my eyes began as I wiped the first tear escaping and fleeing down my cheek. Frustrated, I swallowed hard, choking back the tears. *Stop this and toughen up already.*

I stood still for a minute, trying to appreciate the scenery just outside the window, trying to take my mind off the sadness I was feeling. Still holding my hand under the faucet, I felt the water finally start to warm up. Slipping one plate after another into the warm soapy water, I began to feel better.
It is just not how I imagined it. This is our dream house. This should be a happy time, and I should feel happy. I thought.

WATCH: Chapter 7: ALONE IN THE HOUSE-Day One
SCAN QR Code - KEEP OPEN

Just as abruptly as I felt inundated with sadness, I was overwhelmed with the feeling someone was watching me, an overpowering sense someone was coming at me, staring at me.

Then, I heard the recognizable sound of Jim's house keys jingling in the hallway. I smiled.

Oh, he must have forgotten something. I heard his footsteps coming down the stone hallway.

"Too hard to leave me, isn't it?" I shouted, rinsing the soap from my hands.

I could feel him right behind me now

"What did you forget? Just need another hug goodbye?" with a big smile, I quickly whipped around with my arms outstretched to greet him.

A cold shiver spontaneously rushed through me when I saw no one was there. A sinking feeling in the pit of my stomach, as if I were falling fast in a runaway elevator, quickly began to engulf me. I could only stand there at first, my eyes darting from one side of the room to the other. The cold fear poured over me, and I could feel the hair on the back of my neck stand up. I was sure he was there. I could hear him even feel him standing behind me.

I could always tell when someone had come up behind me. I have had an acute awareness of my surroundings since I was 12 years old. Whenever I had this feeling in the past, someone was there. "Jim?" I said in a soft awkward voice.

I felt stupid. Here I am, a grown woman, trying to muster up the courage to move. I walked into the hallway. Slowly I checked the door and window locks; everything looked normal.

I heard the door open, I heard his keys shit, and I even heard him walking into the room. I ran different scenarios through my head, testing and discarding each one. *Perhaps the water hit the plates, making them sound like car keys. Maybe the plumbing in the house creates something sounding like the front door opening.* I put one of the plates in the sink, trying to replicate the sound, but it did not work.

Desperately trying to shrug off the eerie feeling, I opened the kitchen cabinet I had dedicated to coffee and all coffee accessories. Pulling out the giant red canister, my hands shook.
Nervously I finished pouring water and scooping grounds into the coffee maker. I leaned against the counter, still scanning the room and wondering what had just happened.
Glancing over to the big blanket on the floor, I let out a loud laugh. Peeping out from under the blanket were those little puppy faces staring at me. They looked so cute and so tiny wrapped inside the oversized blanket.

Barkley and Briquette had started crying every time I would leave the bedroom, so Jim had thrown a giant bedcover on the tiled floor for them to cuddle in when I was working in the kitchen. They looked adorable, with their tiny heads popping out of the large blanket.
Smiling at the little dogs, I said. "It's just being in a new place, puppies; we're not used to it all yet, that's all it is" I stopped smiling and stood there staring at the dogs who looked frightened. "You're okay, puppies; we're okay," I said.

I picked up the box labeled fragile and removed the contents one by one. Carefully opening each piece of crystal from its newspaper covering, I gently placed them on the side of the sink. The last item in the box was the container encasing our wedding glasses, prudently packaged in bubble wrap. Cautiously I washed and rinsed each crystal glass and placed them on the counter.

There is so much cabinet space here. I looked around, deciding where to store the expensive crystal goblets and wedding glasses, and selected the built-in china displays.
This is so nice; now we can see them instead of hiding them away in the closet.
I reached up to open the tall cabinet door when a freezing blast of air on my right arm made me stop. As if someone had blown right on my skin. Not moving, my arm still in the air, I looked in the direction of the door.
That was crazy. Where did that come from? If anyone had come into the house, the dogs would have barked? I set the glasses inside the cabinet and walked to the front door.

The temperature inside the house was comfortable all morning; there was no air conditioner on, no heater, and no open window. Now the whole place seemed to fill with the chilly breeze.

I unlocked the front door and stepped outside; it was overcast but still warm. Promptly I turned back into the house and bolted the door.
I examined the windows and found everything remained in its locked position from earlier. I walked back into the hallway and checked the thermostat; the setting was in the off position.
Stepping up to the loft wall, I peered over into the downstairs foyer but found nothing to explain the sudden shot of cold wind.
"It's warm outside, so where is the cold air coming from?" I said, looking at the puppies.
I marched back into the kitchen and abruptly picked up another box. While the coffee maker made its all too familiar gurgling sounds, I rinsed the soap from the glasses and placed them on top of a soft dishtowel.

I'm just tired. I will call the kids later; we can have a nice long talk. It will make me feel better, and Jim will call tonight and then.... Knock! Knock! Knock!
The knocking startled me, and I let out an almost silent scream.

Immediately I felt stupid. Jim had mentioned there may be deliveries this week, his company would be sending packages, and I would need to sign for them. I walked over to the living room window to peek out before opening the door but could see no one at the door and no car in the driveway.
I walked to the front door, rechecking the knob to ensure the lock was firmly in place.
"Who is it?" I yelled, leaning into the front door.
"Hello?" I yelled again.

Something must have fallen over, and it just sounded like a knock at the door. The dogs did not bark if someone were at the door; the dogs would have barked for sure.
Looking around, I saw no reason for the knocking; nothing had fallen from the stack of boxes piled high in the dining room. The dogs and cats were all sleeping; there was no explanation.

Houses make noises, of course, but this sounded just like someone knocking on the door.
I made a cup of coffee, grabbed my cigarettes and lighter, and sat at the kitchen table. Thank god he bought this kitchen set before he left. The wooden table and chairs enabled me to have a place to sit down until the movers arrived with our furniture.

Quietly looking out the large arched windows at the stunning view, I took a deep breath. The house was so quiet I could hear the dogs breathing under the blanket.

"I must be so overtired puppies I'm just hearing things; if you guys did not hear it, it must be my imagination."

Snuffing out the last of the cigarette, I went to the sink and bumped the water knob in the hot position again. Water slowly began to stream out, tinkling on the dishes; I picked up another plate and began to rinse the soap off.

KNOCK! KNOCK! KNOCK!

I dropped the plate into the sink, shattering it against the others. Both dogs barking and growling, ran through the main bedroom, straight to the bathroom.
Panic washed over me. *Someone must be outside; someone is trying to scare me, maybe kids playing a game, and they think the house is still empty. What if this is not kids playing a game? What if there is just some addlepated person outside or someone trying to get me to open the door?*

I ran into the bedroom and removed my handgun from the bedside table. The only real furniture we had been able to bring with us. *Maybe it is just one of the neighbors coming over to introduce themselves. Yeah, I do not want to meet the person who thinks it is okay to knock on my bathroom window to say hello!*

Pulling the thick velvet curtain aside, I inspected the yard to find nothing there to explain the sounds. The two little dogs still barking made my head hurt.

"Calm down, shhh, be quiet! Whatever it was, it's gone now; come on, puppies."

I started to put the gun back in its resting place in the bedroom, a drawer at the bottom of my nightstand.
I opened the drawer and promptly slammed it closed again. "Hell no! Even if I'm paranoid, I'm keeping it with me."

I had never thought to grab my gun in the old house, and I never needed to. A sound like this would have quickly been attributed to neighborhood kids playing outside, bouncing a ball on the side of our home, or playing Ding Dong Ditch. There was no sign of any person or animal capable of creating these sounds, and someone walking up an acre of steep driveway seemed unlikely since neighbors were so far away. The rest of the afternoon, I organized the kitchen with the small 22-caliber weapon resting by my side.

All the cabinets had clean new shelf liners and freshly washed dishes. I unpacked half of the boxes stacked in the adjoining room. My back was starting to hurt by sundown, and I felt too tired to make any dinner. I set up the coffee maker, grabbed a box of crackers and my gun, and walked into the bedroom.

Sitting on the side of the bed, reaching for the television remote, Then, I remembered no television. Rural areas like this could not use cable, and the satellite installer would not be here for another week. I glanced at one of the boxes next to the T.V. and saw the stack of movies sticking out. Thank goodness Jim had put aside a few of my favorite DVDs. He was always so thoughtful, the best husband any woman could have. I chose the one sitting on top, opened it, and slipped it into the player.

I had completely put the strange events out of my mind and almost fell asleep when the phone rang. I checked the caller ID and saw nothing.

"Hello?"

"Hello? Hello!" I repeated.

"Is anyone there? I can hear you breathing; say something!" I demanded.

I pushed the off button on the cordless phone and set it down, only to have it instantly ring again.

I answered again. "Hello?"

The heavy breather, now even louder, made me feel angry.

"Hello! Say something!"

A raspy male voice quietly said something through the static, but it was difficult to understand. I could only make out a few words "Sybil's Pale."

I could feel my heart starting to beat faster. "You have the wrong number!" I shouted, quickly hanging up.

As fast as I set the phone down, it rang a third time. I checked the caller ID, and still, there was nothing. Frustrated, I answered the phone again.

"Hello, hello!"

Just as I was about to end the call, I could hear him.

"Hi, my sweetheart, can you hear me? How was your day?"

"Oh hi, honey, did you just call?" I asked.

"Well, yes, but the phone just kept ringing; everything okay there?"

" Everything is good," I lied. "How is your trip going?" I asked.

"Great, everything is going great. I'm tired, but it's still great. I love this job. How was your day?"

"My day was good; some weird stuff happened."

"What do you mean weird stuff?"' He asked.

I paused, not sure how to explain anything that had happened.

"Nothing, I'm just being silly." trying to avoid the conversation.

"Okay, tell me what happened." He said in the funny way he did when he talked to the kids.

"I heard knocking, I thought was coming from the front door, moments later I heard the knocking from our bathroom window, but there was no one there."

There was no way I would attempt to explain; hey, you were here, and then you were not; I could hear you walking into the house when you were not here. I could not find an explanation, so how and why the hell would I ever try to explain it to anyone else. I was sure I already knew what Jim's response would be anyway, and sadly, he confirmed my belief.

"Are you scared there by yourself, honey?" Jim asked.

"No, I am just not used to the noises in the house. I am sure it's nothing. I miss you so much."

"I miss you too. I will be home again in just a few days. I will call you tomorrow afternoon if I have cell reception on the road, and of course, I will call you tomorrow night before you go to sleep. Sorry, I can't talk long. I have a lot of work to do before a meeting tomorrow. I love you and miss you."

"I love you too, honey, goodnight."

I wanted to scream; I have had a weird day, I am sad, I feel like crying, please come home now. I could have told him; I knew he would drop everything and come back, even it meant losing his job. Putting the phone down on the bedside table, I rolled over and stared at his pillow.

"Oh, god, I miss you. It feels weird in this house." I whispered.

CHAPTER 8

CHAPTER 8
ALONE IN THE HOUSE
DAY TWO

The piercing barking and growling jolted me awake. The dogs wildly jumped back and forth, darting across my legs on the thin air mattress. I had never seen the puppies so upset. I got off the bed, grabbing for my gun. Hesitating for only a moment, clicking the gun's clip into place, I pulled back the hammer to insert a round into the chamber. The only explanation for the little dogs' behavior was someone breaking into the house.

Cautiously walking into the hallway and making my way into the bathroom, I struggled to see the window in the large dark room. The light switch, on the other side of the room, meant walking through the pitch-black bathroom. The dogs, still barking, were now in the hallway just behind me, unwilling to enter the bathroom.

Once the lights were on, I could see no one was there, no burglar, no serial killer who crawled through the window intent on killing us all, no one. I exhaled with relief, realizing I had been holding my breath. I walked back to the hallway and bent down to comfort the little dogs still barking out of control.

"Calm down; what's the matter?"
Together they ran past me into the bathroom. Both dogs seemed to be barking at something only they could see. Whatever it was, it was in the center of the bathroom and at least five feet tall.
"Puppies, calm down; it is okay, we're okay."
Barkley looked up at me, staring straight into my eyes in a way I had never seen before. I reached down, picked him up, and walked out of the room. Still barking and growling, he was no longer looking up but behind me. I turned around quickly, even though I already knew there was no one there.
"It's okay, Barkley."

I placed the small dog on the air-filled bed. I was shocked to see Barkley's little body shaking so violently. I bent down and picked up the little female dog scurrying around my ankles. As soon as I sat down on the bed, they quickly crawled into the covers, laying as close to me as possible.
It was not usual to allow the dogs on our bed, and Barkley and Briquette had always shared their own sleeping space.

Here they had a place on the floor with lots of comfortable blankets and pillows. They had no problem sleeping in the daytime, but they had been unwilling to sleep on their bed at night. Briquette was always a nervous dog with absurd reactions to the most typical situation, so normal behavior for Briquette, but Barkley had never acted this way before. Barkley would only bark at strangers and the occasional stray dog trespassing onto his territory at the other house.

I stared at the hallway that led to the bathroom.

Why are the dogs barking? Maybe there is an animal outside. I glanced at the clock, 2:30 a.m.
I could fall back asleep if I just closed my eyes.

I felt the little dogs shaking under the covers.
"You're okay, puppies; everything is okay. Let's go back to sleep."
Once I was calm enough to keep my eyes closed, I fell asleep.

KNOCK! Knock! Knock!

I jumped up and ran to the bedroom door. Just as the heavy wooden door opened, I snapped out of it.

What in the hell am I doing? Now fully awake, I realized it was a dream; two small children pounded on the front door. An overwhelming urge to get to them, to let them in, made me leap out of bed and start running to the door.

I walked over to the clock 4:48 am. Frustrated, I left the room and staggered into the kitchen.

I stared at the front door.

Snowing, in the dream, it was snowing. The two kids were freezing outside and needed to get into the house.

I reached for my favorite coffee cup, trying to shake the sinister sensations from the dream. I turned on the coffee maker and started for the stairs.

Focus on something else; it was just a dream.

I flipped up the switch for the large wrought iron chandelier. The luminous bulbs lit up this part of the house, which bathed me in a soft, comfortable glow. One of the many things I loved the first time I saw the house. Several things about this house drew me to choose it from the others, the black gothic chandelier, the rock wall fireplace, and the black slate foyer. Even the staircase was a work of art. Midway down the steps, the temperature dropped to what felt like freezing. My steps slowed as I looked around the house.

Out of the corner of my eye, I thought I saw a shadow dart across the darkness from the family room.

Great, I am so tired now I am seeing things.

Stepping down into the foyer, I stood in front of the massive rock wall.

This house is going to be amazing once we fix it up. I thought.

I scanned the log shelves sporadically protruding from the rocks, which spread across the massive fireplace wall. The previous owners had family photos on each log; I thought about all the antiques we had collected over the years and which would display which piece?

 I was tired, excited, and anxious to start the decorating and concentrate on anything reasonable. As soon as I finished my first cup of coffee, I knew I would begin testing paint colors and decide where the furniture would go. I smiled, looking up at the shelves.

We will need at least a twenty-foot ladder to reach those shelves; how are we.... Quickly I turned when I heard the noise coming from the corner of the dark family room. I stood immobile with fear struggling to see into the black space. My eyes instantly drew themselves to the corner next to the water room door. I could feel the hair on the back of my neck stand up. The sensation of someone was standing in the corner staring at me, watching me, was becoming unbearable. I saw nothing, just a sense someone was there.

Backing up, afraid to turn around, I gradually crept back up the staircase, never taking my eyes off the corner as I ascended the wooden steps slowly. Forcing myself to move slowly but wishing to run as fast as possible, panic and pressure were building within me.

BEEP-BEEP-BEEP

I let out a small scream and rushed to the top of the staircase. I could not believe how terrified I felt. Now even the sound of the coffee maker sent me into a frenzy of fear.

I stopped at the top and looked down into the foyer for one last check. There was nothing there to see, but the creepy sensation someone was staring at me now felt as if the room below was full of people watching me.

I quietly made my cup of coffee and went back into the bedroom, locking the heavy door behind me.

I had hoped my working on the house would be easier for me today, and I could make more progress.

Inevitably, when the sun comes up, the eerie atmosphere downstairs will be gone.

Sitting on the bed, I thought about when I was a child. I was always frightened as a kid by nightmares and spooky noises. I felt ridiculous a grown woman, fearing things like a small child left alone in an empty house.

Slowly sipping my coffee, I stared at the bedroom door running the dream over in my head. It was nothing like the dreams of my childhood. This dream was simple and to the point. They are outside banging on the door, frantic to get inside, and I must open the door. They are cold, and the two children would freeze to death outside if I did not hurry. What a strange dream to have in the middle of summer.

I turned on the television, leisurely sipping coffee. *Okay, this is what I need; I will relax here for a while. Watch this DVD and wait for the sunrise.*

I watched the television for a few hours before looking over into the closet. I had scrubbed the walls before putting any clothes inside and planned to paint the walls and ceiling later. The current green color the previous owners had painted on the walls and ceiling made the hallway dark and shadowy.

Even with the light on, Jim had trouble differentiating the shades of his socks when he was packing. After last night, I wanted this closet as bright as possible. I felt like a coward barricading myself in my room, but if I worked on the closet, I would still be making use of my time, and no one but me would know I was too afraid to unlock the bedroom door.

I started pulling out clothes and laid them flat on the bed. I did not remember this room even having this color. When we toured the house, it seemed much brighter upstairs than it was now. I opened the paint can and poured the bright milky white paint into the pan.

Painting the closet seemed to take forever. The pistachio color covered the walls, ceiling, and even the metal brackets holding up the shelves. Every part of this space took three coats before the institutional green color finally stopped bleeding through the new crisp white paint.

My back began to throb, and I looked over at the clock; I was surprised to see it was just after lunchtime. The overcast sky outside gave the impression it was not even dawn.

It would be hours before the paint would be dry enough to put back the clothes still laid across the bumpy air mattress. Timorously I opened the bedroom door and turned on the heater before going into the kitchen. The puppies followed anxiously, looking for their afternoon treat. Picking up the small dog food container, I walked back into the bedroom, through the freshly painted hallway, and into the main bathroom. I filled their bowls with food. I looked back at the dogs; they had stopped just at the entrance to the bathroom.

"Come on, puppies, here's your food."

Briquette started to walk in, let out a cry, and ran back to the hallway. Barkley started fiercely growling, staring into the room.

"What the hell is wrong with the two of you? Okay, Come on, you can eat in the bedroom."

I set the small bowls in the bedroom and walked back to the closet to examine my paint job again.

"Well, puppies, this is much better; the closets are brighter, much easier to see…."

My senseless conversation with the dogs abruptly stopped by the loud sound seemingly inches from my left ear. I hear one loud cough, a man's cough.

I gasped in shock and spun around, and I saw nothing there. I ran into the bathroom, and both dogs started barking, running after me but refusing to enter the bathroom.

There was nothing there. I picked up my gun and opened the bedroom door. I looked around the room, ready to unload the clip, nothing. I sat down in the chair at the kitchen table and lit a cigarette.

It was just one cough, loud and deep, the kind of cough a man with a deep raspy voice would make. Banging and knocking sounds, I could convince myself were the house settling, but this sounded like a person standing next to me who purposely coughed into my ear.

I sat still at the table, listening for other sounds I could not identify. A rattling came from downstairs, a clanking sound from the dining room, and a strange cold breeze blew across my skin. As if the entire house had come alive. I looked down at my shaking hand.

There is no man in my closet coughing, just like the other noise; I will find out what they are later. There is a simple explanation; there is always an explanation for stuff like this.

I reached for another cigarette and the phone.

"Hello," My friend's voice gave me instant relief.

"Hi, Sandy, how are you?" I asked.

"I'm good. How is everything there?" my friend asked.

"Good, just miss you."

"Really? you don't sound good." Sandy balked.

"I must be so overtired and worn out; it's making me hear things."

"Well, what are you hearing?"

"Nothing important, just trouble sleeping, and the dogs seem upset, so they wake me up."

"Hey, I need to go; you going to be okay?" Sandy asked.

"Yeah, I'll talk to you later."

"I will call you back in the next couple of days, and we can have a nice long talk."

"Sounds great, Sandy."

"Okay, bye, love you."

"Love you too." I sighed, setting the phone on the table.

I was determined to keep working. I was going to need to paint every room. The next few hours I spent applying paint shades to the other walls in the house. Paint sample bottles stood like little soldiers preparing for battle on the kitchen counter.

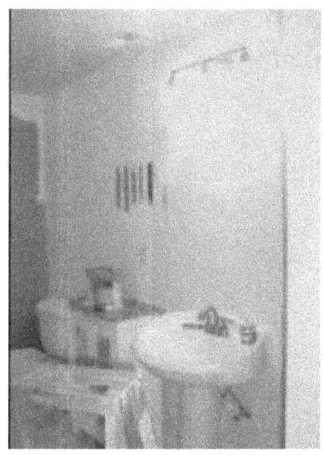

Downstairs Bathroom

Hours later, every wall in the house had a grouping of stripes of varying colors. Most of which were shades of brown we had painted in our old house.

I sat at the kitchen table in the approaching darkness with my back throbbing.

It was still light outside; inside, our home was much darker.

There it was again, the impression someone was watching me, this time from the arch-shaped cutouts in the living room wall.

I sat perfectly, still staring back in the direction of the living room wall. The feeling became so intense, as if there was someone right there just standing there, looking at me. It was almost shocking to look up and not see someone staring back at me. I had this same sensation hundreds of times before, and there had always been someone there.

BOOM-BOOM-BOOM

The sound made me jump, and it sounded like it was coming from the family room below.

My heart raced, and I gasped as I reached for the phone.

"Where's the phone? I left the damn thing right here; where the hell is the phone?"

I jumped from the chair and frantically searched the kitchen counters and table for the phone. "What the hell is going on? Where in the hell is the phone? I left it right here!" I shouted out loud.

Boom, Boom, Boom

I grabbed the gun. Walking downstairs, I angrily flipped on every light switch and walked into every room. There was nothing out of place, and nothing seemed wrong, only a soft meow from the back of the room.

Both cats were hiding inside a bolt of rolled carpet on the side of the family room.

"Was that you two making noise? No, it's stupid you guys can't possibly make....."

BOOM-BOOM-BOOM

I walked over quickly and burst the front door open.

Boom-Boom-Boom

The loud banging was coming from the other side of the river. I could make out earthmoving equipment and see trucks but still could not see people.

"Oh, for crying out loud!" I exclaimed as I slammed the door shut.

Boom-Boom-Boom

The sound seemed to come from the family room again. At least this time, I had an explanation. Sounds from outside were echoing off the back wall of the house.

Annoyed, I went upstairs and continued to look for the phone.

The next time there is a noise, I will open the door and check outside.

"Where the hell is a damn phone?" I checked the bedroom, bathroom, and kitchen.

Frustrated, I leaned on the living room wall, trying to get ahold of myself. I stood frozen in shock when I saw it; the three phones perfectly stacked on the living room floor.

Oh my god, there must be someone here.

My breathing sped up, and I could feel my heart pounding in my chest. I pulled my gun from my clip-on holster and looked around the room. The doors and windows were closed and locked, and I struggled to remember the last time I held the phone.

Wait, I was just talking to Sandy. I was sitting at the kitchen table, and I never brought the phones in here. Swallowing hard, I scooped up all three phones from the floor and dropped them on the kitchen table.

I poured another cup of coffee and sat down.

Dialing Laurel's phone number, I stared at my shaking hand.

I am tired; I have not been sleeping well. Still, I know what I am doing and what I'm not doing.

"Hi, honey, it's Mom; how are you?"

"Oh my god Mom, Are you okay?"

"Yes, why, what's the matter?" I was already shaking and nervous, and her frantic tone almost made me laugh aloud. I was trying to calm down and never expected this panicked response. It felt like one of those holy shit moments when things keep coming at you, and there is nothing else to do but laugh.

"I have been calling the house for the last few days with no answer. Your message never comes on, so I could not leave a message, and I was so worried."

"You're kidding; I have not heard the phone ring at all. I am so sorry you were worried; I've been here the whole time. Your Dad had trouble; something must be wrong with the phone line."

"So, how is the house? Did you get it cleaned up yet? Dad called me earlier and said it was a mess when you got there."

"I am working on it; it's much better than it was when we first walked in. It was crazy; someone left fingerprints and mud everywhere."

"What... Mud? How gross. How is everything else?" Laurel asked.

"Good, I guess."

"You sound funny, is anything wrong?"

"I am just on edge, jumpy, or something. I do not think I am getting enough sleep, and maybe it's just making me weird."

"Mom, what's going on?"

"I don't want to talk about it right now. Everything is okay."

"Mom, should I call Dad? Are you sure you're okay?"

"No, no, I am fine. The house is great, just weird noises and stuff."

"Like what?" Laurel asked

Suddenly I just rattled out what I had intended to keep to myself.

"Knocking and banging sounds and the phones were in a different place, I mean, I just don't remember putting the phones there and...."

Laurel's frantic voice interrupted. "Mom, what are you talking about? What happened to the phones?"

"I was talking to Sandy, and I set the phone on the kitchen table.

At least it is what I remember doing when I went to get the phone to call you, and it was gone. I found all the phones on the living room floor, and I just don't remember putting them there."

"That's kinda weird; what's the knocking and banging about?" Laurel asked.

"I keep hearing what sounds like someone knocking, but there is never anyone there."

"Oh, the house is probably haunted."

"What? Laurel, there is no such thing as ghosts."

"Mom, yes, there is, well, I believe there is. Tell me what else is happening."

I laughed. "You know what? I feel better already. Actually, I would rather have a ghost in the house than just be losing my mind. I think if I get a good night's sleep, I will feel much better. Let's talk about when you are moving up here."

"Looks like five months at the most! Is there a nice room for me to stay in?"

"No, but there will be in five months. I love you. I'll call you tomorrow."

"Love you, Mom; call me if you get spooked again."

"Bye. Love you." I sighed

All the events from earlier just made me feel silly.

I walked into the hallway and into Jim's side of the closet to touch the walls. Dry, okay, I can put everything back and take a break.

Stretching over the bed, I gathered the first clump of hangers holding Jim's dress shirts.

I'm just tired; there can't be someone else in the house. I just need a good night's sleep. Then I felt it again, someone standing behind me, standing right behind me! As if someone were standing only a few inches from me. I swung around, still holding the shirts by their hangers, and saw nothing.

Stupid, this is stupid. Just get a hold of yourself!

All the shoes were put back on their shelves, and clothes on hangers neatly hung; the last items were the guns and ammo. I knelt, opened the sizeable grey ammo box, and pulled out two more boxes of ammo for my handgun and two more of twenty-gauge shotgun shells, setting all four right on my nightstand.

If anyone is coming into this house, I will be ready. I laughed when I realized how much ammo I had taken out.

"Wow, it looks like I am ready for war puppies."

The ringing phone made me jump.

"Shit…Hello?"

"Hi, just calling back to check on you; you sounded pretty sad earlier. Are you okay?"

"Hi Sandy, I'm okay, tired, I guess. I am having a hard time sleeping."

"What's keeping you awake?" Sandy asked.

"The house makes some weird noises, and I am just not used to it yet, and there is other stuff…." I confessed.

"What other stuff? What are you talking about?" she asked.

"It feels strange here like someone is looking at me, almost as if someone is in here with me. I know it sounds crazy. Weird noises keep waking me up, so I am not sleeping well, and I think I am just tired."

"It's just a new place, and Jim not being there, I will visit you soon and…. "

"Sandy, hold on!" I interrupted.

I heard the noise come from what I thought had to be the front door. I whispered into the phone as I set it on the bed.

"Hold on! Sandy, I hear something; hang on a sec."

I put my ear to the bedroom door and heard sounds sending terror slicing right through me. *Running, running, someone is running down the hallway!*

I could hear them running fast, they stopped, stopped in front of my door!

There is someone in front of my bedroom door! Someone is in the house!

I ran to the bedside table, picked up the handgun, and laid it next to the phone.

I could hear Sandy yelling into the phone. "Are you alright? What's happening?"

I pulled the shotgun from the closet and leaned it against the wall. I picked up the phone and whispered.

"Someone's in the house. I heard someone run down the hall."

"Are you sure? Maybe Jim is home." Sandy said.

"No, it's not Jim. Oh my God, I can see shadows moving back and forth under the door; someone is in here." I whispered

I slammed the clip into the handgun. "Hold on; I am going to open my door."

"Wait! We should just call the police!" Sandy shrieked.

"Just stay on the phone with me while I check."

I set the phone down on the bed and slowly walked to the bedroom door.

I will swing the door open as fast as possible and shoot whoever this is. You picked the wrong girl, motherfucker!

I looked down at the crack under the door again and saw the shadows moving back and forth. I reached for the doorknob, turning it as fast as possible. I burst the door open, expecting the intruder to be standing right in front of me, but I saw nothing.

I walked out into the hallway, turning on as many lights as possible. Walking down the hall, I expected someone to jump out at me any second. There had to be someone here. I walked through the kitchen, checking all the rooms upstairs; there was no sign of anyone, no sign of any break-in. Doors locked; windows secure.

There was no one hiding in the corners. I walked back into the bedroom and picked up the phone.

"Sandy, are you still there?"

"Yes, of course! What is going on?"

"I don't know. I don't see anyone. I will take the phone with me and check the rest of the house. Can you stay on the phone?" I asked.

"Of course, But maybe I should call the police."

"Just stay on the phone. Please don't hang up!"

I walked back out into the hallway, slowly approaching the stairs. I quietly lifted the switch to turn on the iron chandelier. The bulbs from the big black hanging lamp bathed the room in light.

I checked every room and closet, and there was no one there, no sign anyone had been there.

"Sandy? There is no one here, and everything is okay. Sorry, I worried you."

"What was that?" Sandy asked.

"I heard someone running down the hallway. I saw shadows under my door, and I was sure someone had broken into the house. I guess I am overtired. I am sorry to have worried you; I feel like a nut."

"You are not a nut! Try to get some sleep, try not to work too hard, and take care of your back. I am sure you are doing too much, and you need to be careful. Most of all, get some sleep!"

"Okay, talk to you later. Love you."

I shut the bedroom door hard and locked it. Standing at the door with my ear pressed against the wood, I listened for other sounds. I could feel my body shaking, and the sudden cold became unbearable.

It must be the night light in the hall, and it must just look like shadows.

Stepping back, I looked under the door, but the shadows were not there now.

I pressed the #1 on speed dial and stood still at the door until I heard his voice.

"Hi honey, good timing. I just finished the dinner meeting. Is everything okay? Did you have a nice day?"

"Hi, I just wanted to hear your voice," I told my husband.

WATCH: Chapter 8: ALONE IN THE HOUSE-Day TWO
SAME QR Code

CHAPTER 9

CHAPTER 9
INTRUDER INSIDE

I woke up to the rain beating on the roof and tapping against the windows. I burrowed deep into the warm blankets and felt the puppies brushing up against my leg. Impulsively I turned on the T.V. to check the weather report and remembered we still had no television reception.

View from the house

Gazing out the window, watching the rain, I started to cry.

Why am I crying? Why am I so sad?

I am not the kind of woman to cry for no reason. I missed Jim and missed the kids, but I could not grasp why I was crying. The sadness was overpowering. Of course, I would feel a little lonely in a new house, and I would expect to feel sad about missing Jim and the kids, but this was different. I felt vulnerable and anxious, as though I was waiting for something horrible to happen.

I wiped tears from my face as the deep hoarse voice resonated in my head again.

"Why the fuck do they always cry!"

I looked up to verify I had locked the bedroom door. My whole body started to shake the way it does when I'm running a fever. Then I smelled it. A repulsive odor seemed to blow across the bed from the opposite corner of the room. So disgusting, I jumped off the bed.

The dogs under the mound of blankets frantically started scampering out from the covers, feverishly barking at the corner of the room. The odor was disgusting, so intense it made bile come up from the back of my throat.

I ran into the kitchen, searching for cleaners and sprays capable of removing whatever was causing this horrible stench. Barkley and Briquette were barking so loud from the bedroom my ears hurt.

Leaning into the cabinet under the kitchen sink and searching through the containers, I jumped straight up when I heard the bedroom door slam shut.

Standing up, I stood still for a moment, looking around the room.

The wind did not slam the door; no windows were open.

Oh god, the guns are in the bedroom, and there is someone in this house!

Slowly I started to approach the room, the hair on the back of my neck stood up, and chills covered my body. The door had crashed closed with such a force I expected to see the door torn from its hinges. The dogs were not barking anymore now; they were crying.

Cautiously I opened the door only about a foot and tried to look inside. Both dogs bolted from the room, running to their big blanket positioned under the kitchen table. I went inside. The smell was gone; the room seemed normal. I looked toward the French doors; they were locked. No windows were open, no air conditioner, and I had shut the heater off the night before. There was no explanation for this.

I don't understand what is happening. I cannot be imagining this.

I skimmed the room searching for the cause of the putrid smell but found nothing.

Walking to the kitchen, I felt the same feeling of someone watching me, now following me. I pressed start on the coffee maker and sat on the floor with the puppies. Both dogs crawled into my lap as I wrapped my robe around them. I sat on the stone floor, looking up towards the bedroom door, looking at the spot where I felt someone was looking back at me, expecting someone or something to materialize right before my eyes.

Well, this is crazy. I know I'm not imagining this. There is a logical explanation, so what is it? There has to be someone in this house! There is someone else here.

I sat still there on the cold tile for almost half an hour. My back and neck felt stiff and sore, and I felt crazy and confused. There had to be some explanation, and I was not the type of woman to get scared like this.

I looked down at the dogs, still hiding under my robe, and both were staring straight at me.

"Hey, are you guys okay. Puppies, are you okay?"

I cupped my hands around their tiny heads, looking into their faces. I never remembered the dogs looking this way, sad as if they were saying, *'we feel scared here; we want to go home now.'*

Slowly I got up, made some coffee, and grabbed a bottle of water.

"Come on, puppies, for the rest of today, we can relax; we can lie around and watch the rain."

The bedroom felt normal, with no smells and no weird noises. I was starting to think I might have imagined it all. I stretched out on the bed, placing the gun under Jim's pillow just in front of me, and reached for the phone. Anxiously I dialed Laurel's phone number.

"Hello."

"Hi Laurel, uh, I miss you, so, so how is everything going? "

"Great, but you sound weird again; what's going on?" our daughter asked.

"What do you mean I sound weird? "

"You don't sound right, and your voice sounds shaky?"

"I feel a little shaky. I have had a weird morning," I said.

"What happened?" she asked

"Not sure I want to say; you might think I'm a little crazy," I said nervously.

"I don't think you're crazy at all, tell me!" Laurel demanded.

"Okay, well, first, there was a weird smell in the bedroom. I went into the kitchen, and the bedroom door slammed shut; I don't understand why. Last night I heard running in the hallway, and I thought I saw shadows under the bedroom door. I told you, it's crazy; I'm just tired."

"Wait! What? The doors are slamming by themselves. That's ghosts Mom. It has to be ghosts!" Laurel shrieked.

"That's silly. I don't believe in ghosts, and I'm just tired."

"Mom, just because you don't believe in ghosts does not mean they are not real. These things cannot happen because you are tired, you have been tired before, and there was no ghost. I think there is a ghost in your house. I know you do not believe this, but I believe places can be haunted. Have you checked out the history of the house yet?

"No."

"I would be happy to check for you; what else has been going on?"

"It feels like someone is watching me almost all the time. See, this sounds crazy; just forget everything I said."

"No, Mom. Sounds interesting. I am going to start looking this up for you. So how are you feeling besides all this?" Laurel asked.

"Okay, I guess. I just wish I could get some sleep. I wish I could sleep longer than just a few hours at a time."

"Why are you not sleeping?" She asked.

"Something wakes me up; either the dogs will just start barking for no reason, or there's a banging or knocking sound waking me up. I will be sound asleep, and it sounds like someone is banging on the doors and walls or knocking on the front door."

"Well, Mom, if it's not a ghost, what do you think it is?"

"I am wondering if it might be kids or something. You know, maybe people don't realize someone is living here now," I said.

"Yeah, I could see that, but Mom, this still sounds like a haunting."

"It's just my imagination, just stress. I love you. I will talk to you later."

I clicked the off button on the phone. I was sitting perfectly still with only my eyes moving to scan around the room, thinking to myself how silly this all had been.

There are no haunted houses, and there are no ghosts! I thought to myself as I looked around the room.

The ugly green walls made me cringe, and the handprints on the ceiling made my stomach feel sick. Then I noticed a mark in the ceiling above my side of the bed, the kind you would make by throwing a knife into the plaster. *Everything about this place is starting to get weird.*

I turned on the television and pressed play on the DVD. Soon I began to feel better. The dogs were calmer, and when I looked at them now, they seemed to be their old selves, tails wagging and happy. Watching the funny sitcom had taken me away somewhere else, where I was laughing aloud and feeling comfortable again.

Jim would be back tomorrow, later in the afternoon, just before dinner. I could not wait until he came home. I knew I would not tell him everything. Maybe I would share bits and pieces of my days alone in the house, but I would not mention everything. I did not want to admit it, but I started to wonder if this *was* possible. Is this house haunted?

How completely silly and typically female, I thought to myself.

Being "A Typical Neurotic Female" was what my father used to call it.

No, I would not be one of those. This is only happening because I am overtired and in pain; my imagination is just getting away from me.

I went into the bathroom and started the tub, pouring my shampoo into the water to use as a bubble bath. I would make a note to pick up some on our next shopping trip.

I hung my bathrobe and towel on the hook and tested the water with my hand. I carefully climbed in and slipped myself down into the warm soapy water.

I closed my eyes and tried hard to relax again.

The loud bang of the door replayed in my head.

How could that have happened? How could the door just slam like on its own?

No, No, No, don't think about it; you are getting yourself scared all over again!

I closed my eyes again and let out a deep sigh. I kept my eyes closed for only a few seconds. I had to open them now; I could feel it again, the watching, someone was watching, staring at me.

I looked around the room, and looking down, I laughed. "Barkley, so cute; why are you in here?"

I looked at his little brown and black face. *He is such a sweet dog with such a gentle spirit.* I held my hand out to pet him, but he would not move. He stayed in place as if he were a soldier ordered to keep his position.

"Barkley, what are you doing? Come here, Barkley."

Still, he would not come; he sat looking at me, turning his head toward the hallway and then back at me again. Watching him started to give me an unsettled feeling. I pulled the plunger to release the water from the tub and stood up. Reaching for my bathrobe, I looked down at the little dog again. He never moved from his position, and he stayed fixated on the hallway and closet.

"Barkley, honey, you need to get out the way, move, please."

"Barkley, move!" I shouted

I did not make a practice of yelling at the puppies, and they were so tiny and so easily frightened, it would just be cruel. The few times I did yell while witnessing potty training accidents, they ran from me, terrified, and peed all over the floor.

"Barkley, Move!"

This time Barkley backed up a few inches and sat at attention again, facing the hallway, and started to growl.

I climbed out of the tub and grabbed my towel.

"Barkley, what's wrong with you? Are you okay?"

I wrapped myself up in my bathrobe and slid into my slippers.

"What is it, buddy? What's the matter?"

The little dog's growl grew louder and more aggressive. I felt my heart beating faster. Fear engulfed me once again as one of the bathroom lights started to flicker. Briquette ran from her dog bed on the floor and stood at the opposite entrance to the hallway, looking up, barking at ear-piercing levels.

"What's the matter?" I asked in a low, shaky voice.

Barkley moved closer to the hallway entrance.

Standing at attention in the hall from different positions, both dogs continued looking up in the same area and barking. As if they both could see something standing in the middle of the hallway.

"Calm down. There's nothing there." I was starting to believe otherwise. I could feel the room getting colder and my body shaking. I thought about every haunted house movie I have ever seen. I always found the stories entertaining but never believed they were real. The flashing lights, cold spots, and unexplained noises I always felt were all figments of someone's imagination. Now it's all happening in my house.

I walked straight into the hallway and my side of the closet and got dressed.

"This is ridiculous; there's nothing here. Go get on the bed, puppies!" I yelled.

Both dogs ran into the bunched-up blankets on the air mattress. I sat next to them and examined the hall and closets.

There is a logical, rational explanation for all of this.

I laid down next to the puppies, wrapped my arm around the blanketed mounds, and began to cry.

I woke up startled by the little dogs barking again and shocked I had even fallen asleep.

"What, what's the matter!"

Both dogs were wildly leaping over me, barking in the direction of the bathroom. I fought to get off the bed quickly, with my back was throbbing with pain.

"I'm sick of this; puppies, knock it off!"

I walked into the bathroom and looked around the room.

"There is nothing here; you're barking at nothing! You two are freaking me out. Stop barking!"

I grabbed a pack of cigarettes and opened the door to the deck. Barkley and Briquette ran out, almost tripping me. The rain had stopped, and the two camping chairs were now dry. I sat in the chair and lit a cigarette.

The air smelled clean, and it was surprisingly warm, even with the thick clouds masking the sun. I watched the tall trees lightly sway in the wind, looking out at the river. It was beautiful. The scene from the deck looked like a landscape painting, and the view of Mt. Spokane made the whole scene dreamlike.

View from the house

"I can't believe we live here. It's so pretty." I said, looking down at the puppies.

It was peaceful and quiet. The dogs curled up at my feet were calm now.

I closed my eyes and tried to focus on all the animal sounds. Ducks flying over my head, neighboring farm cows mooing, birds whistling in the trees, and squeaky squirrel sounds made me smile.

I opened my eyes to see what was causing a rustling sound just below the deck. I was amazed to see a young buck deer had walked right into our yard and was heading towards the secret garden.

"Wow, this is so cool," I whispered as the deer disappeared into the thick brush.

I closed my eyes again and focused on the sounds and the air.

In the distance, I could hear talking, two, maybe three people, a man and possibly two women.

They must be down by the mailbox. I thought.

It took only a second to realize this did not make any sense. There are no sidewalks on our street, and anyone standing by our mailbox would be standing in the road.

Why would they be standing by our mailbox? All our neighbors were far away; no house or other mailbox was close to us.

I struggled to hear what they were saying. The talking became louder, but not enough to make out the words.

Suddenly, I realized it was not coming from in front of me at all. Not coming from the mailbox down the hill and not from the front of the house. The people talking were behind me.

The sound was coming from inside the house.

I got up from my chair and stood in the doorway of the open French door. I could hear the voices louder now, but still unable to make out what they were saying, I walked straight into the bathroom. I peeked out the window timidly at first.

I threw the curtains open and checked the backyard. The talking stopped.

I went back out onto the deck and looked around.

"Come on, puppies, let's go back inside."

The phone ringing made me jump.

"This is ridiculous! Hello," I answered.

"Hi, Mom, how are you?"

"Hi Joshua, how are you doing?"

"Good, Mamma, I miss you. Do you have time to talk?"

"Yes, please, I would love to talk; what's going on, Josh?"

We talked for over an hour about his job and his girlfriend. I thought I would not mention the sound of the people talking or anything else in the house, even though I wanted desperately to talk about it.

It was hard to focus on what he was saying. I decided the talking I had heard earlier had to be the same as the banging from the other side of the river. Sound must bounce from outside into the back of the house. The banging was loud, so hearing the muffled version inside the house made sense. Hearing the voices get louder inside the house seemed different.

There must be some other explanation for it, I thought.

"So, Laurel called and told me some weird stuff was going on over there, and she thinks the house is haunted? Tell me what happened." Josh asked.

"I can't believe your sister told you that. Well, there are a lot of strange things happening, but I am sure it is not because it's haunted!" I assured him.

"Well, like what?" He asked.

I tried to explain how sound from outside seemed to echo into the house. I told him about the people I heard down by the mailbox and how their voices seemed to come from behind me in the bathroom.

"Maybe it's a type of sound refraction, Mom."

"Not sure I know what sound refraction is."

"Well, like sound waves can bounce off things or can be redirected. Sometimes it can be from weather changes or even the walls. And sound can travel, be blocked, and be redirected somewhere else."

"Maybe the house design has something to do with it," I replied.

"Now, I don't understand."

"Okay, so this house has two floors, two front doors, and an attic. The top-level is pretty standard. The downstairs has the other front door, and it opens to the front of the house. The back of the downstairs is underground, and then there is a mountain behind us." I tried to explain.

"Okay yeah, the fact the house is partly cut into a hill could make sound waves react differently. So, what else is going on? Laurel told me about doors slamming and weird smells? You think the house is haunted?"

"I know there is a logical reason for it; I just don't know what it is yet."

"Well, call me if you get scared or hell; call me if anything weird happens."

"Love you, Josh."

WATCH: Chapter 9: INTRUDER INSIDE
SAME QR Code

I smiled as I grabbed the ingredients to make a sandwich. Counting the months until Josh would be able to visit. I imagined how much fun we would have in our game room, picturing us playing darts, poker, and chess with the kids, and I could not wait for Laurel to get here.

Slicing pieces of cheese, I decided to make the guest room more of a priority as soon as our furniture arrived. Unexpectedly the man's voice repeated in my head. "Why the fuck do they always cry?"

I dropped the small knife on the floor.

This time the sensation I was not alone was stronger. Someone was standing behind me. I stood facing the counter for a moment as fear flooded me inside. My mind raced to figure out how I would defend myself.

Oh god, I know there is someone there. Oh God, please do not let there be someone there.

The knife still on the floor behind me and the gun in the other room, I took a deep breath and turned to face the direction of the eyes I could feel burning into me.

Nothing, oh, thank you, God.

I took a few more deep breaths calming myself down.

What is this? What in the hell is happening to me?

All of this is so stupid for a grown woman to be afraid of nothing.

Anger welled up in me. I tossed the small package of cheese back in the refrigerator and marched down the stairs gripping my paper towel-wrapped sandwich.

At the base of the stairs, I saw the water room door open. In an instant, I went from anger to fear and finally landed on frustration. It was absurd I was allowing myself to be this frightened. Looking at the door, it seemed even more likely someone was coming and going in the house.

"What the hell," I whispered.

I charged angrily to the door, slammed it, and yanked on the handle as tight as I could muster to ensure it shut tight.

CHAPTER 10
UNEXPLAINED

I rolled over and looked at the clock, shocked to see it was 10:00 am.
I had not slept late in years, and the night before had left me shaking for hours.
"Coffee would be good." I sluggishly said out aloud as I crawled off the bed.

Reaching for the bedroom doorknob, I suddenly stopped.
Tap, tap, tap

It sounded as if; someone was on the other side tapping on the wooden door with one finger

Tap, tap, tap

Differing scenarios began ruminating in my head. *Maybe a squatter?* I thought, *what if there is some crazy person in the house, perhaps so crazy now he is tapping at my bedroom door. It's a ghost. Good, a spirit would be better. Having a ghost is always better than some insane person in the house.* Grabbing my gun, I slipped it into my robe pocket.

I knelt at the side of the bed and said the same morning prayer I have done every morning since I got sober. Only adding, "God, please help me understand what is happening here,"

I walked back, pulling the heavy door open as fast as possible. There seemed to be no reason for the tapping sound.

I filled the coffee maker, pressed play, and went off to the dining room to choose what I would unpack today. Only a few boxes left meant I would be painting walls until the movers arrived. I set them on the kitchen counter as the coffee gushed into the pot.

Kitchen Upstairs

Opening the cabinet, I retrieved my favorite coffee cup and turned toward the drawer filled with silverware. I gasped, dropping the cup and smashing it into pieces onto the floor.

A sinister chill went through my body. I stood in awe, staring at the opposite side of the kitchen.

The drawers were open. Three side-by-side drawers all open in the same way. Even in my state of exhaustion, I knew I was not responsible for this.

No, this cannot be right. I could not have done this; I would not have done this!

I have almost an obsessive need to leave the house in the best condition possible before bed. An open cabinet or drawer would be a disaster.

This is crazy. I know I did not do this; there must be someone in the house. Someone must be coming in when I am sleeping. I could not have done this.

There was no reason to open these drawers. Two of the drawers contained a few of the cooking utensils we had brought with us, and I had chosen the one on the far end for spices. There was nothing to put in them until the movers arrived, so there was no reason to open them.

I frantically glanced in the upstairs rooms for evidence someone had been there. Searching for anything else disturbed or moved, I found nothing. Leaning over the loft wall clutching the gun nestled in my pocket, I listened intently for any sound coming from downstairs.

Both puppies came running into the kitchen, making me gasp, "Oh god, puppies, you scared me!"

I leaned against the small wall and stared at the drawers until Briquette's irritating high-pitched yipping shook me out of it.

"Okay, okay, stay on your bed while I clean this up."

Picking up the pieces of the shattered cup, I could feel the angst Serena always referred to as my "Fight or Flight" response. My breathing was growing stronger, my heartbeat faster, my muscles tensed up. I took deep breaths to try to calm myself down.

"I think I saw this in a movie once. One of those ghost movies where all the kitchen cabinets opened at once, but it must have been me. I guess I just don't remember. Unless you two did it," I looked over at Barkley as he glared into the empty hallway; I stared at him, wondering.

What in the hell was he looking at?

I pulled a new cup from the cabinet and quietly made my coffee.

Standing motionless, I listened for any noises in the house. The ringing phone echoed like an alarm in the quiet.

"Hi, girl, it's me."

"Hey, Sandy, calling to check on your crazy friend?" I quipped.

"You're not crazy. I just wanted to see how you are doing. Did anything happen last night?" Sandy quickly shot back.

I saw out of the corner of my eye. Then another shadow appeared on the opposite side of the kitchen, and shadows encroached upon me from all sides.

"Are you there?"

"Sorry, I thought I saw something; what if I am going crazy?"

"You are not crazy; stop saying that!" Sandy yelled.

I told her about the night before. How strange the noises sounded, how odd it was to watch Barkley trying to attack an invisible something. I explained how shocked I was when I did not find anyone in the room.

"I was so sure someone had broken in, the dogs were going crazy reacting to whatever it was, and it felt like…." I paused, trying to understand it myself.

"Felt like what?"

"It felt like someone was there. I could not see anyone but Sandy; someone was there."

"Okay, check the whole house! I will stay on the phone with you. If you find anything, we will call the police."

Slowly I descended the stairs, struggling to juggle the phone, gun, and hold the handrail.

"Hang on," I whispered.

I checked all the rooms and closets, apprehensively opening the water room door last.

"I don't see anything, but someone must be coming in here, a squatter or something. I was certain there was someone in the house, and the dog was trying to attack it."

"Okay, let's set up some kind of trap or things he would have to move to come into the house? Put tape over the front doors. The seal will have to be broken to come inside." Sandy said.

"Good idea, I will do that. Sandy, what if remembering the guys in the truck is starting to make me crazy. What if I am going insane?"

"No, you're not insane," She laughed. "You remembered those men from the truck in California, and the house did not make sounds like this. Besides, crazy people do not think they are crazy." She laughed. "Listen, after my sister died, one of the lamps in my bedroom started going on by itself. It scared me at first, but then it was comforting like my sister was still with me. Maybe there is something in your house."

"Do you believe that?" I asked.

"I think so, it's still happening, but I am not scared anymore. Maybe something is going on in your house, it does not mean you have to be afraid, or you're insane!"

"I really don't believe it's ghosts; I'm not sure I can believe in ghosts."

"Not sure you have to, you believe in God, you believe in spirituality, there are many things we don't' understand. This could be from your state of mind since remembering those men. Now you add the stress of moving, leaving the kids, and living in a house you only saw for thirty minutes! It could be those things, but I think there is something more. Over the years, many things have happened, and you never said things like this before. Maybe there really is something there. Just because you have an experience you have not had before does not make you crazy."

"I feel better just talking about it. Thanks, Sandy; I'll talk to you soon."

"Okay, call me whenever you need to."

Setting the phone in its charger, I rubbed my cold hands together.

"Puppies, this house is freezing cold, and it's still August."

I pushed the open drawers closed and poured another cup of coffee.

"Okay, puppies, I'll make you breakfast, and after you guys eat, I will unpack these boxes."

Just as I had set the dog dishes on the floor, I could hear the sounds coming from downstairs

Knock, Knock, Knock.

I leaned over the loft wall and peaked into the foyer. I could see through the glass that there was no one at the downstairs front door.

Knock, Knock, Knock.

Then it sounded as if someone was rattling a locked door.

Loft Wall

The sounds grew louder, but I could see through the glass no one was there.

Two cameras captured the same blue mist

"Hello, Hello, is anyone here?" I whispered. I could barely hear my own words as I felt the warm breath of my whisper escape my lips.

I could feel my heart beating faster. Rattling noises clamored from my right.

Backing up into the kitchen, I watched my closed bedroom door softly shaking back and forth. The dogs intently barked directly at the door.

"Stop it, puppies. There is nothing there; stop it!" I screamed.

I could feel my anger growing inside.

"If there is someone here, you picked the wrong house, mother fucker!" I yelled as I wrapped my fingers tighter around the small-caliber weapon I had kept close to my side all morning.

The rattling door instantly stopped. Lingering in front of the door, trying to summon the courage to check the room, slowly, I turned the knob.

Hastily walking in and scanning the room, only to find nothing. There had been an off chance the door had been shaking from an open window, immediately discarded once I saw the windows still closed and locked.

"It's stress, puppies; it's all just stress. Just a new house with weird noises; we are not going to pay attention to it anymore!"

To my relief, the rest of the day was uneventful, although I could not forget what happened earlier in the morning. Occasional glances at my bedroom door or the kitchen drawers kept breaking my concentration. I forced myself to focus on the house. The dogs remained quiet, and the house felt like just another house. Everything was exactly the way it should be. I unpacked boxes, organized cabinets, and finished unpacking the rest of Jim's clothes. Neatly I arranged his shoes and boots on the top shelf.

This was the way it should be: no unexplained tears and sadness, no thumps and bumps, just moving into my new house unafraid.

As soon as the phone rang, I smiled. "Hello." I cheerfully sang into the phone.

"Hi honey, you sure sound happy. Are you having a nice day?"

"Hi, yes, I am having a nice day," I felt overjoyed to hear his voice.

"Great, well, I'm on my way home. Make me a list of the things you need my help with. I will be home for a few days so I can help you."

"Wait, a few days?" I murmured.

"Ah yeah, sorry, honey, there is a meeting in California, and I have to be there. Just make me a list to knock out some stuff for you before I have to leave again. I will pick up dinner on my way in, and I should be home in an hour."

"It will be so nice to see your face again," I said.

I was disappointed he would be leaving again so soon. I ran into the bathroom and turned on the shower. The water felt warm and relaxing, making it a struggle for me to want to get out.

I shut the water off and wrapped the fluffy bathrobe around myself.

Walking out of the bathroom, I stepped through the doorway into the closet's hallway just as pair of Jim's work boots fell from the shelf and landed just in front of me, making a loud boom when they hit the floor.

Hallway from the bedroom to the bathroom camera moved on its own

My heart began to race so fast it was hard to catch my breath. It was not that the boots fell from the shelf frightened me; it was easy enough to understand. It was the way they fell, landing side by side, left to right. The way they would be if someone were standing in front of me wearing the boots.

I had placed them on the shelf earlier in the day with the toes facing the wall. It seemed impossible for them to fall, flip around, and land, side by side, in the hallway just in front of me.

I stood there for a long while, just staring at them. *I am not going to move them. I want to show Jim when he gets home. No one would be able to understand how weird this is. You have to see it.* I thought.

The cold finally shook me out of it, and I scrambled to get dressed. Finishing my hair and makeup, I proceeded slowly back into the hallway.

I stared at the boots again as cold air once again brushed on my face.

Again, there was the impression someone was right in front of me. As if someone were blocking the way, daring me to pass. I stood still for a moment, almost waiting for whatever it was to communicate with me. My attention broke away when I heard Jim's truck coming up the driveway. I grabbed the boots, stuffed them back on the top shelf, and rushed to greet my husband.

CHAPTER 11
REPUDIATION

With Jim being home, everything felt normal again. The dogs stayed quiet through the night. There were no strange noises, weird smells, or unexplained shadows. I was sure now; it had all been in my head. Maybe it was stress. Perhaps it was something even more straightforward. Just a lack of sleep, but I found this odd since I had never been someone who had trouble being alone, and I had never been someone who had imagined these kinds of things before. Whatever it was, there was a simple explanation for it all. My anxiety seemed to disappear as soon as he arrived.

Upstairs Front Door

We relaxed in the morning, talking for hours. I never talked about what was happening in the house; it would have been embarrassing. I knew it was just me, and there was no reason to worry him.

"Let's walk around the property and explore this place. I have not seen everything outside yet." I said.

"All right, make sure you wear your boots; there's a lot of weeds and brush out there." He said.

Jim neatly set his slippers just inside the hallway and put on his work boots.

"After we walk around, I'm going to take care of a few things around the yard. When I knock out some of those projects, I will tackle the list you made. Hey, by the way, did you find a travel-size container of foot powder. I was going to pack it for this next trip, but I can't find it."

"No, I never saw it," I said.

"I think maybe they might have confiscated it at the airport." Jim laughed.

Now outside, the fog was thick. The temperature was much lower than I expected.

Wrapping my jacket around me tighter, I followed closely behind.

We investigated areas of the property we had not seen before. Down by the shop, we found a sink, a large amount of window glass stacked against the side of the outbuilding, and an assortment of old tools.

Jim walked the large trashcan down the steep driveway while I walked up the steps to the spot we called "The Secret Garden." Old tractor parts and farm tools peaked out of the mud and weeds. I stood on what was left of an old path and surveyed the amount of work we would need to do. Trees and shrubs were so overgrown the trail disappeared into them.

I turned to walk back over the bridge as the hair on the back of my neck stood up again, and the same chilling fear I sensed in the house now crawled across my skin. I rushed back over the bridge and looked back into the once tended garden. Staring into the tree limbs and brush swaying gently in the wind, I felt the dark eyes of someone staring back at me. I decided I was being stupid and rushed to meet my husband.

"Let's go back up and check out the mountain," I said. We walked back up, stopping to check things out along the way; bits of trash, beer cans, and rusty tools hidden in the shrubs, and small paths made by animals intertwined in the bushes.

Once we were at the mountain base, Jim used his machete to open a path. I tried to follow but stopped short as my back throbbed in pain.

"You, okay? Is it your back?" Jim ran over and grabbed my arm. "You should go lay down, and I will be right in."

I limped back to the house and crawled onto the air mattress.

A few minutes later, Jim walked in with a cup of coffee, a donut, and a big smile on his face.

"Here you go, my honey," Handing me the plated donut, he laughed, "Pretty cool to eat on actual dishes again."

"Sure is. Thank you."

I smiled at him as I watched him walk into the closet and remove his work boots.

"I finished almost everything on your list. When you have more heavy stuff to move, just put it on another list, and I will take care of it for you."

Suddenly, he laughed hard. "Oh, that freaked me out for a second; pretty cute, honey!"

"What's cute?" I asked.

"The foot powder," Jim exclaimed.

"What?" I questioned.

"You put the foot powder inside my slipper."

I giggled. "What the hell are you talking about?"

"You put the foot powder inside my slipper." He said in an annoyed voice.

"No, I didn't; I told you I never saw your foot powder!"

"Well, how did it get into my slipper? These are the slippers I took off this morning. You must have done it, honey."

"Maybe it fell into your slipper?" I asked.

"Well, it's pushed up into the toe; you didn't do this?"

"No, I didn't do it, but I will tell you, a few weird things are going on around here. So this thing with your slipper doesn't surprise me."

"Like what? You mean the knocking you heard?"

"Yeah, just weird things seem to happen here." I suddenly felt anxious.

Don't talk about it; you will sound crazy! Just forget it.

"New houses, make new sounds, that's all" I just wanted to forget, pretend nothing ever happened. There was no evidence of an intruder, and nothing was happening while Jim was home.

A break from the house, anxiety over my mental health, and a break from guilt over leaving the kids was what I needed. Soon I was able to convince myself none of it had ever happened at all.

After hours of talking and watching movies, I felt relaxed and comfortable and drifted into a deep sleep.

Knock, Knock, Knock

I opened my eyes wide and labored to see the clock, 3:00 am.

I looked over at Jim, who still slept soundly.

He did not hear the knocking. I must have been dreaming.

I snuggled next to him and tried to go back to sleep

Knock, Knock, Knock!

This time the sound sent me straight up in bed.

I am not asleep; this is not a dream! Why in the hell is he not waking up?

Slowly I stepped off the bed and tiptoed to the bedroom door. I was opening it as quietly as the old heavy door would allow.

I went out into the hallway. Unable to find the light switch, I grappled to see in the dark.

From downstairs, a door slammed, then another door.

BOOM, BOOM

Banging noises came from all the walls.

The dogs started barking the cats began crying.

I tried to scream, but no sound would come out. I squeezed my eyes shut tight, trying to scream for Jim.

I opened my eyes and looked over at my husband, sleeping soundly.

The clock now showed 3:20 am.

A dream, it was only a dream.

At six in the morning, I could feel the cold nose of one of the puppies touching my toe.

I wrestled to get up off the air mattress.

Glimpsing over to see if Jim was asleep, I was surprised to see what I thought was my husband was just a lump of blankets.

"Honey, where are you?" I asked.

For just a moment, I thought, *what if this is another horrible dream? What if I am not awake? Oh, no, what if....*

"You want coffee?" echoed from the kitchen.

"Yes, please," I shouted with a smile.

It felt so nice he was home. Everything seemed peaceful and relaxed.

I opened the bathroom curtain and peered outside. The backyard was beautiful, full of pine trees and wildflowers, and I could hear the birds and squirrels in the trees.

"Your coffee is on the table, so how did you sleep last night?"

"Good, I guess; how about you?" I yelled from the bathroom.

"Not so good; you were rolling around and making weird noises most of the night; were you having nightmares?"

"Yeah, sorry," I said.

"I had a few weird dreams myself, but I can't remember anything."

I felt concerned, not that he had a bad dream, but that it made me happy. I was pleased to know it was not just me; even sharing a bad dream made me feel less alone.

I sat at the wooden table and sipped my coffee, excited that the satellite dish installers would arrive this morning. Internet access and television I have missed for so long would finally be a reality, and I would be in touch with civilization again. Something was comforting about having access to the outside world.

It took hours before the satellite dish was installed and the house had working television and internet access.

I felt like myself again. I simply forced all my concerns about the house out of my head.

Jim and I laughed at the local commercials. We watched the news for the first time. Stories about a barn burning down and a stolen car seemed so different from the more gruesome news we had always watched in Los Angeles.

It was only a few days home, and it was time for Jim to leave again. He would be flying to California, and once done in California, he was head straight to Montana. This trip meant nine days away; my husband assured me this long trip was unusual. I could not stop the tears early in the morning when he walked to the front door.

"I'm going to miss you so much," I said sadly.

"You are going to be so busy there will be no time to miss me. The movers should be here tomorrow afternoon with all our stuff, and tonight you can watch TV. You're going to have fun figuring out where all the furniture should go."

"I'm still going to miss you," I said.

"I'm going to miss you like crazy. I will call you tonight, sweetheart. I love you." Jim said.

I stood on the deck, waving at his truck as he left.

"I love you," I whispered and ran inside to answer the phone.

"Hello"

"Hi, Mom"

"Hi Laurel, Oh, I miss you so much," I said.

"I tried to do some research on the house, just using the internet…."

Laurel explained how she had searched for information on our house, town, and surrounding areas.

I sat down at the kitchen table and lit a cigarette.

Excited to hear what she had to say, I held the phone closer to my ear. Not because the house might have some strange history. It was nice to talk to Laurel; the subject did not matter.

"Okay, tell me what you found," I interjected.

"In the United States, Father's Day is celebrated on the third Sunday of June. Its first celebration was in Spokane, Washington, on June 19, 1910. Learning this information doesn't give me anything to explain away the reason why your house is haunted." Laurel laughed.

"Laurel, your being silly there is no such thing as ghosts; there can't be."

"I know you don't believe it, mom, but it still doesn't make it not true. So anyway, there's more history to your area, and a lot of weird stuff is going on in Washington State."

Laurel read a long list of chilling events, Indian massacres, a teenager who killed the family dogs with an ax, and a list of serial killers. She read the names of people she found who seemed to be associated with the state. Ted Bundy, James W. Canady, John R. Grasser…

My mind wandered as Laurel continued her list of names. I wondered if her focus on the evil part of the world was something *I* had nurtured in her.

Childhood should be fun and filled with fairytales, but I had always warned her of the darker side, never talk to strangers, never tell anyone but the police where you live, never speak to anyone! I snapped my attention back to Laurel.

"Yates is known to have murdered at least 13 women, and Jack Owen Spillman, the 3rd, is a serial killer from Spokane, Washington. He is also known as The Werewolf Butcher!"

"Oh my god, Laurel, how horrible. Betcha can't wait to move here now."

Laurel laughed. "I'm excited about moving to Spokane, Mom, and I'm ready to do some ghost hunting in your house!"

"Oh, so silly, I love you. Talk to you later, honey."

I set the phone on the table and smiled. It was comforting to know Laurel would move to Spokane and live just minutes from our town. I looked over at the paint cans stacked in the hallway and sighed. I had so much to do before the furniture came. I focused first on the walls where the movers would place the more cumbersome beds and sofas.

There will be no chance of my dripping paint onto our furniture if I paint the walls before the movers arrive.

Living Room Upstairs

After hours of painting walls and part of the living room ceiling, I set my paintbrush down, remembering I had internet access now, and I could check my email.

"Okay, puppies, I am going to be in the office, you guys take a nap, and I'll be back" The little dogs looked up at me as if they had understood and agreed.

I scooped up the cigarettes, lighter, and phone heading to the office. I stopped at the bottom of the staircase; the feeling was dreadful.

Foyer & Downstairs front door

Immediately I checked the water room door, closed. I still had the creepy sensation; I was not alone. The air became colder and colder, and I started to shake.

Water Room Door

I forced myself to walk through the room. Just as I put my hand on the office doorknob, a cold breeze lightly brushed against my neck and face.

Office

I quickly walked back upstairs, slipped the brush into the can of paint, and called the dogs.

"Hey, puppies, let's go work in the bedroom for a while." The little black dogs scampered out from under the blanket and followed me to the bedroom.

I locked the door, opened the bedside table drawer, and stacked the extra boxes of bullets on the table.

CHAPTER 12
INTO THE PARANORMAL

It was exhausted from all the cleaning and painting, but it was the constant stress and lack of sleep taking its relentless toll on me.

I fell asleep instantly after my call with Jim. I slept soundly, but only for a few minutes; a loud noise jolted me awake.

At first, I thought I was dreaming and ignored it, and it happened again. Every time I entered the transition from awake to asleep (known as the Hypnagogic State), a loud bang would snap me awake.

Later the loud banging changed. It was the screaming that made me check the house twice the night before, and it repeatedly happened until the early morning. I have never told anyone about the screaming (until now), and I was too afraid of how crazy it sounded.

I cannot stay asleep because I hear screaming?

After three cups of coffee and a shower, I finally started to feel alert and rushed to the door when I heard the truck outside.

I instructed the movers to place all the boxes and furniture in the downstairs family room. Each room still required some paint and flooring, so it was easier to stack everything up in one place. Only the upstairs furniture was to stay on the upper floor.

It took hours for the movers to finish, but once done, I was elated. Tonight, I could sleep in our bed. With all our furniture and things in the house, it would feel better now. The same place that gave me the feeling I was an unwelcome visitor would now feel more like home.

Waving at the big truck as they drove off, I was astonished at how they effortlessly maneuvered the big vehicle down our steep driveway.

As soon as I shut the front door, uncontrollable tears rushed down my face. I knew why I was crying the minute I shut the door. I felt it while the movers were in the house. The all too familiar feeling that I am not alone. The same sensation someone is in the house, staring at me. I was surprised I felt it even with my attention focused on the furniture movers. It was easier to ignore with people in the house, but still, it was there. Now I was alone with it again.

I walked into the bathroom, stood in front of the sink, and looked in the mirror.

Get a hold of yourself; everything is okay. I splashed the cold water on my face hoping it would snap me out of it.

Main Bathroom

I stood straight up and turned toward the sound coming from the bathtub. I swallowed hard as I watched the water faucet and the shower handle turn by themselves. Water now poured onto the floor.

"What the hell!" I rushed over and turned the handles to the off position.

Grabbing a towel, I blotted the water from the floor, sighed, and walked back into the kitchen.

I just didn't turn the shower all the way off. I thought.

"This house is weird, Puppies" The little dogs looked up at me, seemingly to acknowledge my statement.

Upstairs Livingroom

I stared at the walls in the living room, trying to visualize where our paintings and decorations would go. Admiring the way our sofas looked in this room. I fought to make the scene in the bathroom leave my head.

Why would it take all day before the water came on? I turned on the sink, and somehow it made the shower go on. Great, I have solved the challenge, a plumbing problem.

I pulled my gun from the kitchen drawer (where I had hidden it when I heard the movers) and went to the office.

Shivering in the cold room, I searched for answers on my computer. I needed sleep and solutions, and I found what I was looking for in just a few attempts.

Exploding Head Syndrome, the name made me laugh aloud.

A type of Hypnagogic Auditory Hallucination:

A rare and relatively undocumented parasomnia event where the subject experiences loud crashes, bangs, doors slamming, even gunshots at the onset of sleep or within an hour or two of falling asleep.

Attacks may change in number over time, with several attacks happening in the space of days or weeks. Sufferers may feel a sense of fear and anxiety before and after an attack, accompanied by an elevated heart rate. Also reported are an inability to vocalize sound and even mild forms of sleep paralysis during an attack. There is no known treatment.

I thought back to when I was a child, and I would wake up from the sounds of slamming doors and screaming. As an adult, I figured my family was acting insane after a night of drugs and alcohol or even my young subconscious just screaming for help. Over the many years I have been sober, I had nightmares preventing me from sleeping, but I have not experienced the screaming again until now.

I knew I would not tell anyone about this, and I felt silly enough, and I would not discuss anything related to the word hallucination with anyone, at least not yet.

I just wanted to go to sleep. I called the puppies into the bedroom, looked at the bed, and sighed.

My back was agonizingly painful, and I had thrown all the bedding in a pile on the bathroom floor to clear the room for the movers.

I bent to pick up the blanket and sheets, distracted by the overhead light, as it flickered on and off quickly as if it were speaking to me with Morse code. Gently I backed out of the room with the bundle of sheets in my arms.

Quietly I made the bed. I stepped and moved as soundlessly as possible while listening for any noise. I was nervous that at any minute, something else would startle me. Immediately when I finished, I crawled under the covers and pulled the blanket close.

That night, it was not the same sounds keeping me from sleeping; it was more as if something else kept me from even being able to close my eyes. A sensation I am not sure I can adequately explain.

I remember having the experience when I was younger, the first time I was eleven years old.

Living with my father, I would be home alone, everything would be normal, and a sudden rush of fear would wash over me. You would have the same type of anxiety watching an unexpected scary scene in a horror movie. I could hear a whooshing noise as if I were standing in front of a train coming at me at full speed but with its volume turned low. I would become increasingly terrified but with no explanation. I would sit still, literally *hearing* impending doom. Panic would wash over me; it would feel hard to breathe. My stomach would turn over in fear, and then I listened to the front door open; my father was home.

Now here it was again, the certainty someone or something was coming.

I knew this was in no way part of *exploding head syndrome*.

Exploding head syndrome explained those noises ripping me from my sleep, but I only experienced what I termed 'The Train Sensation' when I was wide awake.

I set the gun on the bed just in front of me, and I would be ready for whatever was coming.

I sat awake for hours before I fell asleep.

In the morning, I woke up exhausted.

I leaned against the counter, sipping my coffee, and moaned at the sight of the ladder and paint cans still in the center of the living room. My arms and legs were so sore, and all I wanted to do was go back to bed. I walked back into my room and tried to watch the news. After an hour of small-town news and the monotonous droning voice of the anchorman, even painting the house seemed more exciting.

I got up, refilled my coffee, and walked into the living room. The puppies popped their faces out from under the blanket as if they were checking in on me.

I picked up the ladder, positioning it under the last section of the ceiling that needed cleaning and painting. Unsteady on the ladder and with nothing to grab onto, I struggled to keep my balance

KNOCK-KNOCK-KNOCK

The sound was so loud and sudden I almost fell backward. I could feel my legs starting to wobble as I slowly stepped down. I set the paintbrush on the ladder and wiped my hands clean with a rag. I was only a few feet from the front door, so I knew no one had knocked on the door.

It was impossible, but it had sounded like someone was knocking on wood right behind me. I stood still and waited to see if it would happen again.

I looked over the loft wall at the door downstairs. With its glass insert and large windows on each side of the door, I could tell no one was there without ever going down the stairs.

I went back to the ladder; the puppies started growling before my foot touched the first step.

KNOCK-KNOCK-KNOCK

This time the sound was drowned out by the little dog's high-pitched barking.

There was still no way to tell where the knocking had come from; I was just relieved that this time the dogs reacted to it.

Knock – knock – knock

Spinning around, I looked toward the bathroom. This time the knocking was softer, almost timid. Walking closer to the window, I heard the knocking sound again. Now the sound was coming from the kitchen. I rushed into the hall.

Knock-Knock-Knock

I hurried from room to room each time I heard the knocking sound, with Barkley and Briquette running behind me.

The feeling of dread and fear washed over me as I stood in the hallway listening to the knocks coming from each window.

The little dogs retreated but continued the growling from under their big blanket.

"Okay, puppies, it's okay. It's just animals outside."

I knew it was not true, but I needed to convince myself this was a normal occurrence out in the woods. I wiped the tears from my eyes and unloaded one of the boxes. Pulling and tearing the newspaper from each item, I filled bag after bag with the crumpled paper, cautiously placing our favorite things on the sofa.

Tap-Tap-Tap

The dogs barking and howling made it impossible to hear anything else. I stepped into the hallway slowly.

Tap-Tap-Tap

"Shhh puppies, please be quiet." It sounded as if someone was tapping on the downstairs front door.

I cautiously walked closer to the loft wall but saw no one.

I grabbed my gun and went downstairs; I searched all of the rooms and found nothing.

I looked back to make one more check before heading back up the stairs. I saw the water room door standing open again. I battled my lack of sleep, trying to remember when I had closed it last.

Was the entrance to the creepy room closed? When I first came downstairs, I did not notice it was open. Did I open the door while I was checking the other rooms?

I walked over and peeked inside; everything was normal. I firmly closed the door and went into the office to find a paper pad and a pen, and I scribbled the time and a quick note.

8:35 am water room CLOSED

I could not find any reason for the tapping sound. Both the cats were sound asleep. I opened the front door, no noises outside.

I started back up the stairs and heard a man's voice murmuring. I could not make out what he was saying. I looked up at the a/c vent on the wall.

Okay, it is someone outside; the sound is coming from the outside.

I opened the front door again, but it was dead silent. I shut the door and stepped back onto the stairs. I stood still for a moment; then I heard talking again. The man was talking, not whispering, but it was hard to hear what he was saying. A chill went through me, my body shaking uncontrollably, and even my teeth began to chatter. I remained on the stairs looking around. I was trying to determine where the voice came from; it seemed close but quiet at the same time. As if someone were playing a tape next to me but turned the volume down so low, I could not understand.

The minute my eyes caught it, I whispered, "Holy shit."

The door to the water room had opened again. I was filled with fear and anger. All I could conclude was there had to be someone in the house. It felt as if someone was trying to drive me crazy. I marched straight to the door and pushed it shut. I turned and stood in awe as I watched

the staircase light flicker. I quickly walked up the stairs, my hands shaking as I tried to hold the handrail.

The phone ringing made me burst into tears.

"Hello, Hello!" I said with tears streaming down my face.

"Hi, Mom, are you okay?" Laurel asked.

"No, I'm not okay," I answered in a soft but shaky voice.

"What happened?"

"If I had to guess, I would say I am losing my mind," I answered.

"Oh my god, mom, what is it?"

"There is a door in the house, and I cannot keep it from opening on its own. The dogs bark all the time at nothing. I just heard a man talking, but I can't see where it's coming from; I think there is someone in the house. This house is making me feel kinda crazy, and of course, nothing happened when your dad was here."

"What, man!" Laurel shrieked.

"Even though it sounds nuts, I think I heard a guy talking on the staircase,"

"What did he say?" Laurel asked.

"He was talking, but I could not understand the words. Like the volume was turned down, I don't know it does not make any sense. I can't understand it; I just heard it."

"Mom, I'm going to call you back."

Abruptly Laurel just hung up. I looked at the phone, shocked.

I grabbed the notepad and pen:

8:40 am -man talking on the staircase

8:41 am -water room door opened -I CLOSED IT AGAIN!

I set the pad and pen on the kitchen counter and went back to painting the living room. The rest of the day was uneventful and quiet, and I fervently worked until dusk. By evening, empty boxes were scattered across the kitchen floor among the paint cans and wrinkled plastic tarp. The house was so quiet; I could hear the water drops dripping from the rinsed paint rollers and brushes tapping the stainless steel sink. The complete quiet made me uneasy, and the sudden phone ringing made me cringe. Before I could finish getting out the word hello,

Laurel fanatically yelled.

"Okay, not to freak you out, but you have a lot of the signs!"

"What signs?" I asked with an irritated tone in my voice.

"Well, I did some research for you, but I want to ask you a couple of questions first."

"Okay," I said in a sarcastic tone.

"Do you hear footsteps or walking?" Laurel asked.

"Is this about your ghosts again?"

"Yeah, I know, I know, just humor me. I know you don't believe in this stuff, but just let me read this to you, and let's just see if you have some of these."

Frustrated, I said. "Okay, go ahead."

"Footsteps or walking, doors opening and closing, do you have that?" Laurel asked.

"Yes, but it is a new house, and we just moved here, so I am not used to the noises the house makes. Yes, one door keeps opening, but I don't see it opening. Either I am leaving it open, or the cats are pushing it open…."

"Well, it says something about doors opening here," Laurel began to read.

"The experiencer either hears the distinct sounds of the doors opening and closing, or the experiencer will return to a room to find a door open or closed when they are confident it was left in the opposite position. Very rarely will the experiencer actually witness the phenomenon taking place."

"The phenomenon! Honey, this is just silly; there are no ghosts in the house. I am sure it is kids playing a game. Teenagers who did not realize someone lives here now. The real estate agent said the previous owners had not lived inside the house for a long time. My real concern is some homeless person has been sneaking in here, and I'm just really tired!"

"Okay, sorry, Mom."

"Love you, honey, thanks for calling."

I pressed the off button on the phone and looked over to check on the puppies. I turned on the TV to drown out the clicking sounds coming from the window. I was frustrated; believing in ghosts seemed silly; there had to be another explanation.

I was exhausted and sore from the awkward positions painting put one's body in.

I went to bed, knowing at least one more task was completed.

CHAPTER 13
THERE ARE NO GHOSTS

I awoke to the phone, singing our daughter's ring tone.

"Mom, I'm sorry I upset you yesterday."

"I'm just tired. I know you are trying to help. What were you trying to tell me?" I asked.

"Well, I want to finish asking you the questions first. Would that be, okay?" Laurel asked.

"Sure, just hold on a sec." I put my robe on as fast as I could. The room was freezing as if it were the dead of winter, but fall had not even arrived yet. I rubbed my cold hands together and picked up the phone.

"Okay, what would you like to ask me?" As I walked into the kitchen, I glanced to check the room for anything out of place.

"Do you hear footsteps in the house?" Laurel asked.

"Yes, something does sound like footsteps and running," I said as I reached for a cup and turned on the coffee maker.

"Running? You are hearing running?" Laurel asked.

"Yeah, I thought someone was running down the hall; I thought someone had broken in."

"Wow, okay. Next question, things are disappearing and reappearing in another place?"

"No," I answered.

"What about the phones?" Laurel asked me.

"Okay, yes. I have that also."

"Doors, cabinets, and cupboards opening and closing, or electrical disturbances," Laurel continued.

I nervously swallowed, "Well, yes, I guess so?"

"Okay, let me read more. It says dinner plates sliding across the table; pictures flying off walls; doors slamming shut with great force, furniture sliding across the floor. Didn't you tell me you have a door constantly slamming shut?"

"Yes, the bedroom door slammed, but there is some rational explanation. If pictures start to fly around, I am leaving."

"Which one is it, Cupboards opening and closing or electrical disturbances?" Laurel asked.

"Yes, I have both of those," I answered her softly as I listened to the sounds coming from downstairs.

"What, wow! You have both. What else has happened since you last talked to me? Has more stuff happened?" Laurel yelled.

I took a deep breath. As a mother, it felt wrong to discuss this with our daughter. A Mom should always be the one to send the spooky things on their way. I had consistently told the kids when they were young; there was nothing to fear when it came to ghosts and monsters under the bed. They were not real, just part of childhood imagination.
Laurel was a grown woman now, and it was comforting she was so opened-minded. I knew I would never hear her say; Oh, it is just your imagination. So, I explained as best as I could what had happened. I told her everything I could remember.
She listened intently and asked if anything else had happened.

"I was making coffee, and I saw the kitchen drawers were open. Obviously, it was me, and I just don't remember ever opening them. As far as electrical disturbances, if it means lights are flickering, then yes, sometimes the lights flicker. So are you finished asking me questions?"

"Well, the rest of them are: feeling of being touched, physical assault, seeing apparitions?" She quickly announced.

"Well, I am not being assaulted, and I have certainly not seen a ghost; if either one of those happens, I will be checking in to the nearest…."

 "Animals reacting weirdly, hot and cold spots?" Laurel interrupted.

"Oh definitely, the animals are acting weirdly, not sure about hot and cold spots, the whole house seems colder than it should be in summer and …."

Laurel interrupted again, her voice higher and excited. "Unexplained noises, knocks, something being dropped, banging, rapping."

My stomach turned the minute she said the word *knocks* and then *banging*.
"Yes," I answered

"Feeling of being watched?"

"Yes," I said as a chill ran through my body.

Shouting out the next item on her list, Laurel continued firing off questions,

"Unexplained shadows and unexplained smells?"

"Yes!" I said, thinking back to the unexplained smell in our room.

Cries and whispers or the feeling of being touched, do you have these?" Laurel asked.

"Cries and whispers I have not heard, not really the feeling of being touched, but the feeling of cold wind blowing over me or on my arm."

"Okay, let me read the explanation. Feelings of being touched - the feeling of being watched is one thing, and feeling like you are being touched is quite another. Some people feel something brush past them, something blowing on them, something touching their hair, or "a hand" on their shoulder. Some feel a gentle poke, push, or nudge…."

"Okay, then yes," I interrupted.

"I know you don't believe there is a ghost in your house, but you have all but one of these. Mom, you have all but one! The house is haunted!"

"Well, It is kinda creepy hearing your list, but I know there are logical explanations for everything here."

"Oh, okay," she answered sarcastically.

"Really, honey, there is no ghost, just a nervous person living in a new house. I love you. I will talk to you later. Can you email me this list you are reading?"

"Really? Well, yes, of course!" she said.

"I'll check my email and call you later, okay?"

"Love you, Mom; try to have a nice day."

I set the phone on the kitchen counter.

There is no such thing as ghosts, but how sweet of Laurel to go to all this trouble. I smiled, poured coffee, and walked into the bathroom.

The old bathtub looked like it belonged in a haunted house. Apprehensively I turned on the water to start a bath. The conversation with Laurel rang through my head as I put the stopper into the drain of the clawfoot tub.

Sounds as if someone is breaking into the house,

I scrutinized the water facets waiting for them to move on their own as I poured the iridescent liquid into the water.

Both puppies came running into the bathroom and curled up on the bathmat.

"Hello, little puppies, scared of the ghost, are ya'?" I laughed, walking into the bedroom and locking the door.

Relaxing in the sparkling soapy water made me feel at peace again. The room was quiet except for the dog's gentle snoring.

Over half an hour later, I pulled myself from the warm, comforting bubbles.

In bathrobe and slippers, I silently walked down the staircase as if I were going to awaken some sleeping monster downstairs.

The office was freezing; the thermometer read 40 degrees; I trembled as I sat in the office chair. As soon as the email loaded, I opened the attachment and printed out what Laurel sent.

Without shutting the computer down, I walked quickly from the office and took the papers upstairs.

Sitting on my bed, I tried to read the list.

THE SIGNS OF A HAUNTING

These may be indications that your house is haunted. True hauntings are rare occurrences, and it may be difficult to determine whether any strange phenomena you are experiencing in your home might be due to a haunting. Here is a partial list of phenomena that might indicate that your house is haunted:

I could only get through the first paragraph before I set the paper in my bedside table drawer. *This ghost crap is ridiculous none of this can be real.*

After I dressed, I took the puppies outside for a walk. It was peaceful and smelled like flowers and Christmas trees in the yard. I walked around the property with the little dogs following close behind.

On the far end of the yard, a group of dead bushes stood over five feet tall. I walked to the garage to find the garden tool resembling a giant pair of scissors we had jokingly named 'The Lopper Ploppers.'

I cut the bush's base, intent on removing the dead tree-like weed. The thick stalk fell, drooped over, and hit me in the head. I struggled to pick it up and throw it off to the side. I leaned down to cut another stalk and noticed a few of the brown flowers from the tree had stuck in my hair.

Quickly I stood up to pull them off my long ponytail as I realized this was not a flower at all. The rounded dead blossom was a thorny burr about the size of a Ping-Pong ball. Recklessly I pulled at it, ripping my hair out in long strands. When I reached up to touch the top of my head, I let out a small scream. What felt like twenty burrs were stuck together on the top of my head, all entangled in my hair. Frantically I began ripping them off as fast as I could.

Tears ran down my face as I saw large strands and chunks of my hair coming out with them. Once I had pulled them all out, I ran into the house to take a shower.

I winced as my soap-filled hands touched my head. My fingers were bleeding from the small spikes still stuck in my skin. Blood trickled down my face as I rinsed out the shampoo. I cautiously stepped out of the tub, almost tripping over the dogs. Both dogs looked up at me with sad faces.

"What's the matter with you guys? Nothing happened to you," I said.

Standing in front of the mirror, I pulled the last spikes from my fingers and brushed out my wet hair. I looked back into the mirror and saw the small trickle of blood running down my forehead. I stared at it, just watching it slide down my face and drip off my chin into the sink.

Another line of blood came down from my scalp as a sudden sense of fear and Déjà vu surged inside me.

I remembered having almost the same experience when I was much younger, staring into the mirror and watching blood running down my face. The disgusting feelings came over me again, and I could feel every part of my skin crawling with the sickening pain and repulsion. I thought I would be sick and grabbed the edge of the sink.

BANG- CRASH

The loud sound shook me out of it.

"Oh, Shit!" I yelled, rushing into the hallway, nearly tripping over the puppies wildly barking and running towards the living room.

It sounded like a box full of glass had shattered to the floor. I searched through every room upstairs and found nothing wrong. The dogs continued to bark at the entrance to the living room, but there was nothing there.

I must have looked like an insane person, blood running down my face as I screamed at the two tiny puppies who were indeed only trying to protect me.

"Shut up! Shut the fuck up! Shut the fuck up!"

I picked up my gun and walked back to the bathroom to stop the bleeding. I was confused and scared but aware the reliving experience had ended. I tried to slow my breathing to calm myself down as I wiped the blood from my face.

As soon as I was calmer, I finished getting dressed for the second time and walked into the kitchen to check on the puppies.

"I'm sorry I yelled at you guys," I said to their little puppy faces as I struggled not to cry.

As soon as I patted them both on the head, I walked straight into the other room and started painting the baseboards. Other than the quick pauses I took when I heard unexpected noises, I did not put down the brush until Jim called to say goodnight.

CHAPTER 14
VALIDATION

Days had gone by, with the only disturbances happening at night while I tried to sleep.

The first of many storms had come through Spokane and into our town, coating the house in gloomy darkness. Thick dark clouds moved in the sky. The giant trees surrounding the house seemed almost sinister. The natural protective fortress now swayed back and forth like a threat as the heavy winds slammed into every window.

I was relieved that Jim would be home soon. A well-deserved break from painting and setting up the house was just what I needed. I spent days painting walls and ceilings and removing the strange wallpaper in our new dining room. From morning to night, I worked on the house. I painted walls, unpacked boxes, and re-arranged furniture.

Nothing seemed right. The whole experience was frustrating. In the other house, decorating was one of my favorite things to do. This house was different; it was never right, no matter where I put it.

Some of our furniture seemed an even better fit in this house, and I thought it would be easy to decorate. Still, it always looked off, wrong somehow, no matter what I did. As if I were taking some test and failing at every attempt.

Jokingly, I had told Sandy the house did not appreciate my decorating skills since many of the pictures would fall to the floor after putting them up.

In the kitchen, it took me an entire day just to arrange knick-knacks and antique canisters in the spaces above the cabinets. On my last attempt, I stepped down off the ladder and backed into the hallway to check the arrangement. To my surprise, it not only looked right, but it looked familiar. Like I had seen this before, it looked nothing like the previous owner's setup or any house I had lived in before. Still, it seemed familiar.

I grabbed a pair of pliers and walked toward the living room. Hanging the paintings in this room would be difficult since two of them were as large as I am. I sighed and picked up the smaller paintings leaning them against the wall.

Slamming the nail with the side of the plier, I missed and hit my finger. "Damn it!"

Jim had bought me a lightweight hammer to keep in the house, which seemed to disappear days before. I was sure I had set it on the stack of boxes in the dining room, right next to the package of nails; when I went back, IT WAS GONE; just the open box of nails remained.

Oil paintings, decorative shelves, and a sizeable substantial mirror having once graced our prior formal living room leaned against every wall. It seemed daunting, as if I would never finish this house. Boxes were still stacked high in the dining room, and the entire downstairs was in chaos. At this rate, I would not finish for months.

I tossed the pliers on the couch, "Time for a break, right puppies?" The little dogs looked up at me from inside the blanket.

"Go outside?" The small dogs hastily ran to the front door, looking like cartoon characters with tiny, animated legs. I knew I should put leashes on them, but they had so much fun running in all this space I simply opened the doors and walked out with them. The air smelled clean and not nearly as thick as it seemed inside.

I sat on the steps and just stared into the foggy landscape.

Being outside made me feel lighter and happier, even with the ominous weather.

I sighed as the puppies ran to me, frightened by the wind and ready to go back in.

"Okay, we'll go back into the house," I said reluctantly.

As we stepped inside, the painting slid from its resting place against the wall and slammed onto the floor.

The dogs ran for cover under their blankets.

I stood in the doorway, staring at the painting, trying to understand what made it fall. I set it back against the wall and opened the glass storm door again, nothing.

I closed the glass door and walked in again, thinking the floor must have moved, still nothing.

I felt ridiculous; I do not remember any time in my life when I would have thought to question something like this. If so many other strange things had not happened, I am sure I would never give this a second thought.

I picked up the painting, hanging it in position on the wall.

I backed to check if it was straight; it was as if I had backed up into a refrigerator, the air around me so suddenly cold it was startling.

"Hello?" I said aloud, glancing over to ensure I had closed both the storm door and the wooden front door. Both doors were closed. There were no windows open. I walked out of the living room and headed towards the coffee maker as Laurel's words repeated in my head. *Cold Spots*

As I poured a cup of coffee once again, it felt as if I was not alone.

"Come on, puppies, come on."

Dread showered over me, and I rushed to the bedroom door and took one last look, scanning the kitchen and hallway before I locked the door.

Chills went streaming across my skin.

What in the hell is wrong with me? Nothing like this has happened before. I looked down at the little dogs curling up on the pillow.

"Well, you guys are not upset, so that's good."

I sat on the bed and reached for the phone. It was early evening, and I had no reason to keep working on the house. There was never much light penetrating the house during the day.

The large trees outside blocked the sun and shaded almost every window, but, at night, the house would become so dark, even with all the lights on, it was difficult to see.

I will start again tomorrow.

"Hey, girl," hearing Sandy's voice made me instantly feel better.

CRASH - BANG

The sound seemed to come from somewhere downstairs. I felt my entire body tense up.

"Sorry, Sandy, I have to call you back."

"Wait, what was that noise…." I could hear her yelling just before I ended the call.

I opened the drawer where my handgun and ammo were stored, checking the chamber and clip; it dawned on me that Sandy had heard it! She had heard the noise too!

I walked carefully to the bedroom door and turned the handle as quietly as possible.

A horrible screeching sound emitted from the door opening as it seemed to open the rest of the way on its own.

Walking through every room, I began what was now my new routine, searching every room with a gun in hand, looking for the phantom intruder. Just yesterday, this made me feel irrational and paranoid. Unsure if I just heard things. The dogs did not seem to react to some of the sounds. This time was no different; they slept through undisturbed, not noticing I had left the room.

Sandy heard it over the phone; this was not just another noise I might be imagining. That was real.

My heartbeat was fast as I crept down the stairs expecting to see the trespasser any second. There was nothing; there was no one. The sound had been so loud I was sure someone had broken in. I checked all the windows and doors again before I hurried back upstairs.

"Okay, puppies, we are okay" The dogs remained on their bed, still unaffected.

If Sandy had not heard the sound, this would have made me question my sanity again. I exhaled, trying to calm down, opened the bedside drawer, and set the gun just inside.

Sandy heard it. Finally, someone else heard it.

I anxiously grabbed the phone. It was a huge relief to hear Sandy talking about what she heard. Finally, there was a reprieve from my concerns; it was not all in my head. I was not just an over-imaginative, frightened little ninny who jumped without her strong man beside me.

"Oh yeah, I heard it. It sounded like a crashing sound; what did you find?" Sandy asked.

"I didn't find anything wrong or out of place, and nothing fell or broke. It was nothing again!"

"What does Jim think?" she asked.

"I haven't told him much at all."

"Why?"

"I don't want him to worry, and truthfully, it scares me a little to tell him about this stuff; it makes me feel crazy," I confessed. Not understanding myself, why was I apprehensive about talking about the unexplained occurrences with my husband.

"You don't give him enough credit. Tell him what's going on, tell him I heard it too, and stop being afraid you are crazy you are perfectly sane."

"Maybe, but hearing noises coming from nothing I can find still makes me feel unbalanced. I want to make sense out of it." I confessed.

We talked long into the night, reminiscing about happier times before her sister passed away and before I had moved to this house. I missed my friend.

CHAPTER 15
NOT ALONE

Jim would be home for the whole week, working in Spokane and the surrounding urban sprawls. We would be able to spend our evenings together, eat dinner together, and sleep together. These everyday actions for most couples had become significant events for me. Now I would be able to talk to him. I wanted to tell him about some of the abnormal situations in the house while he was at work, but I had mixed feelings.

I logically knew I could trust him not to belittle or dismiss me. He never treated me with disrespect or as if I were irrational. I kept telling myself I did not want to worry him, but the truth was I was embarrassed. It is important to me to be a strong woman, not given to things as silly as bumps in the night. My deepest fear, I would sound crazy.

After his latest long road trip, the first whole weekend we had together was exhausting. Saturday errands took forever, and stores were so far away that it took almost forty minutes to get to town. It was hours before we were home. Jim knew I was still afraid to drive alone into Spokane, even though I never admitted it to him.

Sunday, we spent installing floor tile. It was hard work but fun. It was fun having him home, and he made me laugh with his jokes and feel safe in his presence. Even the puppies did not seem disturbed anymore.

Jim popped his head in the bathroom the next morning,

"I should be home early. Do you want to go out to dinner tonight?"

"Do I! Yes, please!"

"I'll be back as soon as I can, love ya."

"I love you too."

I did a few light things in the house, emptied more boxes from downstairs, and hung a few more pictures. I did not want to do too much work. If I made my back worse, I would be unable to sit in a restaurant. Quitting early and taking a nice long shower seemed the best idea.

I stepped from our strange claw foot tub and wrapped myself up in the fluffy robe.

As I dried my hair, I could hear the music. I turned the blow dryer off and went into the bedroom. The television was off, and the windows closed. I returned to the bathroom, turning on the blow dryer again.

"La-La-La-La-Laaaa"

I saw something move in the mirror. Whipping around to see who was behind me, the music played now from the other side of the room. "La-La-La-La-Laaaa"

I shut the hairdryer off again. This time the music did not stop all at once. It played for a moment in the quiet room, fading away like shadows in the early morning. I turned on the dryer again. Chills went up and down my spine as I looked back and watched the faucet handles turning on their own and the bathtub water go on by itself. I timidly walked to the tub and turned the handles back, making sure they were in the off position as far as possible.

Main Bathroom

After I dressed, I heard the bathtub water again and turned in disbelief. I heard Jim's truck coming up the driveway and quickly ran to turn the water off.

Within an hour, we were driving into town; it took another forty minutes to get to the restaurant Jim had chosen. We had a fantastic night out; we laughed, talked, and had a wonderful dinner. I wanted to tell him there might have been such a thing as ghosts, and perhaps they live in our house. I wanted to ask him if he had ever heard music in the bathroom, but instead, I suggested we may need a plumber.

Over the next week, every day was peaceful. We relaxed each night, having dinner at home together, watching our favorite television shows. We talked well into the night about his job, things we would need for the house, and what we could do with so much property.

Soon it was time for him to leave on another trip. Time seemed to fly by when he was home, and now he was going again.

In the morning, he kissed me goodbye and gave me a long hug.

"I love you. I will call you tonight," he said.

"Love you too. I'm going to miss you."

I waved as he drove down the driveway and disappeared into the trees.

"Well, shit, here I am again. Okay, it's just you and I, puppies,"

I marched into the dining room and ripped another corner of the wallpaper down.

The kitchen was still the only finished room in the entire house, and every other place in the house required hours of work to make it our home.

The morning passed quickly. I pulled and scraped the paper from the wall, painted the baseboards, and drank as much coffee as I could stomach.

By four-thirty, it was starting to get dark. I stepped back to look at the large wall, now free of the antique-looking wallpaper with its purple grapes and giant green leaves. I felt the familiar cold breeze, and the disgusting man's words rang in my head again,

"Why the fuck do they always cry?"

My body tensed up, and the fight or flight feeling washed over me again. Thoughts ran through my head, seemingly all at once.

Should I be afraid of the man's words or the unexplained cold breeze touching me?

Is the cold breeze that man? Why do I keep hearing him talking?

Does something trigger it, or is he standing next to me? Is this going to be another reliving?

"Okay, puppies, ready to go have dinner and watch television with me," I grabbed a bottled water from the refrigerator and a platter of cheese and crackers and headed to the bedroom.

As if the cold breeze was the signal to announce, it was someone else's house now.

I answered the ringing phone as it echoed through the house.

"Hello"

"Hi, Mom"

"Hi, Laurel, how are you, sweetheart?"

"I'm good, getting ready to move to Spokane! I should be there by the end of November or early December!"

Enthusiasm and joy leaped through my mouth as I exclaimed: "So soon, great!"

"I can't wait to see you, Mom, and can't wait to stay in the haunted house."

"You're silly; there is no such thing as haunted houses."

"Well, since we are on the subject, I was thinking about the voice you heard."

"The voice?" I asked, confused.

How did she know? I had not told her about the men in the truck, about their conversation. I never told her how they spoke so calmly about what to do with my body once they finished. Laurel did know a lot about what had happened to me, but I would never share these details with her.

"The man on the stairs? Mom? Are you still there?" she nervously questioned.

I had forgotten all about it. The panic started to drift away, and I sighed with relief.

Instantly it occurred to me that maybe this was all psychological deflection.

The memories I did have of the men in the truck were terrifying, and my brain chose to give me amnesia regarding the rest of that night. Maybe all of these unexplained events in the house did have something to do with those memories.

"Mom?" Laurel asked again.

"I know it doesn't make sense; I'm sure it was my imagination," I answered.

"You imagined a man talking to you? I don't think so, Mom."

"Maybe, there is an air vent on the staircase; maybe somehow the voice is coming from somewhere else and coming in through the vent.

"Well, maybe not, Mom; I thought, what if…."

"What if what?" I asked.

"What if you record it?"

"What?" I asked.

"Record it, and you can turn up the volume and hear what he is saying"

I could not concentrate on what she was saying. I knew she meant recording the man's voice on the staircase, but all I could think of was; *What if I record the men from the truck?*

"No, it's nothing. I...." I stammered

"Oh, sorry, I wasn't trying to scare you, Mom."

I was overwhelmed; *How did Laurel hear how scared I was? Why the hell am I so scared?*

"I'm not scared! I am going to go take a long hot bubble bath and watch bad T.V. I will talk to you tomorrow, okay."

"Sure, Mom, and sorry I scared you."

"I'm not scared! I'll talk to you tomorrow."

I never ran the bath. Instead, I headed straight downstairs and went into the office.

As soon as I sat in the office chair, it hit me; this was the first time I had ever been downstairs after dark. It is not an inviting place to be, but at night, it seems as though I am the trespasser.

With the computer on, I tried looking up scientific reasons to explain what was happening in the house.

What I found consisted of ridiculous websites with bats and spooky music. One site even had a flying witch. Even more, websites displayed photos of the paranormal experts sporting facial tattoos, bizarre piercings, and pentagram necklaces. As soon as I found something not resembling a Halloween site, I printed the page and left the room.

Halfway up the staircase, the dogs started barking from the bedroom. I felt the air get colder, and the room got darker. The staircase lights dimmed, so much so, it was hard to see the steps. I ran up the remaining stairs and into my bedroom.

"Puppies, calm down. Shhh." I said in my quietest voice while closing the heavy door. Both dogs immediately stopped barking and slipped back under the blanket. I lit a cigarette, sat on the bed, and read the paper in my hand.

The following definitions may or may not support various beliefs, but ghosts are spiritual remains of the deceased—some entities with basic reasoning and communication abilities.

Parapsychologists attribute hauntings to the spirits of the dead and the effect of violent or tragic events in the building's past, such as murder, accidental death, or suicide.

I do not mean poltergeists, and I am talking about spirits that haunt old buildings, cemeteries, and other peaceful areas.

People have reported a glowing orb, a misty apparition, a transparent, or a fully formed human.

They are not always silent. There are times we can hear the spirit speaking without the aid of a recorder. You may even see, hear, or feel the presence in the immediate area.

You do not recognize this being as anyone you know. You have no idea what is happening, and you need answers. You must deal with your situation directly and ask what it wants from you.

"Oh, for crying out loud," exasperated, I threw the paper off the side of the bed and went to sleep.

CHAPTER: 16

CHAPTER 16
SIGNS OF A HAUNTING

I stood in front of the window, watching the last leaves fall from the branches. The property had many deciduous trees whose foliage turned brilliant red, orange, and fire yellow in fall, floating lazily to the ground at the start of winter. The Tamarack Pines now looked like giant golden Christmas trees.

The deer came into the yard to graze on grasses more frequently now, and raccoons visited every evening like little thieves sneaking up to the house. The nightly visits from Raccoons gave me a sense of calm. At least I could attribute nightly noises to them and not my imagination running away because it was Halloween.

Rational explanations like this were always at the forefront of my mind. Something moves; I could spend hours investigating the source. Occasionally I would find what satisfied me as a reasonable explanation. Walking back and forth on a specific part of the bedroom floor would make the armoire move and, on occasion, could make the bedroom door move. These revelations always gave me a brief sense everything was normal. Momentary peace is inevitably followed by the next inescapable questions.

Who moved it when I was not in the room or when we were sleeping?

Why did the door and furniture not move the same way the next day?

Only one answer appeared unwavering; the acoustics in the house were very bizarre. Sound from one room would amplify in another. Single incidents such as my screwdriver rolling off the table downstairs would register upstairs as a crash, sending me on a terrifying quest to locate the cause.

My talk with Josh about sound refraction sent me on a mission to find answers online. It was comforting when I read articles regarding sound entering a room at an angle causes the sound wave to bend. Therefore, the sound created in one place may register in different areas of the house.

I still wanted to know why the screwdriver rolled off the table in the first place.

It was not the debunking of paranormal activities; verifying I was not hearing things made me feel better. Understanding I was not crazy was my true motive in trying to perceive what was happening.

One afternoon, I set up our new desks in the office; the printer and the paper shredder suddenly cranked into life. The loud sound of the paper shredder was so intensely shocking I jumped from the floor and banged my head on the desk.

I stood up and grabbed my head. With the room spinning, I watched as the printer lit up and made its distinctive chime. I bolted from the room as the paper shredder went on again. I had never touched them; there was nothing to explain what had happened. I was just sitting on the floor, merely tightening one of the drawers, nowhere near anything electrical.

There were always events like this in the house. Daily occurrences left me puzzled and amazed. I had lost count of how many times I had uttered the words,

"That cannot happen."

We had been in the house for months now, and a surplus of repairs and deliveries had kept me busy. Couriers brought in new appliances, and technicians checked the electricity and plumbing.

The washing machine seemed to explode one morning, sending a waterfall into the downstairs family room. This incident required Jim to spend his entire weekend ripping out the water-soaked carpet and dragging it down the steps to the shop.

The refrigerator leaked water all over the kitchen floor one morning.

Another morning I woke up and came out to make coffee only to find ice cubes all over the floor.

The microwave shut itself off one afternoon and never worked again.

The built-in ovens refused to heat on the *bake* setting.

Light sockets would not work one day and then perform as designed the next day.

The bathtub continued to turn on by itself. Occasionally while relaxing in a warm bath, the shower would turn on by itself and blast water into my face.

Broken machines were not at all alarming; the washer, dryer, and refrigerator covered in mud when we first arrived, were mistreated, so breaking down was not surprising at all. It was the timing as if everything in the house was falling apart all at once. Although these were inconvenient costs, I was thankful and happy to have the new appliances. However, the electrician and plumber gave us no relief at all.

The electrician found the electricity to be in perfect working order, and the plumber could not explain the bathtub and shower.

The second electrician to check the house also tested the attics Radon Fan located above Jim's side of our closet. The fan, designed to pull the radioactive gas from beneath the home, had stopped making noises just two days before. Immediately I started searching the internet for the effects of the gas on the human brain; I was sure I would find answers about audio and visual hallucinations.

Radon is a radioactive, colorless, odorless, tasteless noble gas, occurring naturally as the decay product of radium. Chronic (long-term) exposure to radon gas in humans may cause lung cancer, acute leukopenia, anemia, and leukemia in children.

I also asked him to check the ceiling fan above our staircase before leaving. I showed him the remote attached to the loft wall explaining that we had replaced the batteries countless times. I described how my husband had precariously balanced himself on the barely six-inch platform trying to make it work.

I screamed out loud the day he climbed the loft half-wall, his legs shaking as he pulled the chain and flipped the switches back and forth. As if he were trying to find the missing sequence in a video game. Nonetheless, and to no avail, neither of us held the capacity to make the fan do our bidding.

"Well, Miss, I went up and found that fan was never hooked up. The wires run into the attic, but they ain't attached to nothin'. The crawl space at that end is too small to get at. I don't got the supplies here to take it down and rewire it, but yer radon fan is all fixed up. She was just running slow, nothin to worry about."

The plumber simply looked at me as if I were insane. In the most condescending voice I had heard in a long time, he said, "Well, dear, I don't think that's able to happen. At least not the way you are describing. I tightened the handles, and I am sure that is all it was. Nothing is wrong with your pipes or plumbing."

Later the very same evening, I could hear water running in the bathroom. When I investigated, it stopped just as I entered the room.

The water room door still opened on its own.

Often, I would find lights on in the house that should not be on.

One evening I went downstairs to check on the noises and saw all the lights on.

Our electric bill had increased to such a large amount the electric company sent us notices to let us know we were using more power than the combined neighbors were.

I found our monthly bill would go from eighty-five dollars to four hundred with no explanation.

There were some brief periods of calm in the house, only to have it start up all over again.

I spent weeks working on the guest room, all other work on the house adjourned, Laurel would need a comfortable, clean place to stay in, and she would be here soon.

With the dark green carpet already removed, installing a new floor tile was next on my list.

I'm not fond of carpet except for decorative throw rugs, and I have always thought it was unsanitary if pets are in the house.

It took almost two weeks to finish the floor in what would be Laurel's room.

While fixing up the house, everything seemed to take longer than it should.

Removing wallpaper would take hours, not the actual removing of the paper but stopping to check the source of the noises, crashes, and bangs while I worked.

The guest room was one of the worst. With no furniture inside the room, unexplained creepy sounds, moans, and crying echoed through the room, making my skin crawl. It was disturbing to think our daughter would be sleeping in this room alone, and I do not believe I would ever have the nerve to sleep alone in this room unless there were other people in the house.

I was exhausted, and I worked extra hard into the night to get everything finished.

Sighing, I turned on the television and sat on the bed. Turning to the program guide to see if anything was interesting, I heard the commercial playing in the background.

"There is no greater feeling in the world like moving into your new house...."

I laughed and turned off the volume.

I reflected on the first day we had moved into the California house for a moment. A nice feeling slipped over me as I thought about all the excitement I felt while organizing and decorating the home in Mountain Cove. The warm memories of creating something new from a clean, fresh canvas.

My pleasant memories were quickly interrupted by Barkley's low growling as he stared at our bedroom door. I sat still, watching the dog and the door, waiting for the barking frenzy to start again. A strange sound right outside the bedroom door made me tense up as Barkley seemed to relax.

As if whatever it was had left. I opened the drawer my handgun was stored in and saw the two papers from Laurel's email months before stuffed in the back.

I set the articles on the bedspread and went to check the hallway.

Peeking out the door, I just looked around and saw nothing.

Looking into the kitchen, I could feel the hair on the back of my neck standing up again. Closing the door hard and locking it, I went back to the papers on the bed.

Contemplating ghosts and hauntings were not even something I had done as a child. Real-life was scary enough. I always loved movies about ghosts and haunted houses, and I enjoyed scary movies involving unrealistic and improbable occurrences. Ghosts were frightening in the theatre; that was the appeal, fun, and scary in the moment but undoubtedly not real.

There were days when I was sure our house was haunted and felt open-minded to the idea. Each day I would come to a different conclusion. Some days it was ridiculous, and I would explain away what was happening no matter how unlikely or complicated the explanation was.

Today it seemed possible, the idea of ghosts.

I sighed again, reaching for my reading glasses, and wrapped the blanket over myself as a cold breeze from nowhere blew across the bed.

THE SIGNS OF A HAUNTING:

These may be indications your house is haunted. True hauntings are rare occurrences, and it may be difficult to determine whether any strange phenomena you are experiencing in your home might be due to a haunting. Here is a partial list of phenomena potentially indicating your house is haunted:

Unexplained Noises: footsteps; knocks, banging, tapping;

scratching sounds; sounds of something dropped. Sometimes these noises can be subtle, and other times, they can be quite loud.

Electrical Disturbances: switching off lights. This can also happen with TVs, radios, and other electrically powered items.

Doors Opening and Closing: the experiencer will return to a room, only to find a door, cabinet, or drawer open or closed when they are confident it was in the opposite position.

Items Disappearing and Re-appearing: Objects borrowed and returned unexplainably. Sometimes, for days or even weeks, the items not returned, but when they are, it is in an obvious place. Items returned, showing up in the most obvious places.

Unexplained Shadows: the sighting of fleeting shapes and shadows, usually seen out of the corner of the eye. Many times, the shadows have vaguely human forms.

Strange Animal Behavior: a dog, cat, or other pet behaves strangely. Dogs may bark at something unseen, cower without apparent reason, or refuse to enter a room they normally do. Cats may seem to be "watching" something cross a room

Feelings of Being Watched: this is not an uncommon feeling and can be attributed to many things, but it could have a paranormal source if the feeling consistently occurs in a particular part of the house at

Cries and Whispers: on occasion, muffled voices, whispering, or crying can be heard. Sometimes it is music from some unknown source, and people can even hear their names whispered into their ears.

Cold or Hot Spots: cold spots are classic haunting symptoms, but any instance of a noticeable variance in temperature without a discernible cause could be evidence.

Unexplained Smells: perfume, cologne, smoke, or bad odors you do not have in your house. This phenomenon comes and goes without any apparent cause and may accompany other phenomena, such as shadows, voices, or psychokinetic phenomena.

Other Physical Evidence: unexplained writing on paper or walls; handprints, fingerprints, and even footprints.

Moving or Levitating Objects: dinner plates sliding across the table; pictures flying off walls; doors slamming shut with great force; furniture slides across the floor.

Mild Psychokinetic Phenomena: hearing a door open or close is one thing. Actually, seeing it happen is quite another. Similarly, seeing the light turning on or off by itself is greater proof that something unexplained is happening. Doors and windows are locked or unlocked. Some people report that they can feel and/or hear something sitting next to them in bed.

Feeling of Being Touched: the feeling of being watched is one thing, and actually feeling like you are being touched is quite another. Some people feel something brush past them, something touching their hair or "a hand" on the shoulder. Some feel a gentle poke, push or nudge. Some people describe this as cold air brushing against them.

Physical Assault: scratches, slaps, and hard shoves. This kind of personal assault is extremely rare but obviously highly disturbing

Apparitions: the physical manifestation of a spirit or entity. These phenomena are also very rare and can take many forms: human-shaped mists or forming mists of some indistinguishable shape; transparent human forms disappearing quickly, and most rarely, human forms looking as real and solid as any living person but disappearing into a room or even melting away in front of you.

After reading the papers, part of me felt as if this was the stupidest thing I had ever read, and it seemed impossible even trying to be open-minded to something I had always thought was absurd.

However, there they were, all those words, jumping off the page, describing our house.

Unexplained noises,

lights turning off and on, doors,

cabinets and cupboards opening and closing,

unexplained shadows,

muffled voices,

cold spots,

unexplained smells,

doors slamming shut, doors opening,

strange animal behavior, items disappearing and reappearing,

Feelings of being watched,

sometimes it is music from some unknown source.

Looking down at Barkley and Briquette snuggled in their blanket, I smiled at them.

"Okay, puppies, we certainly have unexplained noises and lights turning on and off. Doors, cabinets, and cupboards opening and closing, we have that."

I read number 4. again.

Items Disappearing and Reappearing: Objects borrowed and returned unexplainably. Sometimes, for days or even weeks, the items not returned, but when they are, it is in an obvious place. Items returned, showing up in the most obvious places.

Chills went across my back as my memory flashed on what I saw just minutes before I locked the bedroom door. The hair stood up on the back of my neck again.

"The hammer, the hammer!" I yelled.

"Oh my god, the hammer was there, right there in front of the coffee maker!" I said, almost shouting to the small puppies now hiding under their blanket.

I struggled to try to remember if I found the hammer earlier today.

I must have put it there, but the last time I saw it was so long ago, Months ago!

I could feel the hair on the back of my neck stand up again. Chills ran across my skin. A wave of fear seemed to pour over me, so intently frightening that I was unable to move anything but my hand wrapping around the pistol grip.

"Why the fuck do they always cry?" the deep voice spewed from my head again.

God, please don't let me go crazy," I whispered.

WATCH: Chapter 16: SIGNS OF A HAUNTING
SAME QR Code

CHAPTER 17
MOVING OBJECTS

Time seemed to rush by once I changed my focus to Laurel arriving. I was eager to show her the beautiful property and the surrounding forest.

The guest room was clean and painted with finished floors. The furniture was set up and the bed made. I wanted to make the place pleasant for our daughter, to feel homey and comfortable. I tried to hang pictures to liven up the room, but nothing seemed to help. Still, the room had a bleak and lonely feeling to it. I rummaged through the remaining boxes of knick-knacks, searching for anything I could add to the walls or tables.

Secretly I could not wait for her to experience some of the occurrences in the house, and she might have some idea what some of it was.

I thought about the previous weekend. Jim had been home for longer than usual, and I had finally decided it was time to say something about the house. The conversation replayed in my head all morning. His reaction surprised me. He sat quietly at first, listening to me intently as I explained some of the events over the last few months. He abruptly ended the conversation with, "This house is not haunted!"

I had casually mentioned a few more occurrences over the next few days, but his response was out of character. He seemed defensive, not defensive of himself but the house!

Older haunted house movies played through my head, the ones where the husband turns into someone else and becomes possessed by the haunted home. He was not the open-minded man I knew. He was now reacting in a way I had not experienced before. I assumed his frustration was with me since nothing ever seemed to happen in the house when he was home. I often wondered what was going through his mind at that time. *Did he think I was crazy?*

That morning he seemed so irritated when I woke him up at 4:30 am.
"Get up, get up! Please come into the kitchen and see this! You are never home when this stuff happens, and you have to come and see!" I shrieked.

He strolled into the bathroom and leisurely slipped into the kitchen from there. I wanted him to hurry and see it before it stopped. "What is it, honey? What's so important I could not sleep for another hour?"

"Look!" I yelled, pointing up at the ceiling fan turning on its own. "How is this moving? It's been turning for over an hour now."

"Yeah, that's something." He said, unimpressed.

"There's no electricity; it's not hooked up! You don't think this is weird?" I shouted.

"There is some explanation; something is probably wrong with the electrical," he said as he started his morning coffee.

"But it's not hooked up to electricity," I said quietly.

His reaction frustrated me. It was the first time he was there to see something unexplained happen, and he did not seem to care. I had been through months of unexplained incidents, and I had waited for this for so long.
I sighed, thinking that one day, something would happen that would capture his attention—forcing him to experience some of what I had. He would finally understand what I did; something was different about this house. Then we would share our experiences, the events that felt miraculous, and more importantly, the ones that just scared the shit out of me.

I pushed the morning out of my head and visualized Laurel shivering in this ice-cold room. I took one more look and closed the door with a deep sigh. I had done my best to make the room comfortable, but nothing I did made the creepy ambiance transform into a home.

I would not want to sleep in there. Maybe it is just me; maybe Laurel will not think it is as creepy as I do.

I glanced over to the sofa and felt sad. Our cats were now reacting to me as if I were a stranger. I had approached Trinity the day before to rub her ears, and she hissed at me the way a feral cat would in the wild. She used to follow me constantly and now I was afraid to go near her. I shrugged it off the best I could and opened the door to the office.

I stood still at the doorway; after a minute, I laughed; it was ridiculous to stand there waiting for the printer to go on, merely waiting for some ghostly encounter to happen just because I opened the door.
I walked to the computer, hit the power button, and grabbed a pad of paper from the drawer.

I typed my question into the search engine. Scanning the answers and looking on the internet for some natural causes was even more frustrating. Most of the information I found put me in one of two categories, an uneducated idiot or a crazy person.

WHY DO PEOPLE EXPERIENCE PARANORMAL EVENTS? Mental Illness- Low I.Q. - Only poorly educated people have a propensity for belief in the paranormal.
I tried it again, re-wording my search.

NATURAL CAUSES FOR PARANORMAL ACTIVITY: Limitations of human perception and ordinary physical explanations can account for ghost sightings; for example, air pressure changes in a home causing doors to slam or lights from a passing car reflected through a window at night. According to research in anomalistic psychology, visions of ghosts may arise from Hypnagogic Hallucinations, "waking dreams" which are experienced in the transitional states to and from sleep.

I felt exasperated. There were no windows open when the doors slammed.
I saw no lights from passing cars; we could not even see the street from our home.
I was not stupid; I checked the possible causes hundreds of times. Hypnagogic hallucinations were off my list; I was awake. All the explanations I was finding were all talking about seeing an apparition. I had not seen a ghost, just occasional shadows, things out of the corner of my eye. They were frightening as if I was witnessing someone run past me, but when I turned to look, of course, there was never anything there.

I clicked another link:

....CAUSES PEOPLE TO EXPERIENCE PARANORMAL EVENTS? A study of two experiments into alleged hauntings (2003) concluded that people consistently report unusual experiences in 'haunted' areas because of environmental factors. Some of these factors included "the variance of local magnetic fields, size of location and lighting level stimuli of which witnesses may not be consciously aware. Some researchers in Canada have speculated that changes in geomagnetic fields could stimulate the brain's temporal lobes and produce many of the experiences associated with hauntings.

After about an hour, the cold in the room made my body shake.

I shut down the computer and went upstairs. Wrapping my robe around me, I made a cup of coffee and picked up the phone.

"Hey girl, I haven't talked to you for a while. Did you get my messages?" Sandy answered.

"No, sorry. You left messages?" I said, confused.

"Yeah, well, your calling now; how's it going up there?"

"It has to be geological something about the area is creating some of this. It does not explain all of the signs in Laurel's list, but…."

"What signs?" she quickly asked.

I realized how irrational I was sounding and took a deep breath. I had not even asked how Sandy was, and I just could not focus on anything else.
"Laurel emailed me this list of 16 signs that your house is haunted."

"Hmm, do you have it there? Can you read it for me?" Sandy asked.

I read the list feeling like an idiot for even considering this at all. "So, which ones do you have?" she asked in a voice that put me at ease right away.

"Unexplained noises we certainly have. The list says some unexplained noises are footsteps, knocks, banging, and the sounds of something dropping. Lights flickering and doors opening, we have that for sure. Unexplained shadows and strange animal behavior, we have for sure as well. Muffled voices and the feeling of someone watching me, yup, got them. Cold spots, unexplained odors, handprints, doors slamming, and maybe the feeling of being touched."

"Wow, that's a lot, hun. How stressed are you feeling?"

"Pretty stressed; going crazy stresses everyone out. The dogs and cats are acting weird, very weird. There still has to be explanations for it all. I read an article online about the theory that one cause is magnetic energy affecting my brain. Maybe it's geological? I'm still not sure there is not someone breaking into the house, but I cannot figure out how an intruder would get in and out of here. There has to be a reason for everything happening here; I just do not know what it is yet. Unexplained noises, lights turning off and on, doors, cabinets and cupboards opening, and closing can all be explained another way, right?"

"Sure, if you want there to be," Sandy answered.

"I was using the hammer, and it seemed to disappear. It has been missing for months. I saw the hammer resting in front of the coffee maker, and you know how much coffee I drink. There is no way I would have missed it. It just was there, Sandy; there is no way I put it there, no way!"

"You don't seem open-minded to this, but it sounds like the house is haunted."

"That can't be true; this can't be real; what if I'm crazy? There has to be another explanation!"

"If you want there to be, then yes, there is another explanation. For people who believe, no explanation is needed. For people who do not believe no explanation will ever be good enough. It sounds like you may have to decide which one you are"

"I miss you, Sandy," I said.

"Miss you too; the kids are here, so I have to go; we'll talk soon?"

"Of course. Thanks for talking with me. Bye, Sandy."

I stared at the phone in my hand, thinking about the afternoon I talked to Josh. I heard a woman shouting, "Hello." Assuming a neighbor had come over to introduce herself, I quickly walked to the front window to see who was there. I walked the entire perimeter of the house searching for this woman, but there was never anyone there. Best of all, Joshua heard the woman too.

I sat back against the pillow wishing my friend could stay on the phone longer.
For the first time in my life, I did not enjoy being alone. My life had been such a struggle that I looked forward to my time alone. I love spending time with friends and family. I missed the kids and

Jim, but typically I am okay alone. Many people have told me if they were in my place, they would go crazy being alone like this. I was not lonely; I was unsettled about being alone; there is a difference.

Since we moved in, I felt like someone was watching, staring at me. Never before had this feeling been so strong; it was as if someone were right behind me, in every room, and following me everywhere I went.

Chills went across my arms as I suddenly identified what I was feeling; *I'm never alone.*

I picked up the list.
"Hey puppies, it says strange animal behavior. I think they are talking about you."

Before I could re-read the following sentence, I saw movement out of the corner of my eye and glanced toward the window, the first snow. I loved the snow, and I sat up and rushed into the kitchen.

Standing at the sink, I stared out the window, watching the large snowflakes fall.

Almost immediately, my stomach turned as if I was on an elevator ride that had dropped out of control. I tried to stay focused on how beautiful it was, how happy the snow made me feel just seconds before. The breathtaking diversion shattered as I stood still and quiet, subjugated with fear.

It does not feel like someone is just watching me; now, it feels like someone is staring me down!

CHAPTER 18
THE FIRST RECORDING

I walked through the house, giving each room a quick scan to verify I had not forgotten anything. I needed to make sure everything was safe and felt like home. Jim was picking Laurel up at the airport on his way home. I checked and re-checked each room.

This house was far different than our home in California.

There was always light coming through the many windows in the other house, even at night.

Here no next-door neighbors, no outside lights, and the strange darkness that always blanketed the rooms made clearing everything more than just important.

The positioning of light switches was challenging, necessitating someone to walk into the darkroom and locate the light.

Checking the guest room one last time, I smiled to myself. *Laurel will be here soon!* I thought.

My smile vanished as I looked into the cold and uninviting guest room. As I looked around the room with our familiar belongings hanging from walls and set on tables, I sighed. As hard as I had worked on this space, it still felt like someone else's room. It struck me as I closed the door; it was not just this room. It was the entire house; no matter how hard I tried to make it a home, this house felt like it belonged to someone else.

I stood at the base of the staircase, looking toward the guestroom hallway. Wrapping my sweater tighter around, even with the heater on, it was freezing. Cold breezes seemed to come from nowhere; no windows were open to explain it. I folded my arms in front of me, rubbing my elbows in an attempt to warm up.

"What do you want?" I said quietly to the empty hallway, where I could feel the presence of someone else. My attempt was quickly interrupted as I heard the truck maneuvering up the steep driveway; my heart soared.

I bolted up the stairs and out the front door running to meet them, tears streaming down my face.

Laurel emerged from the truck, dressed in her California clothes. I shook my head and smiled as I watched our daughter's sneaker-clad feet sink deep into the snow.

"Oh, Laurel, I can't believe you're here! I missed you so much; come on lets, go inside and warm you up."

I took her arm and led her inside. I could feel Laurel becoming anxious when we entered the halfway point of the entrance hall.

"Oh, Mom, it's so pretty in this room," In a shaky voice I had not heard before.

"You, okay?"

"I guess the plane ride made me tired."

"Okay, let me show you the bathroom and your room; I just finished it today. You can lie down and rest if you want".

I led her to the staircase, turning to watch her expression as we descended each step.

"Mom, I can't believe how big the house is, and these rooms are huge and, umm, freezing."

I opened the guest room door as a cold blast of air escaped from the room.

"Oh my god, it's cold!" Laurel said.

"I know it is cold down here; we made sure you had a lot of blankets in your room; oh my gosh, I need to start dinner and go hug your Dad; you get settled, and dinner will be ready in a bit. I'll turn up the heater. Are you going to be okay?"

"Sure, I'm so happy to be here. I'm fine. Mom, go ahead."

As I walked up the stairs, I kept my eyes fixed on our daughter, waiting to see her expression as she entered the guest room. Once I reached the top of the stairs, I could hear the faint voice from below.

"Geez, it's cold."

I hugged my husband hard and prepared a quick dinner. We sat in the unfinished dining room, laughing and talking for hours.

"Mom, I feel tired. I think I want to go to bed now." Laurel said.

"Were all exhausted; I'm so happy you're here. Let me know if you need anything."

After a big hug, I watched Laurel sink down the stairs and disappear into the guest room.

"Thank you, honey, for getting Laurel here; it's going to be nice to have someone around when you're out of town. I missed her." hugging my husband tight.

"No problem, so when does she start work?"

"In a month, silly," I laughed.

"I'm happy she is here. I missed her too, and it makes me feel better knowing you won't be alone."

I was up by five am to hug Jim and see him off on another trip. I watched his brake lights disappear into the snowy trees. I let out a lonely sigh as I poured a cup of coffee and sat at the kitchen table.

Anxious to get started fixing the house again, I moved quietly; I knew any sound I made would echo through the rooms and wake Laurel. Organizing the rest of the office would be productive and would not disturb our daughter. I poured another cup of coffee and walked downstairs.

I glanced over at the closed guestroom door and quietly walked into the office. I stood in awe as I watched Jim's printer lit up as soon as I opened the door.

Timidly I sat in the chair and moved the keyboard closer. I had started keeping track of what was happening in the house, quickly scratching out notes on pads of paper and the backs of napkins. I gathered all the little pieces of paper and began creating a list, unsure of what I was doing or why. Chills ran up my spine as I typed.

8:35 am - Water Room Closed

8:40 am - Man talking on Staircase.. There has to be an explanation; check vent

8:41 am – The water room door opened- I CLOSED IT! I closed it again jiggled the handle to make sure cats could not push it open

10:00 am – Man talking on the staircase; I cannot understand what he says.

Before I could finish, I heard the distinctive happy voice. "Good morning, Mom!"

I jumped up to greet her. "You're up early; how did you sleep?" I asked.

"Not good. I had so much trouble staying asleep. I think your ghosts were trying to say hello to me last night."

"Oh silly, there is no ghost," I said.

I was delighted to have someone so open-minded to talk to about the house. Laurel is not just a believer in the paranormal but has had experiences since she was young.

It's interesting that although I did not believe in ghosts, I did believe her. It would not be until much later that I realized that I also had experiences when I was young.

Perhaps my own life was so scary that there was no room for anything else.

We walked upstairs, and I poured her a cup of coffee. Laurel asked question after question. "Where did you hear the banging?"

"Which lights went off and on?"

" Tell me about the voice you heard."

"What happened in this room?"

Despite my feelings concerning the paranormal, Laurel's questions made it all seem routine and comforting.

In the first week, other than my daughter's inability to sleep through the night, everything else was seemingly uneventful. Laurel had put down a deposit on an apartment in town while still in California. I was excited to find out the manager had let her know the apartment was unavailable for another two months and her job would not start for another three weeks. So we would have lots of time to tour the town and spend quality time together.

For weeks, we painted walls together, laughed, watched movies, and talked while I waited for something to happen. Ultimately, it did.

"Mom!" Laurel screamed from the staircase.

I bolted into the kitchen, "What! Are you okay?"

"Look! I thought you said it did not work?" Laurel said, pointing to the ceiling fan spinning wildly out of control.

"It doesn't, "I whispered.

I watched the fan swinging left to right from the force of the blades swirling at dizzying speeds.

"Laurel, come up here in case it falls off the ceiling."

We sat in the dining room, watching the blades turning violently and listening to the strange sounds coming from downstairs. The dogs were softly growling as they looked up at the fan, and the cats cried out from one of the lower rooms.

We both looked at each other in silent agreement; *'this was not normal.'*

"You all right, Mom?"

"Yes, of course, it's weird but not a ghost…."

"Oh, okay, yeah, there's no ghosts. I forgot. Since there is no ghost in the house, I say tonight we try to talk to it."

"What?" I asked

"Yeah, let's talk to it. Dad is gone; we don't have anything else to do tonight. Do you have a recorder?"

"Yeah, come to think of it, I do. Alright, but I think it's silly."

I did think it was silly until I thought of the man talking on the staircase. If I could record the voice, maybe I could figure out where it was coming from; I wrapped my sweater around me tighter. The house was colder than usual, and the sun had set here earlier than in California. By three-thirty, darkness immersed the house.

I watched my daughter jump from her chair and run down the dark stairway.

"Laurel, I'm brewing a pot of coffee. Do you need a snack or something to go with it?" I yelled.

Laurel reappeared with her arms tightly wrapped around two notebooks, a stack of loose papers, and a fist full of pencils.

"Mom!" she shrieked, "You can't eat or drink anything while we are talking to the ghost!"

"Who says?" I asked.

"I looked it up on the internet. It said no eating or drinking, and there can be no other sounds at all. We have to be very quiet. Please, Mom, no coffee until after we are finished."

"Well, if you read it on the internet, it must be true!" I laughed.

"Oh, Mom, before we start, we have to think up some questions to ask."

"Questions?" I asked with a smile.

Watching my daughter drop the pile of papers and notebooks she had been cradling in her arms as the pencils scattered across the dining room floor.

"Well yeah, we have to ask questions!" Laurel exclaimed.

"Okay, what should we ask?"

I smiled, watching Laurel feverishly numbering the pages and scribbling questions. She seemed so excited and carried herself with new confidence I had not seen before. As senseless as I thought this was, I could only observe in amazement with a smile on my face, amused by her level of excitement.

"Question one: Did you die in this house?" Laurel announced.

"How about, why are you here? What do you want?" I suggested.

"That's good. And number three: Are you upset people are in the house?"

Laurel explained how she had read up on communicating with *The Entities,* as she called them.

I smiled, watching her set up and light the candles. I giggled to myself as I watched her tediously setting the pads of paper and pencils on the table like a place setting for dinner.

"We need your camera too." She squealed.

I went to the bedroom to find the recorder and camera. Checking the camera for batteries, I glanced at Laurel's notebook and skimmed over the questions.

Is there anyone here who would like to speak to us?

1. Do you live here?
2. Why are you here?
3. What do you want?
4. Are you upset that people are in the house?
5. What is your name?
6. Did you die in this house.
7. Are you the one making noises?

"Okay, mom, do you have the camera and tape recorder?"

I giggled." Yes, Laurel, I am all ready to catch the ghost!"

"Okay, let's turn out the lights and begin," Laurel said in her most serious voice.

I tried not to laugh with the house dark and candles glowing; it felt like a movie set.

"Is the recorder on?" she asked

"Yes," I answered.

"Okay, time is 9:30 pm." Laurel proclaimed.

In her most serious voice, Laurel asked her first question.

"Is there anyone here who would like to speak to us?"

Sitting still and quiet for so long, I finally felt compelled to break the silence.

"How long do we wait for Mr. Spooky to answer us?" I asked sarcastically.

"Mom, you have to take this seriously. The website said not to joke around; it makes them mad." Suddenly Laurel began to giggle herself.

"Okay, okay, your right, it is kinda funny. Okay, let's try again." Laurel laughed

"Is there anyone here who would like to speak to us?" I asked

We both sat quietly for about two minutes.

"Do you live here?" Laurel asked.

Another few minutes passed, and Laurel motioned to my notebook.

"What is your name?" I asked.

We waited

"Are you the one banging and knocking?" Laurel asked.

A low growl came from the kitchen. I looked at Laurel; her startled face almost made me laugh, reminding me of her cute expressions when she was little.

"Are you okay?" I asked.

"Mom, Shhh," Laurel said.

"Are you angry we are here?" Laurel sheepishly asked.

Both puppies jumped from their beds, running into the dining room, barking, and growling. Their persistent snarling grew louder.

Laurel looked at me with eyes big as saucers. "Oh shit, Mom!"

"It's nothing they've done this before. Puppies, calm down."

"When?" she asked, "I have never seen them act like this."

"Laurel, maybe we should stop," I yelled over the growling.

"Oh yeah, I'm good with that," Laurel said.

I stood up and flipped the switch to the chandelier. The second we stopped, the recorder and the room flooded with light, and both dogs instantly stopped growling and barking.

"Let's check and see if we have anything here." Laurel grabbed the recorder.

"Now, I'll make coffee." I walked into the kitchen, watching the little dogs prancing back to their bed.

"Okay, ready, Mom."

I could hear Laurel's voice echoing from the little box,

'Okay, time is 9:30 pm.

'Is there anyone here who would like to speak to us? '

How long do we wait for Mr. Spooky to answer us?'

A background noise I attributed to the refrigerator began to rumble out of the recorder.

'Do you live here?'

Silence.

"Guess not!" I laughed from the kitchen.

'What is your name?'

'Are you the one banging and knocking?'

I looked up the minute I heard it, "Wait! Laurel, rewind it."

Laurel backed up the recorder and turned the volume up this time. The machine echoed the all too familiar sound of the little dogs barking and snarling as the audio playback filled the room.

A distinctively different tone, a higher-pitched female child voice ominously played back.

'Uh Oh!' the young female voice surrounded the room.

Laurel rewound and played the sound again. "Mom, that sounds like a little girl's voice."

"It does. That was kind of creepy; I wonder what it was." I said.

Laurel turned the player back on.

'Are you angry we are here?'

'Yap yap bark bark bark--- I DON'T' GIVE A FUCK! --- Yap yap bark bark.'

"Oh my god, Mom, did you hear that?"

I had heard it. The man's voice sent chills up my spine, but I did not want to react. I could feel my entire body tense up. *The man from the truck almost sounds like the man from the truck!* Hearing the voice made me question the sound, was it reproduced from the recorder or was it all just my mind and me.

I brought in the coffee cups and sat down. "What did you hear, Laurel?"

She looked at me with a shocked expression. "You didn't hear that?

"It was hard to hear with the dogs barking so loud. Play it again."

I was unwilling to discuss the idea that this sounded like the voice I had been remembering. I looked into Laurel's eyes, and I could see she was getting scared. I wondered if she could see I was even more frightened.

"Okay, listen!" Laurel shouted.

'Are you angry we are here?'

'Yap yap bark bark bark--- I DON'T' GIVE A FUCK! --- Yap yap bark bark.'

"Well, what do you hear?" I asked again.

"It's a man saying, I don't give a fuck. You can't hear him!"

Laurel yelled.

In an instant, I realized my concern over learning the identity of this man's voice; I had readily accepted the idea we had recorded a man talking in our home.

"Yeah, it does, and it's probably just a noise that sounds like a man," I said.

Frustrated, Laurel picked up the recorder and walked to the kitchen.

"Mom let's turn it on and just leave it in here and let it play. Let's see what else we can get." her eyes big and her voice shaking.

"Okay, let's go to my room and watch T.V. for a while." I was trying to make light of the whole thing so as not to scare her anymore.

I never expected to record voices, but this voice sounded familiar. The accent, the way he enunciated his foul language.

It was hours before I was able to fall asleep.

I had to stop thinking of those men and that night. That horrible night, the doctors had told me it was just too terrifying to remember.

Oh my God, am I starting to remember?

CHAPTER 19

CHAPTER 19
SOMETHING IS HERE

The weeks seemed to fly by like days.

Laurel started her job. I missed her during the day but was thankful I was not alone at night.

The unexplained noises were not reserved for the dark. Things were just as frightening in the light of day as they could be at 2:00 am.

One night Laurel returned from work to see the fan slowly turning again.

"When did that start moving again?"

"About an hour ago. I tried to stop it, but it started again."

"Why is it moving?" she asked.

"I don't know."

"Mom, turn on the camera; how did you stop it? What did you use?"

"I used the mop."

Laurel ran to the closet to retrieve the mop and held it up to the slow-moving blades. The fan came to a complete stop. She put the mop away, nonchalantly requesting.

"If you're a ghost, move the fan again."

I backed up to get the whole fan in the video as the fan slowly moved.

"Can you make it go faster?" I said impulsively. Immediately I felt embarrassed. I knew Laurel would not judge me; I was judging myself. *How could I be this person? I don't believe in this stuff.*

I continued to video the fan in awe as it seemed to respond to Laurel's commands.

"Move the fan faster?"

The fan seemed to respond and increased in speed. It was very subtle, but it was moving faster.

"Faster," Laurel said.

"Faster!"

Again, it increased just ever so slightly.

"Mom, let's replay the video."

I loaded the digital camera card into my computer.

The movie showed the fan reacting to Laurels' commands.

"Mom, it's like it's listening to me. It's really doing it!"

WATCH: Chapter 19: SOMETHING IS HERE
SCAN QR Code - KEEP OPEN

"Well, it can't be responding to you. Not possible, but your right; it looks like it can hear you." I giggled.

"Are you at least willing to record some more?" Laurel asked.

I went to the bedroom and retrieved the tiny recorder. Walking back in, I was surprised at how quickly Laurel had set up the table again. She lit the candle in the center of the dining room table.

"Put the recorder on the loft wall so we can record from the center of the house. We should be able to record anything happening from this vantage point."

"Okay, silly," I said.

"Mom, this is not silly!" Laurel snapped.

"Honey, relax; there are no such things as ghosts; there can't be," I said.

"Why, Mom?" Laurel retorted. "Is it because you don't believe in it? How do you explain it?"

"Wait, What was that?" she whispered as a strange moaning sound came from the other room.

"I don't know. Are you sure you want to do this? I don't want you to be scared." I said.

"Mom, come on. Now we are supposed to be quiet for a while and focus, and we can start asking questions again once a few minutes have passed."

Laurel tore the page of questions in half.

"You ask these," She tossed the torn paper at me.

My daughter seemed so intense it almost scared me. At first, the whole thing seemed adorable and funny, watching my daughter's passionate interest in something so foolish, but it was not cute anymore. It frightened me to see her acting like this, but at the same time, I also understood. Things happening in this house were, at times, so incredible it had become an obsessive interest of mine as well.

After forty-five minutes, we had read all ten questions. I turned on the lights and brought the recorder into the dining room.

"Great!" Laurel's face lit up with excitement as she held the recorder to her ear.

"You play it back. I'll make dinner. Don't hold that thing too close; the dogs barked so loud it will hurt your ears."

I watched her with concern as I pulled the plates from the cabinet.

"Hear anything?"

She looked sharply over at her mother with annoyance, "Mom, shhh!"

I pulled the pan closer and sliced two pieces of chicken as I kept glancing at my daughter

"What?" I asked.

Laurel's eyes opened wide. "Mom, we recorded someone again."

I scooped the potatoes onto each plate and left them in the kitchen due to my overwhelming curiosity.

"Can I hear it?"

Laurel leaned over close to me, set the small recorder between us, and pressed play.

'Are you upset people are in the house?'

The recorded barking was so loud it was hard to listen to, but I could hear the man behind the ear-piercing sounds from the dogs.

'Bark bark FUCK IT! Bark bark FUCK THIS! Bark yap yap bark.'

"Well, we can both hear it. Maybe it has something to do with the dogs barking, and it just sounds like…."

"What!" Laurel screamed. "Come on, Mom, you heard it too! You heard this person talking on the tape before. You heard the little girl; even Dad said it sounded like a little girl's voice. How much evidence do you need?"

"I think we are just hearing sounds so unfamiliar to us our minds are trying to make sense of it. I did some research on it. It's called The Pareidolia Effect; our brains tend to recognize patterns in random things. It's why sometimes people see a face in the clouds or Jesus on their toast. There is also Audio Pareidolia, so maybe our brains are just trying to reconcile what we are hearing. With the barking in the background, we just can't be sure it's a person."

"What about the lady you heard say hello, and the guy *we both* heard talking on the staircase?" Laurel shouted.

Just a week before, we had been heading up the stairs to start dinner. As we rounded the staircase landing, we both heard a man talking. Neither of us could distinguish what the man was saying, just an inaudible couple of words. It led us to try to record something downstairs. We heard nothing with our ears during that time, but when we played the tape back, we both listened to a man with a very raspy voice say, "SYBIL'S PALE." I remembered hearing that before.

Months ago, I called the phone company to complain about what I thought was a party line. A caller breathed into the phone and simply said, "Sybil's Pale."

"I don't know, sound refraction like your brother said. All I do know; is you have no reason to be scared."

"So, why do you keep your gun loaded?" Laurel asked.

"Because most of the noises in this house sound like someone is breaking in. I am worried about it being an intruder, not a ghost!"

"I think it's haunted, Mom; the house is haunted!"

"I know you do, and maybe it is, but maybe there are other reasons we don't understand yet. Let's just eat dinner" I walked back into the kitchen and slid the plates into the pass-thru.

We sat at the table quietly, eating dinner.

Tap Tap Tap

Followed shortly by what sounded like a door closing downstairs and, just as random and quick, a knocking sound.

"Haunted, it's haunted, Mom," Laurel said, not even looking up from her plate.

"No, it's…."

"It's haunted!" Laurel laughed. "Why is this so hard for you to accept? We are both hearing and feeling the same things."

"Laurel, I'm getting pretty tired. I think I'm going to bed. Are you going to be alright?"

"Sure, I'm going to stay up and listen to this with headphones."

In bed, exhausted, I knew it would be some time before I would be able to sleep. Laurel's question rang through my head *'Why is this so hard for you to accept?* 'My denial of what was happening remained secret even to myself. I sat up in response to the timid knock on the door.

"Mom?" the door creaked as she opened it slowly.

"If I blow up the air mattress, can I sleep in here on the side of your bed?"

Before I could answer, Laurel rushed in with a pile of blankets and pillows. I giggled at the sight of my grown daughter, who now resembled the seven-year-old version of herself.

"I brought my headphones; I want to listen to the rest of this tape." Laurel snickered.

"Good night, sweetheart." I closed my eyes and thought, *How wonderful it felt having her here.*

Such a relief not to be alone. I am no longer alone in believing we are not alone. I smiled and closed my eyes.

The next morning, I found Laurel sitting at the kitchen table anxiously perusing her notebook. Before I could utter a good morning, my daughter excitedly instructed me

"Mom, you have to sit down; there was a lot of stuff on the recorder. Like a lot of people, you have to hear this!"

"Okay, coffee first."

Laurel pressed play, and instantly the recorder bellowed out a man's voice.

"What the hell is this?" Laurel asked.

"Who is that?" I asked

"I never heard this before; I don't know. I listened to this tape last night, and I never heard this." Laurel said in a frantic voice.

Can you play it again? I didn't understand what he was saying" I asked. I sat at the table, sipping my coffee as Laurel replayed the recording.

The voice was male and unintelligible except for the words

'Hell No.'

We both stared at each other in amazement.

"I don't understand how this could be on the recorder." Laurel said with a frightened look on her face.

"So, can you tell me what you were listening to last night?" I asked

Laurel read the questions and explained what she documented as the perceived answer as she read aloud.

"It sounds like more than one person is talking, and then it sounds like different people are answering the questions. Some of them are hard to hear but listen." Laurel picked up the recorder to replay the previous night's recordings for me.

"Oh shit, shit! I think I deleted it. Can you get it back?" Laurel screeched.

"No, but it's okay. Can I see your notebook?"

"Shit! Sorry, Mom," Laurel slid the book to me.

"It doesn't matter. I will load it into the computer right away next time. Has anything else happened, anything weird?" I asked as I slid her notebook to my side of the table.

A look of wild excitement engulfed her young face, "Hell yeah!" Laurel shrieked.

I turned the pages of notes she had made—five pages of what appeared to be people talking amongst themselves.

"Can I ask you some questions?" I asked as I made a note at the top of the empty page.

"Sure," Laurel said.

I quickly scribbled the list of some of the strange things she had experienced in the house.

Laurel:

1. Footsteps (three times) sounded like heavy boots stomping on the floor with pacing.

She thought her dad was getting out of bed, then remembered he was not home.

2. She could hear someone in the kitchen; things were tapping like someone was looking for something. She thought we were in the kitchen until she came up and realized we were asleep.

3. Walking sounds, up and down the stairs. She thought maybe cats but saw cats sleeping, and the steps were too heavy.

4. Eerie feelings when she approaches the office door- like someone is staring at her.

5. Banging on the walls, always different walls and different places, sounded like someone was kicking the walls from outside.

6. The far corner of the living room feels like someone is staring at her.

7. When she walks past the window by the staircase, her hair stands up, and she feels creeped out.

"I expected to see someone walking around the living room, but there was no one there!" Laurel exclaimed.

I wrote as fast as I could.

8. The closet doors in the office moved on their own.

9. Feels like someone in the office is staring at her into the window from outside

10. Too cold in the office, and it feels like the wind is blowing, but no windows open.

11. Feeling like someone was right next to her in the guest room, and a man whispered into her ear. "Hey hey," and Laurel ran out of the room.

I was shocked for a moment as I heard Laurel's voice change. I wrote one more entry.

12. Laurel is now almost in tears(telling t me) – every night after going to sleep within thirty minutes, she feels like someone is standing over her staring at her.

"Mom, I know you keep saying it's not, but this house is haunted. I can feel it, Mom; there is something here. I'm not crazy!"

I looked into my daughter's eyes and realized I could no longer do this. The more I denied and made excuses for what may be happening, the more I watched my daughter question *her* sanity. My denegation intended to keep Laurel from being scared had created the feeling I knew too well. It is more frightening to see these things and fear your judgment and mental stability than to fear a ghost.

I hesitated for a moment and said what Laurel had been waiting to hear.

"I can feel it too. No, you are not crazy. Neither of us is crazy; something is here."

Security Camera Captures Movement

CHAPTER:20

CHAPTER 20
ORBS

Temperatures had gone down to nineteen degrees below zero. Every day we shoveled snow off the roofs and deck. After finishing the backbreaking chore, we huddled with hot cocoa or coffee near the fireplace. Even with the cold outside, it was almost impossible to stay indoors. The piled-up snow on the trees was breathtaking. The sun shined on the white blanket covering our entire property; everywhere, the snow glistened like diamonds. The winds had blown the snow onto every surface. What had been a forest of dozens of shades of green was now a land of pristine pure white.

The house continued to make strange noises, banging-tapping-knocking; one day, while I was alone in the house, I even heard someone sneezing. My camera was nearby, and I was able to snap a picture in the direction of the sound. I was already in the practice of taking pictures to check paint colors, capture the snowy landscape, and show Sandy and the kids the progress on the house.

One night Laurel and I heard a loud bang near the office.

Frantic and immediately engaged, Laurel yelled, "Mom, quick, take a picture!" I grabbed my camera and took one image of the hallway next to the office door.

Not giving much credence to the photo, I waited to look at the image the next day. I thought it was silly, but this particular picture changed my mind.

I had already taken dozens of photos and never saw anything like it, a large pink and purple circular spot.

I went through past pictures and found the one I took when I heard the most unexpected sound downstairs. The sound was someone sneezing, and two bright white circles near the ceiling showed up in the picture.

Most of the house pictures seemed normal, although some had misty shapes I could not explain.

We do smoke, so at first, I thought the irregular forms were simply due to cigarette smoke or particles in the air from smoking. Later I attempted different experiments with smoke and photos, and nothing came out with any results even closely matching, and there was the fact we were *not smoking* inside the house at the time.

These matched what people refer to as orbs or light anomalies. I remembered hearing a long time ago; that some ghost hunter had dismissed the idea of Orbs because they had proven to be dust or moisture in the air. I never gave it much thought or cared about any of it. Of course, it would be dust; that made sense to me at the time.

Along with the smoke experiments, I also did a series of dust and mist tests. The one thing I found that stayed consistent was dust and mist orbs moved in the same direction (as long as there was no air source). While doing these tests, we discovered that from 1:00 am to 2:30 am; our security cameras would pick up the sphere-shaped objects as it would for an intruder- We called it the Orbing Hours. The camera recorded them coming through the windows and moving in strange directions. At that time, everyone was asleep, and we turned off the a/c or heat before bed.

The strange round lights and other images we have captured are typically called Light Anomalies.

WATCH: Chapter 20: ORBS
SAME QR Code

When we took a photo in the location of an unexplained sound, there was a striking difference. I thought perhaps it was just a coincidence, so I started leaving cameras close so I could grab one if I heard an unexplainable sound.

I still was not sure if I believed this was paranormal or not. I did not know what I thought anymore. One thing I knew, all our pictures seemed reasonable unless there was an unexplainable noise. If one of us could take a picture quick enough, crazy-looking forms and translucent balls of light would appear. Sometimes there would only be one, and it was usually the size of a large pizza or car tire. I had seen small orb-like things appear in pictures before, but I still had never seen anything like the strange things in these photos.

A few days earlier, Laurel and I started to make a recording downstairs but stopped within just a few minutes after we heard it. The recorder was on, but we were not even ready to sit down yet when we heard what sounded like two women talking right next to us. It was shocking for both of us. We were unsure if this was another language or even gibberish, but it precisely recorded how we heard it. The camera was already on, and I took a picture almost instantly. I expected to photograph maybe two women standing beside us. When I reviewed the film, it was another giant pizza-sized orb. The orb situated itself right in front of one of the chairs. If it were dust, then surely there would be more than one. Later, when I slowed down the tape, it was mind-blowing. What we thought was two women was one woman saying, 'Get in the chair now.' I couldn't call this a coincidence or dust. I have chills writing about it now.

One afternoon I heard strange sounds coming from all over the house, then music from the staircase. I took a few quick pictures, and there were dozens of orbs as if they were descending the stairs.

If this were dust or moisture, something still needed to be the cause. What stirred up the dust? Where did the music come from? A few so-called experts told me not to call them Orbs, and they are meaningless. My experience in this house tells me differently. The staircase has never displayed that gathering of orbs again.

Laurel and I made a tremendous amount of progress on the house and got it ready for Joshua to come and visit. The sounds in the house continued, knocking on doors, walls, and windows. Occasional talking seemed to come from nowhere. Icy cold blasts of air arrived without explanation, and then there were the lights….

First, it was the Christmas lights on the staircase.

It started the first day I set them up. I carefully wrapped the thick pine garland and Christmas lights to the handrail and banister. At first, I thought the lights were broken or shorting out. Each time I approached the lights, they would flash off, but they turned back on as soon as I walked away. Once I got my camera and started recording it, they did the opposite. Turning on when I got close, but they turned off as soon as I walked away. This strange game went on for about ten minutes and stopped. (not to happen again until the following year.) Of course, the first thing I suspected was a short in the wiring or even the socket, but it stopped as if someone just got tired of playing this game.

Lightbulbs were dying; some exploded into a wave of glass fragments, the remaining lights seemed to flicker whenever they felt like it.

We had a fantastic time together at Christmas, just an average family celebrating the holidays. Jim was home, Joshua flew in from California, and Laurel gave him the guest room and stayed in the office. We stayed up late talking and laughing every night; we watched movies, played cards, drank tons of hot cocoa, and ate every meal laughing at the table. The house felt calm and peaceful, like almost every Christmas we had in our other place.

Very soon, things changed. Our conversations were almost all focused on the house, strange noises- smells, and moving doors. Josh told us he had shut the closet door, and when he went back into the room, the door was open every time. The knocking and banging sounds were keeping him awake. By the second night, she was unable to sleep in the office.

She insisted the closet door in the room would shake by itself, and the room would get even colder than its average 50 degrees. She heard noises, saw shadows, and started saying, "I know I am not crazy!" I knew that feeling all too well. As the words come out of your mouth, you can feel the self-condemnation flooding you. I knew just what to say to them to make them both feel better. "I believe you."

Having these experiences together just drew us closer than ever. There is something bonding about it; it also helped me understand I was okay.

While Josh and Laurel were still sleeping, I baked a cake for Joshua's sobriety birthday. Jim left to run a few errands, the cake had cooled, and I had spent a long time on my feet decorating it. I went and sat down at the kitchen table to rest my back. The entire house was peaceful. I let out a long sigh. Then, I heard something I had not heard before. Similar to nails on a chalkboard. A loud scratching sound. At first, I couldn't locate where it was coming from; then, I sat in horror as I watched one of the arched windows slowly cracking. It was starting from the bottom, and as if in deliberate slow motion, it slowly splintered to the top.

The glass company could not repair the window in the snow, so we waited until spring to get it fixed. I was so grateful we had double-panned windows. When the workers came out, I asked the supervisor what made it crack and how to prevent this from happening to the other windows.

He just shook his head and said. "I couldn't tell you; I have no idea why this cracked in the first place. Just one of those things, I guess. I wouldn't worry about it happening again."

Things like this happen in all houses. The window cracking was not what surprised me. I had never lived in temperatures like these before, and for all I knew, this was just something that happens when it reached below zero outside. It was the slow and methodical way it happened, an eerie five minutes of the inside pane screeching its way to the top while I sat and watched as if it was sending a message at the time I interpreted as "fuck you."

CHAPTER 21
NEW FRIENDS

Time had rushed by while Laurel was still in the house. Finally, the time had come, and Laurel moved into her apartment. My total focus was now back on the house, repairing it, decorating it, and listening to it. Snow still falling every morning created an ominous quiet outside, while the strange noises inside intensified. Bangs and thumps startled me daily.

Nothing happened the same way or even in the same place. Cold spots would always be in a different part of the house. It would have made sense to me if the cold spots were the same place, but it was always different, on the same day or even at the same hour. One area of the house would seem normal for a while, and out of nowhere, a blast of cold air would send us shivering.

Devices or appliances would flash on and off in one room, and the next day the electrical disturbance would focus on another place in the house. It seemed to be some kind of short in the electrical system. However, the next day it would be on the other side of the house. One day, many of the lights in the house would individually flash off and on as if speaking to us in Morse code. If it were only electrical problems, it would have never occurred to me any of this was paranormal.

The only pattern I could see was it seemed each occurrence took turns. If the fan were moving, nothing else would happen until it stopped. A light in the living room would flash off and on and then stop entirely before another unexplained event would take place. Sandy and I joked if ghosts were making these things happen; they were very polite and never interrupted each other.

The dogs continued to react to something I could not see. The little puppies never seemed to sleep anymore. The barking and growling would happen day and night. It was hard to take the high-pitched barking all day long, but the night was the hardest. Being sound asleep, waking to the sudden loud barking, and repeated growling each night had frazzled my nerves. I would start to relax every time the house went quiet. The sudden snarling and barking reignited my fears and concerns about the house. The dogs were also being affected by their lack of sleep.

I was sure my apprehensiveness would be relieved when we moved the puppies to the garage. Some of this anxiety had to be from lack of sleep. Barkley and Briquette had never adjusted to the house. The nightly barking and growling became too stressful and took a toll on us. Reluctantly, we decided to move them out of the house. Jim built a sectioned-off area with sleeping, food, water, and even an emergency place for potty pads. I filled it with expensive pillows and blankets. It was a temporary place for them; I never believed they would have accepted this, and I was later shocked when they did not want to come back into the house.

"I'm so sorry, puppies; I love you so much." I cried the morning I took them out to their new home. I felt overcome with guilt. These two little puppies had done everything in their power to protect me, guard me, and be my companions when I was alone. I felt I owed them; how could I put them out there alone? Part of me felt like this was so cruel after all they had done.

Watching their little tails wag inside the new house, I could see they were happier here, no more barking all night long, no more shaking in fear.

"I love you guys," I said as I plugged in a night lite for them. I wondered what it would be like now, with no one to look out for me when Jim was gone.

The cats did not want anything to do with me, running for cover whenever anyone came down the stairs.

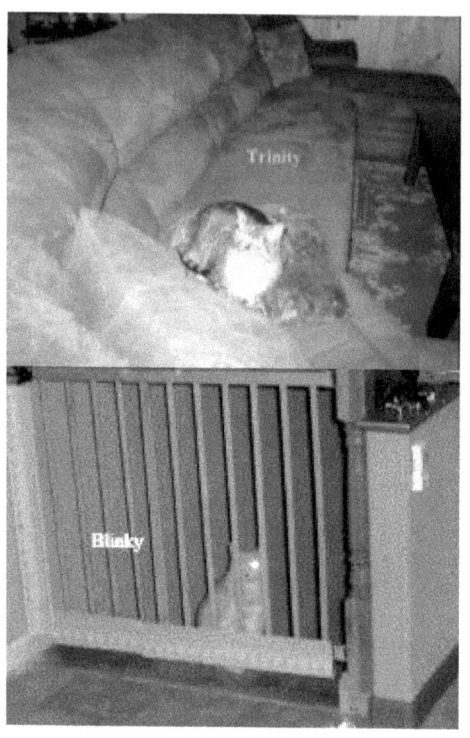

Laurel had moved out, and Jim was only home on the weekends. On the nights Jim was away, Laurel would occasionally come over and spend the night. We would blow up the air mattress, drag in the blankets and pillows from the guest room and drag them back in the morning. It seemed like so much trouble to go through. I had asked her why she went to so much inconvenience, and her answer always remained the same.

"I love you and miss you, Mom; I just want to hang out."

Laurel would not say why, but she did not sleep in the guest room again until many years later.

I told Jim how much I wanted another dog, a dog who would like to hang out with me. Days before, he had told me that he had concerns about my being alone, and he felt another dog might be the answer. I did not share all of my reasons for wanting another dog with Jim.

It was unsettling when Barkley and Briquette would bark and growl at things they could only see. It made the whole thing so much more frightening. I could not fall back on "maybe it was my imagination" when they could hear and see it too. Now I was alone, to hear and see things I had never believed could happen. The cats were so frightened they rarely came out and lived mainly in the room we set up as a gym. As alarming as it was to have the puppies reacting all the time, I realized there had been some comfort in it as well. They were happy now, and I was unwilling to drag them back inside.

Alone in the house, I questioned my sanity once again. After researching dog breeds, I told Jim I wanted a Husky. I had always thought they were beautiful but could never have one in California due to the extreme heat. Now we had the cold temperatures and space a Husky would need. What was the decisive factor for me? Huskies do not bark.

TALA

Jim found me another friend within a week. He drove the dog

home from Seattle. As he walked through the door, almost immediately, he announced, "This girl stinks; she needs a bath now!" and he placed the adorable Siberian husky puppy in my hands. I wrapped my arms around my husband, thanking him for this beautiful gift. After researching names on the internet for days, I decided to name my new friend Tala Dakota (according to the internet, this was Sioux Indian for Wolf Friend).

A problematic new puppy meant my attention was on the dog and not the house. Within weeks, I scheduled an appointment with Lori McCallister, an in-home dog trainer who would soon become my friend.

I watched as the red four-wheel drove up to our steep driveway with ease and smiled as I watched her eagerly waving at me as if we were already great friends.

"Helloooo, I'm Lori." She sang in a bubbly, friendly voice.

"Hi, thank you so much for coming out here."

Before I could reach out to shake hands, she was already giving me a quick hug.

"No problem," she said as I walked her inside.

"What a lovely home you have. Can we sit for a moment and discuss what you would like to get out of this?

"Of course, thank you again for being willing to come out here."

Lori explained how she preferred to train dogs on their territory, and she made it a practice of doing in-home training whenever possible.

"Training in a strange place will make the dog act differently than they do at home. This way, I can see the problems."

I guided her to the kitchen table and poured her a glass of soda. We hit it off right away. I felt impressed by how at ease I felt with this stranger, and her sparkling positive attitude gave me a sense of peace. We focused on the new puppy, and Lori asked more about Barkley and Briquette.

"We had to move them in the garage; for now, they are just not happy in the house."

"What was the problem?"

I did not know what to say. I just sat stunned by the question, feeling the unease brimming up inside. Finally, I found the courage to say something.

"They're uncomfortable and bark all the time at something we… None of us can sleep. We made them a home in the garage. They just did not like it in the house. Some different things have happened here and…."

The moment the words left my mouth, I regretted it. Why would I say this to a total stranger? Oh, my god, this woman will think I am insane.

To my surprise, my new friend responded with no judgments and made me feel as if this was nothing but a typical conversation.

"What exactly do you mean by different?"

"Well, I can't believe I am saying this to a person I just met, but there are a lot of strange things happening here. Our kids think the house is haunted."

She sat looking at me and finally responded.

"Well, I'm so sorry to say it this way, I visit a lot of houses, and your house does have a little different feel to it. This is not like me. I just feel very comfortable with you. I would never say anything like this to a new client or any client! The moment I walked in, I did feel something unusual. It's not really scary in your house only, only that room behind me makes me feel a little uneasy." Lori said.

My stomach turned as I watched Lori point to the arched-shaped cutouts in the living room wall where I had felt the stares of someone I could never see. I shared with my new friend some of the unexplained things I experienced.

We were both astonished by our straightforwardness with each other and talked for another two hours.

"No matter what happens, you have me to talk with, I believe you. I can tell there is something unusual here. If it gets scary, call me. As for your new dog, just work on the things we talked about, and I will be back next week."

"Thanks, Lori; talk to you soon."

"It's probably angels!" Lori yelled back as she climbed into her car. I smiled as I watched my cheerful new friend waving from her car before disappearing into the trees.

CHAPTER 22

CHAPTER 22
IT CAN TOUCH US

Turning towards the living room, I noticed the box of light bulbs now precariously sitting on the edge of the coffee table. I sighed. Jim had seemed aggravated by the weekend rituals of replacing light bulbs. Dragging the new bulbs to the ceiling lamps preparing to replace the blown bulbs, only to discover they had unscrewed themselves.

I had initially thought, perhaps, it was normal for a bulb to do this in colder temperatures.

I mean, with the severe cold comes contraction, and with the warmth comes expansion, right?

I asked Lori how many times she had had this happen at her house, and her response surprised me. *I have never even heard of that before!*

I added it to the list of weird shit we had not experienced before.

I checked online and did find some information:

💡 **Light bulbs may unscrew themselves due to thermal cycling, metal contracting, and expanding from the temperatures of the lamp. Light bulbs would never fully unscrew themselves from the fixture**

That did not explain the night I walked up to our dining room chandelier, and I reached up to check if the seemingly burned-out light had unscrewed itself like the others. Before I could touch it, the bulb fell into my hand. According to the explanations I could find, this was not possible; someone had to unscrew it.

I picked up the box of bulbs, walked into the kitchen, and smiled, thinking of Jim's new attitude about the house. I am not sure if he fully understands what it meant to me to hear him finally say he was having strange experiences also, even if he still felt there was an explanation other than the paranormal. We had talked for hours about the things we had seen. I showed him I had changed my journal of events into a book, and his reaction surprised me. He was proud of me and had no concerns about the book's contents. He encouraged me to keep writing and not hold anything back. He confided in me he thought we would have to move. He had discussed the situation with his boss,

"….if it becomes too much for my wife to be alone in the house, we will have to move and sell."

Instantly I understood what appeared to me to be an unwillingness to talk about it was concern about my being here alone. Jim was more open with me now about his experiences. One afternoon he came out of the main bathroom and announced,

"Well, I have something for you to put in the book. Your husband can hear a little girl talking in the bathroom."

While he sometimes still declared his unbelief and skepticism, he also purchased additional cameras and a new digital recorder.

I placed the box of light bulbs in the cabinet and answered the phone. The next few hours I spent catching up with the kids. Laurel talked about her job, new friends, living in her new apartment, and the frustration of removing snow from her car every morning.

Our oldest son was very busy with art school and work but made time to tell me he was in love, which explained the recent lack of phone calls.

Josh seemed only concerned with my health and expressed his concern I was alone in the house so much.

"No, silly, I'm all right. I have the new dog, the house is still not finished, and there is a ton of work to keep me busy." I said.

"But… you're not scared? There's a lot of weird stuff in that….."

The phone went dead before he could finish his sentence. I tried to call him back; however, there was no dial tone. It rang again minutes later.

Josh's voice, filled with tension and worry, rang out, "MOM! MOM! Are you okay?"

"Yes, why?" I asked, confused.

"MOM!" he bellowed again, "I could hear a man breathing on the phone. Are you okay? You were talking, and it sounded like someone took the phone from you; your voice was far away, and I could hear a man breathing heavy."

"No, the phone just went dead; I'm alone; everything is okay. Calm down."

He was sure someone had broken into the house and taken the phone from me. He kept describing what he heard, my voice in the background and someone else breathing heavily into the phone. It took thirty minutes to convince him I was safe, and no one was in the house holding me at gunpoint.

I set the phone on the table and looked down at Tala, who gave me the signal I had recently interpreted as its time to go potty. I walked all the dogs around the property, practiced some of the training techniques Lori had taught me, and went inside to make dinner.

I was excited that Jim would be home soon. He would only be back for this one night and would have to leave again in the morning. I walked over to the other side of the kitchen and knelt to open one of the lower cabinets. I pulled the mixing bowl out and set it on the counter; still crouching, I searched for another dish to serve the rice. Before I could find it, I heard the strange sound above me. I looked up and gasped in shock.

I stood up quickly and stepped back, watching as the silver bowl slowly spun in a circle.

I stood in awe as the bowl increased in speed. I could not believe what I was seeing, and it took me a few moments to think about filming it.

I slowly picked up the camera from the other side of the room and turned it on. It seemed to take me forever to find the video setting, and I was sure it would be like so many other times when the activity would stop just as I got the camera ready.

I recorded what I could but quickly abandoned the camera down to my side when I heard a noise behind me. I turned around and saw the dog watching the spinning bowl with me. I checked the camera as soon as it stopped. I had filmed a small part of it, but at least I had some of it. I could not wait to show Jim. When he came home, we talked about the bowl and other things recently happening in the house.

I felt my stomach turn as soon as he explained his schedule for this week. I missed him so much when he was gone.

In the morning, I kissed Jim goodbye and walked out onto the deck to wave goodbye. As soon as he drove off, I grabbed the phone to call Laurel. I told her all about the bowl, but she only focused on the sound of my voice.

"I thought you would be more excited about it," I said.

"I am, and I can't wait to see it, but I am more worried about you. You sound sad. Besides, I told you I think the house is haunted. I wouldn't be surprised if you told me things started flying all around the house!"

We made plans for her to come over and spend a few nights at the house.

The rest of the day was peaceful.

At night before I went to sleep, I stopped to listen to the nightly sounds of the house. Each night they were different, and some nights, although rare, there were no sounds at all. The most common was the creaking door sounds and quiet talking. Over the last week, something new had started to happen. The house began to mimic us.

I first noticed it after giving Tala a dog bath in the tub. I had filled three empty and clean plastic milk containers with clean water to rinse the soap from her fur. With her bath done, my back was intensely hurting. After pulling her out of the tub, I attempted to clean up the bathroom. In frustration, I threw the hollow containers into the empty bathtub. They made a distinct sound as they bounced around the claw-foot bath. Two nights later, while I was alone in the house, I almost came unglued when the exact same sound came from the bathroom. The bottles were put away, and the room cleaned up; there was no explanation for the noise. It was precisely the same unique sound.

After that, it happened at least once a week. Everyday sounds were mimicked in the house:

Keys tossed across a table,

Toilet flushing,

Shower curtain opening and closing,

Refrigerator door closing,

Sneezing,

Coughing,

Kitchen cabinets closing,

Coffee maker,

Walking,

The sound of the stairway gate opening and closing

and Tala's nails tapping on the floor and windows.

One afternoon Jim and I were standing at the kitchen window watching Tala chasing birds in the backyard. Tala ran out of our site; immediately, we could hear her nails hit the window behind us. The same sound they always did when she would jump up on the window to see what we were doing. Tala couldn't make it around the house in only a second and be at the window. We both turned to the window, and of course, Tala was not there. We turned back to the backyard and saw her staring back at us. Months later, it would be common to hear her nails on the wood floor as she walked across our bedroom. I would sit up in bed only to see her soundly sleeping.

I continued my ritual as I did now every night when Jim was gone. Lock all windows and doors, place the 22-caliber handgun next to me, and insert the 38' into the leg holster I had attached to the bedpost.

Most of the sounds were no longer frightening to me. Even the house impersonating us was not scary anymore. However, the noises sounded like someone was breaking into the house, still sending terror slicing through me. Having Tala with me gave me a sense of a ceasefire. She did not wake up in the middle of the night with the intense barking and growling. Her only response to the sounds in the house was usually a slight lifting of her head and looking at me. I would quickly assure her we were okay, and she would fall fast asleep again. I was happy to see she could hear the sounds and even more pleased to see her subdued reactions. She did not respond or interact with the house until she was older.

Jim purchased three night-vision hunting cameras with motion sensors, and I set them up in the house. I hoped to capture shadows I saw out of the corner of my eye or anything to explain what was happening here. It did not happen every day now; in fact, the long pauses in between activities kept sending me back into denialism. Just as I decided the whole thing was a combination of coincidence and imagination, it would start back up again.

Laurel and I recorded a few more unexplained voices. We set up the hunting cameras around the house and checked them twice a week. Many times, there was nothing there at all. The nights we heard noises and faint talking, we would always find something in the photos. The cameras recorded the date, time, and temperature, helping us keep better track of the images. We discovered things we did not know when the activity in the house changed, and so did the temperature. The cameras were motion-activated. Each picture displayed temperature, time, and date. The heat could be 65 degrees in one image, rapidly change by one to ten degrees or more in the next photo, and then return to its original temperature, all within three seconds. What we found on those cameras made no sense, and later they would defy all the laws of reason.

WATCH: Chapter 22: IT CAN TOUCH US
SAME QR Code

After my nightly phone talk with Jim, I curled up under the blankets and went to sleep.

I was jolted awake by the poking. At first, I thought Tala was pawing at me. I sat up to find Tala soundly sleeping on the little brown pillow Jim had brought home the weekend before. I lay down again, wrapped the blankets over my shoulders, and closed my eyes. I felt it again, a poking as if someone were poking my thick blankets hard enough to touch my arm. My eyes shot open, but I stayed still. Only moving my eyes, I glanced first to the hallway and then the side of the bed. I watched as the blanket and puffy comforter moved. I could not believe what I was seeing. As if an invisible finger were poking at me. I slowly sat up, turned on the bedside lamp, and slid the gun out from under Jim's pillow.

CHAPTER 23

CHAPTER 23
ANIMALS REACT TO IT

I walked through the front door struggling with the grocery bags. The dogs were fully engaged and wildly barking at my bedroom door. I had brought them back into the house due to the cold temperature outside. The area experienced a sudden drop in temperature no one seemed to expect.

Piling the groceries in a mound on the granite, I turned when I heard a noise from the bedroom. I could feel my stomach turn as I pulled one of the handguns from the kitchen drawer. A new habit I had developed over the last few months was to make sure every room had some type of weapon.

Slowly I walked into the main bathroom, avoiding the bedroom door. Shaking, I held the gun as steady as I could. Stepping into the bedroom hallway, I was astonished to find no one there. The sounds I had just heard sounded like someone was ransacking my room. Even the dogs had reacted to it. I glanced at the window and the French doors; both verified everything was locked. I was shocked to see the closed window. The noises could not have come from outside. It also would have explained the temperature in the room, which now matched the cold outside.

I timidly walked back into the kitchen. Barkley and Briquette had crawled back under the table, hiding under their blankets. I went back outside to retrieve the last groceries and heaved them onto the counter. The room was eerily still and quiet. Then I heard my bedroom door creak. I glanced down the hall to the front door, hoping I had just left it open, and this was an easily explainable wind draft. The wooden door was open, but the glass panes of the storm door we opened in the summer were shut tight and locked.

I turned and watched in terror as the door quickly closed and then opened again. Briquette crawled from her blanket, stood just a few feet from the bedroom door, and growled. I tried to ignore it, but it continued repeatedly, and then I went to get my camera.

The door slowly opened again with the loud creaking resonating through the house. I looked to see Barkley and Tala's reaction, surprised to see them looking at something I could not see in the front living room, not even reacting to the door or Briquette's barking and growling.

"There's nothing there, Briquette; you're okay. Calm down"

Growling and barking with raised hackles, Briquette remained still and fixated on the door.

I could feel it too. The undeniable sensation, there is someone in the house. I could feel the room begin to get colder, and I turned on the camera. My hands were shaking, making it difficult to turn it on. Just as the camera dinged to announce itself ready, I watched as the bedroom door opened on its own, and Briquette backed up away from the door.

Chills rang through my body as I located the video control and started the recording.

The door now only cracked open, gave the appearance of someone inside the room. As if someone is attempting to peek out into the hallway. Recording, I tried desperately to focus the camera. As I approached the door, it lightly closed again on its own.

"Hello?" I said.

The dog's high-pitched noises were drowning out my voice.

"Shhh Briquette be quiet, shut up"

I set the camera on a candle stand in the hallway and backed up to console the dog. The door opened again, and Briquette pulled away from me and growled. The other dogs did not make much sound but now stood at attention and stared at the door.

The door closed, opened, and closed again. The slow creaking of the heavy bedroom door made the whole event seem even eerier. Far worse was the fact I knew with certainty there was no rational explanation, and there was no draft in the house at all.

"Briquette, okay, it's okay."

I was so nervous with tension building around me I yelled at the startled dog, "Briquette, stop!"

I walked to the camera and refocused it.

With the camera refocused, the dog growled louder.

"Stop, relax, it's all right, nothing going to hurt you! Shut up!"

With the camera still rolling, I started dinner.

"Puppies, shhh, calm down."

The sound of the dogs barking and growling sent me more on edge than what was happening with the door. I sighed when I saw the camera flashing its battery light. Frustrated, I went to turn it off and recharge the battery. I nervously finished preparing dinner as the bedroom opened and closed repeatedly and then just stopped.

I portioned out the spaghetti and meatballs as Laurel walked through the door.

"Hi Mom, I'm spending the night. Is that still going to be okay?"

"Sure, I'm happy to have you."

During dinner, I told her about the door.

"Let's watch the film. I want to see it!" Laurel shrieked.

I loaded the S.D. card into my computer, and we both watched silently.

"Wait, Oh my god, Mom, did you hear that?"

"Yes, I'll play it back."

"Whispering, it's whispering; it sounds like the little girl we recorded before," Laurel said.

"I can't understand what she's saying, Damn it, I wish the battery had not died."

"The only thing I heard right before you shut it off was maybe, my name is?" Laurel said

"I know that's what I hear also, but it's so faint. I wish I had been able to leave the camera on!"

WATCH: Chapter 23: ANIMALS REACT TO IT
SAME QR Code

"Let's do a recording tonight," Laurel said.

"All right, but you set it up."

"We need to be downstairs, okay?" Laurel asked.

"Sure"

Laurel ran down the staircase. "I'll set up things; you get the equipment."

I went to my closet and grabbed the cameras and EMF detector. Other items came with the ghost hunting kit Jim had half-jokingly purchased weeks before. An instant-read thermometer and an alarm box that detects movement or changes in temperature. Since it went off with a terrifying screech every time I used it, I decided to leave it. I picked up the thermometer gun and slipped it into my pocket.

Downstairs, Laurel had set up the poker table with candles, pens, and notebooks.

"Okay, let's get started," Laurel said.

"Wait, did you hear that?" I asked.

Right after I said it, we burst out in laughter. We had both been watching a few of the more famous ghost hunting shows, which always included people on the show consistently saying, "Did you hear that?" It had become a joke between the two of us since it all seemed so silly.

"I'm laughing, but yes, I heard it. Mom, stand over there, and I will take your picture."

Laurel snapped a picture in the direction of the sound.

"Mom, we're getting orbs again."

"Can you hold or touch my hand?" I asked in a loud voice.

Laurel snapped a picture as I held my hand out.

"Mom, Oh my god, check it out."

I held my arm out on the camera screen, and five or six orbs seemed to be dropping from the ceiling onto my hand. It was hard to see, but they were there.

"Wow, that's weird; what do we do now," I asked.

"I say let's just keep taking pictures" Laurel sat on the couch and handed me the camera.

"Let's wait till we hear…."

BANG

A loud banging came from upstairs.

Laurel jumped and shouted out, "Oh! Mom, it felt like something touched me!"

"You okay?" I asked as I turned the camera on Laurel.

"I'm okay; it felt like something touched me. I guess it was my imagination, but that's not!" Laurel pointed to the Tri-Field Meter sitting on the table. "It's moving!" She shouted.

"Yeah, I see it; it's not supposed to move at all."

I turned the camera and recorded the little box as it moved.

That's crazy; why is it moving?" Laurel asked.

"I don't know," I said.

"Was that the cat?" I asked, referencing a strange sound we heard.

"I certainly hope so," Laurel said.

I laughed and shut down the camera.

"Let's go back upstairs," I said.

"Okay, but one more thing, I want to try the thermometer here where I was sitting; it's really cold here now."

Laurel checked the temperature, and I flipped the camera back on, taking a photo of the red dot from the thermometer.

"Okay, one last picture, and we go upstairs; it's freezing down here."

I took one last photo and shut the camera off.

"Can I make some hot chocolate?" Laurel asked.

"Of course, but me too, please."

I loaded the camera card into the computer.

"Oh wow, that was so intense. I think we forgot to turn on the recorder," Laurel said.

"Your right."

I scanned through the pictures, shocked by what I saw.

Laurel set the two cups on the table. "Okay, let's check it out."

"Okay, now don't be scared," I said.

"Why, what is it?"

Laurel was sitting on the couch and said something touched her. I snapped the picture right away. She was looking at her arm; there were three small orbs on her arm and shoulder in the photo.

"Mom, look! That's when I said something was touching me!

Look! There are little orbs on me."

"Yeah, I see it." I said as I clicked through the other pictures.

"Here is where I ask it to touch my hand. In this one, I am looking at it."

Both of us sat in awe, staring at the computer. The photos of orbs were fascinating but blurry and hard to see, and I was disappointed we had not used one of the better cameras.

"There is the last one that red light is the thermometer, right?" Laurel asked.

"Yes," I said. "But, I took one last picture."

I clicked to the following picture, and Laurel gasped as she saw the photo of one bright white orb sitting on the couch in the same place she had felt the blast of cold air. I picked up my cup of cocoa and started sipping carefully just as a loud bang came from downstairs.

"So, how's work?" I nervously asked.

"Good. I like my job a lot." Laurel answered.

Another banging sound, and then it sounded like one of the doors downstairs opened.

"You know I'm sleeping in your room?" Laurel said nonchalantly.

CHAPTER 24
A RELIVING

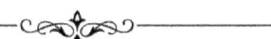

I sat at the kitchen table still and quiet, waiting and hoping it was over. I was breathing deeply, trying to recover from what had just occurred. There was no explanation for what had just happened to me. Now my back throbbed with pain. I looked down at Tala, now curled up in a ball quietly sleeping, and I smiled. Wishing I could emotionally recover as quickly as this dog—just moments before, I had upset her with my screaming. Everything was fine; I was laying tiles in the family room. Spreading glue on the back of each tile and carefully inserting them in the proper place. Stretching over the wet tiles, I noticed the blood almost pouring down my legs. I struggled to get off the cold tile floor and headed upstairs.

As soon as I heard it, I was horrified.

'Why the fuck do they always cry!'

For the first time, more words rang into my head.

'Shut the fuck up, bitch, Shut up!'

Then the pain, first on my face, then my mouth and throat, began to ache. My breathing felt difficult. I made it to my bedroom and crawled onto the floor, where I prayed next to my bed. The violent pain in my legs and arms ached, comparable to someone trying to pull me apart.

I sat on the floor, twisting in pain and sobbing, feeling as if I were under an invisible sexual attack. Not consistent with it happening now, but more like the aftermath of a brutal rape and beating. It made no sense. I sat curled up on the floor, clutching my legs to my chest. The fear was so intense I was surprised I had not had a heart attack.

The pain intensified, and I screamed, reaching for my pillow to drown out the noise. I had trouble moving my arms as if a strong force had been pinning them down. I pulled the pillow down and wailed into it. Even though I was in the house alone, hiding the sounds I made seemed essential. I was terrified. No one was hurting me. There was no one there, yet I could still hear the two men screaming back at me.

'Shut the fuck up, bitch, Shut up!'

"Oh, God, what's happening? It hurts!" I yelled.

I yelled in pain again and again. Then I was overwhelmed with terror as I heard a young girl screaming in sync with my screams. My skin crawled with revulsion as if their hands were still clawing at me. A horrible, repulsive feeling washed over me, and I tried not to vomit. It seemed like it had gone on forever. I reached into the bottom drawer and pulled out one of the handguns.

If this does not stop, I can always shoot myself in the head.

Immediately a sound from the kitchen was so loud and sudden; it sent me reeling into a different type of horror. I knew all the kitchen cupboards had fallen from the walls.

I abruptly stopped crying when I heard the crashing from the other room. Suddenly the pain lessened; I grasped the bedpost and struggled to get up off the floor.

When I was able to stand, I grabbed up the gun and opened the bedroom door. Tala met me in the hallway. She was visibly upset and whining. I scanned the room but found nothing wrong, no reason for the loud smashing sounds. With my entire body still shaking, I struggled to sit on the chair at the kitchen table. I tried to calm myself down, taking deep breaths as tears rolled down my face. I lit a cigarette with my shaking hand and stared into the kitchen in disbelief. I do not know how long THE RELIVING lasted or even how long I sat at the table, trying to understand what had happened. I was in pain and feeling very confused.

I had these experiences before but never this severe.

I have been in therapy off and on most of my life. I understood this to be a re-living.

As if the physical self has kept your memories, your brain cannot stomach remembering

The screaming still haunted me as I sat in the chair, just like the memory of the man's voice. Not an audible sound but a memory so powerful you can almost hear it.

Someone else was screaming! A young girl was screaming!

The bleeding had stopped, and only a dull pain remained. I got up from the table and poured a cup of coffee. As I dispensed the dark overcooked liquid into my cup, I reached for the bottle of aspirin.

With my hands still shaking, I spilled the contents all over the counter.

"Shit!" I quickly scooped up four pills, choking them down with the bitter coffee.

My hands still shook as I prepared a new pot and pressed the brew button. I sighed again and walked into the bathroom to start the bathtub. It would be impossible to stand in the shower with the pain I felt, and I thought maybe the warm water would calm me down. Sitting on the side of the tub, I smiled as I watched Tala prance into the bathroom. Bending over to pet her head, I could not stop the tears from rolling off my face onto hers. I slid down onto the floor, wrapped my arms around her, and cried harder.

"Why is this happening? I am sorry if I scared you. I wish you could talk; I love you."

After the tub had filled, I went into the closet and changed my clothes. Stepping into the warm water, fully dressed with the gun close by on the bathroom counter, I still could not believe what had happened.

After hearing the voice, revulsion crept across my skin. Every woman understands this feeling after a rape, an overwhelming disgust and desire to rip your soul from your body. But, this was worse than it had ever been before, and I wondered how many people had this experience.

I had never spoken to anyone about it at this point in my life, and no one has ever confided in me about having these physical reactions. Even as a drug counselor and sponsor, no one has shared this type of event with me, and I know many people have these experiences.

Perhaps this type of event is only to be shared behind the closed doors of a therapist's office.

Resting in the tub, I watched my wet clothes begin to float above the water and thought about the noise that had shaken me out of the horrible experience.

I was on the floor, in agonizing pain, terrified, and then I thought about the gun. I knew I would not shoot myself; the power of having the choice was all I needed. I realized the very second the thought had crossed my mind that the noise in the kitchen had happened. I was sure the upper kitchen cabinets had all just fallen from the walls. The crashing was so loud; that I heard the glasses and dishes crash to the floor. Now, the house that had frightened me earlier gave me a reprieve from the horrifying memories of my past. As if the house itself helped me.

I stood up, dried off, put on my robe, and tossed my wet clothes into the washer.

In the closet, I looked up at the hallway light now, flickering as if it were sending coded messages. As I stared up at it, I had a feeling of peace come over me.

"Thank you," I said aloud.

I was grateful I was alone. What if Jim were home witnessing all that had happened today? How insane I would look writhing on the floor screaming, taking a bath with clothes on, and now talking to the house itself.

"Well, that's it, Tala, now I really am crazy," I said.

Still in pain and unsettled by what happened earlier, I shuffled into the kitchen.

"Oh my god," I whispered, looking up at the fan slowly spinning.

I grabbed the small recorder Laurel had left on the counter and turned it on.

"Are you trying to tell me something? If you are, try to talk into this. I appreciate your help earlier...."

I stopped abruptly; I didn't understand why, but I started to feel scared again. I turned off the coffee maker, made a sandwich, and went to lie down in my room.

With the pain in my back, I was unable to relax. I reached over and grabbed the laptop Jim had bought me. Opening the saved files from my previous search, a sudden feeling of unease came over me as I read the following lines.

Complex Post-Traumatic Stress Disorder and the Paranormal.
Studies on the severity of childhood trauma and the paranormal.

The person with CPTSD may need to find a way to regain at least the illusion of control. Studies have shown it may be possible to induce Paranormal Phenomena to protect against the anxiety of severe memories of childhood abuse. The study of numerous individual cases reports a much higher percentage of people having paranormal experiences, also sharing the diagnoses of severe Post Traumatic Stress or referred to as Complex Post Traumatic Stress Disorder.

As I read the article, I was stunned. It had crossed my mind hundreds of times. Maybe it was all just me, and it made sense; perhaps I could create some sort of delusion to deflect my feelings from the reliving experience.

Maybe, I have been in therapy too long, laughing to myself

I felt crazy thinking it, but it felt like someone else was there with me, trying to help me. I did not understand anything anymore.

How can I record the voices of people if it's all a delusion?

Reading the article further, I felt confused and sick to my stomach, and I was not clear what they were saying.

Am I imagining it or inviting it?

I shut the computer down and walked to the kitchen. Picking up the recorder I had left playing in the room. I asked. "Is there anyone here? I do not know what is happening, but I do not think I have to be afraid of you anymore. If you want to talk to me, I will listen"

I quietly set the recorder down and went back into my room. I wanted so badly to talk about what had happened, talk to Jim or Sandy, but the fear only overwhelmed me.

What if talking about it makes it happen again. The repulsive sensation I was having earlier had stopped, and I was not okay with possibly stirring this up again on the same day.

I just want to forget.

Then like a signal, I heard the tapping sound at the window and the muffled voices from inside the house. I closed my eyes and fell deep asleep for the first time since moving into this house.

CHAPTER 25

CHAPTER 25
SEARCHING FOR ANSWERS

My opinion on the presence in the house would vary from day to day and even hour by hour. Of course, there was no such thing as ghosts; moments later, something would happen to recreate a belief in something I had always felt was impossible.

I think my hesitancy is rooted in the vast differences between what I experience (in this house) and what the media portrays.

It was not until later an author friend was on a paranormal TV show. He warned me that the show had taken the actual events and dramatized them for ratings, we assumed. The whole reason I enjoyed his book so much was its realism.

I wanted answers, and I wanted to know what was happening in the house and inside me.

I sat in our office for over an hour, searching for information on the paranormal. The more websites and articles I read, the more ridiculous the idea of haunted houses seemed. What was happening in our house was far from the dramatic stories and telling's I was reading, and nothing here was like the TV shows or movies depicting haunted house scenarios. I wondered if some of the mediums, physics, and so-called "paranormal experts" who come up in search engines, comprehend how silly and fallacious they appear. They claim to be experts on the paranormal while wearing black capes, witches' hats, and sporting pentagram necklaces and tattoos.

Although I am not what you would call religious, I believe in a God of my own understanding. I pray twice a day and have absolute certainty God has already delivered me out of what I call hell. I have no interest in devil worship, the occult, or the medieval ideas brought on by numerous religions. Questions about the paranormal should not mean automatically joining the dark side.

I clicked link after link, scanning websites and reading between the lines, searching for explanations not involving someone's agenda. While I tried to remain open-minded, I just wanted to learn about this more scientifically. I read the first article I found without flying bats and witches.

THERE ARE TWO TYPES OF HAUNTINGS

INTELLIGENT HAUNTING: An intelligent haunting is when an entity attempts to make contact with the living by manifesting itself physically or by altering its environment as a means of drawing attention to itself. Most intelligent hauntings are seeking just one thing – attention. They do what they can to get your attention – they open and close doors, move items, turn electronics on and off, try touching you, and make noise. Their intention is often misunderstood; most are not trying to scare you but get your attention: an awareness and an ability to interact with the living or other spirits.

RESIDUAL HAUNTING: A residual haunting is a recording from the past that replays itself. While some residual haunts can be traumatic (if recorded during a traumatic event), they pose no harm. There is no thought, no logic, or recognition involved, and it is not aware of you.

I kept searching, and I came across a report

Exteriorization of Emotion.

Based on Dr. Carl Jung's theory, the article that a person with excess emotions can create energy in motion unconsciously affects their environment. Making things move and creating unexplained sounds. The person experiencing the phenomena has no idea they are causing it.

I clicked the back browser and checked the other links in the search engine. I found another paper connecting PTSD and the paranormal; only this theory quantified excess emotions could invite the supernatural. This theory explains Post Traumatic Stress creates such intense energy; it can open the experiencer to a different spiritual realm. Attracting entities by the energy generated in a post-traumatic event.

A person who has suffered systematic physical trauma or abuse is like a beacon for paranormal activities

My attention was pulled away by the footsteps coming from upstairs, followed by a crash. A loud sound, again as if all our glasses had broken. I closed the computer, picked up my gun, and slowly went up the staircase. I checked all the rooms and found nothing. I knew I would not find anything tangible; I knew it was just the house again.

I picked up the phone and quickly set it back down. Jim, Lori, and the kids were all still at work. Sandy was busy spending the day with her grandchildren. I had family members I could call, but I did not want to go through it again. I was devastated the last few times I had reached out to family members. Their reactions shocked me, and the anger surprised me the most. I feel for anyone else who has experienced this from family and friends. It is heartbreaking when those who claim to love you quickly judge and dismiss your feelings. Those condescending rationalizations they are hell-bent on explicating, even if their explanation creates a barricade in our relationship or ends it altogether.

'Oh, it's just you're house settling.'

'It's just your imagination!'

'Maybe you just need attention!'

'Why would a ghost move your fan?'

'Only people with low IQs believe in haunted houses.'

'There is no such thing; you just don't understand that houses make noise!'

I can only attribute these reactions from people as fear; this great need to let me know that "they know what it is" Seems to be more about convincing themselves.

I never intended to force anyone to believe my house was haunted. I, of all people, understand the internal struggle with believing in hauntings and ghosts. If you tell someone about an experience and the listener has not directly experienced it themselves, the reaction can surprise you. I was looking for comfort; you love me - I am scared - please listen to me.

One of the worst experiences was laughing; as I explained the terror I was feeling; one of my family members just started to laugh. It reminded me of a client I saw when I was a drug and alcohol counselor. Her sister told her parents she saw someone outside her bedroom window. They dismissed her and gave very insulting reasons why she would imagine it. Then one night, when she was alone in the house, she woke up to the man standing over her. She did not attempt suicide because of the rape. She said her parent's comments made her want to end her life.

'Why would he pick you?'

'Did you leave the curtains open?'

'Did you lead him on?'

'It was not the same man you saw outside; that was all in your head.'

My interactions with family and even some friends led me to understand more about the individuals I allowed in my life. I already had amazing people in my life who listened to me with love and compassion, with no need to debate me about my feelings. I am still unsure why I let it go on for so long. Perhaps it was guilt or just hope it would change.

None of these people were evil; they simply fall into what I call:

A Category #1 Type Personality.

If someone says something hurtful and wants to resolve the issue, **The "Category# 1"** person wants to know the exact words said and when they said it. Usually claiming you do not have the right to feel hurt by what happened.

"Category# 2" personalities react differently. With no need to debate the situation; their concern is how you feel. Category # 2 people understand "perception is reality."

I reflected on a conversation I had with Lori just days before. She has always had a propensity for Native American culture and beliefs. She compared my situation to a tribal philosophy. If you enter the wrong tribe, there will be conflict. Each tribe has its views and traditions. There is no reason to have hurt feelings; you are just in the wrong tribe. If we are born into the wrong tribe, we can start our own. Some people hurt you, who can say their reasons, but they are just not your tribe. Your tribe will love and support you and be there when you need them.

So many things were starting to change in me, and one of them was the people who hurt me were simply no longer a part of my life. I had always been afraid to end relationships with hurtful family or friends; now, it seemed natural. It sounds strange, but I think it had something to do with those first few years in the house. The fright I experienced was so intense it was as if I were so full of fear I did not have room inside myself to fear anything else.

A loud noise now came from the office downstairs. I made a coffee, picked up my camera, and headed downstairs. I started to go back into the office, but the noises in the family room stopped me. I set down my cup and turned on the camera. I snapped picture after picture and then changed the setting to video. I recorded for only a few minutes and then started back to the computer. Before I reached the office, there was a loud noise in the gym. The door to the gym began to close slowly on its own. It was always unbalanced, and I used a tasseled curtain tie to keep the door open. This room was where we kept the cat's food and water, so it needed to stay open at all times. As the door was closing, I could see Blinky inside the room staring at me, too far from the entrance to have caused this. He could not remove the tie from the doorknob anyway. After recording it, I retied the door and went into the office.

I turned the computer back on and read information about the paranormal linking with brain wave activity, transcendental states, meditation, and geological explanations. I made some notes and printed them out.

BRAIN WAVE ACTIVITY:

In some cases, theta activity rises in cases of Post-Traumatic Stress Disorder. Many individuals that report having "Spiritual Experiences" or supernatural experiences tend to have more significant amounts of theta activity.

GEOLOGICAL THEORIES AND THE PARANORMAL:

Paranormal activity can manifest as our energy imprints in the place where we live. Go to your county's website and find the geological survey for your area. Look for concentrations of crystalline elements around your home or water tables. Both **can** account for this type of energy storage, like a battery.

It was frustrating not to know what was happening. If it is a "ghost" doing all this, what is the point? What is the motive or goal? What does it want?

Does it serve an ultimate purpose if it is unconsciously manifesting by me? I had re-livings before, and nothing like this ever happened. Was it just this house? Who are the people we are recording?

I knew it was a fact; during the last severe re-living episodes, the house helped me. Real or not, paranormal or coincidence, it helped me get through the afternoon.

I felt confused, exhausted, and aggravated with myself for being so preoccupied with needing answers. This preoccupation was the opposite of the practicing principle,

"Let go and let God," I had learned so many years before.

Today was supposed to be a day I was going to relax, and I felt more depleted than I did on the days I spent painting walls and moving furniture all day. I shut down the computer and spent the rest of the day outside watching the dogs play until the sun went down. Weeks before, we rescued a Sheppard puppy as a companion for Tala. We had been driving down the main highway in town and spotted a man on the corner with his trunk open and a large sign offering -Sheppard Puppies For Sale- I say rescued because it was summer again, and the puppies were inside this man's car trunk looking like they would not live through the day.

Tala loved her, I loved her, but Jim loved her most of all. It was immediately obvious she was his dog. He chose the name Pandora and jokingly said, "Because we may have opened Pandora's box with this one."

Once it was dark, I went inside to make us all dinner. I stood in the quiet of the kitchen, looking around the room, surveying all the work I had done to this house. All my attempts to make it feel like home still left the house cold, and most of the time, I felt as if I was a trespasser. I realized right that moment that our house's layout was the same as the layout of the home I lived in with my mother. The kitchen, living room, dining room, and bedroom were upstairs, just like when I lived in the forest with my mother. My biological mother was ill from drug addiction and mental illness, and her paranoia seemed to know no bounds. Her motherly instincts, I discovered later in my life, did not exist. It was a terrible existence for a child. This house is the only other home I had ever seen designed this way.

After dinner and my nightly call from Jim, I went to bed. The house was peaceful, and the only sounds were the light breathing from the dogs as they sprawled across my bedroom floor, literally dog-tired from playing so hard. I fell right to sleep.

I sat straight up in bed at 2:30 in the morning, sobbing. Tala came over to my side of the bed to see what was wrong. Pandy, still a puppy, seemed unaffected by my crying. I tried to reassure Tala by reaching to pet her head, and I was surprised to see my hands wildly shaking.

In this night terror, the screaming came from a young girl in the back seat of an old familiar white pickup truck.

I saw three people in the front seat, two men with a young girl between them.

They did not seem to know I was there.

Terrified by what was happening to her, the girl struggled to escape the two men.

They hit her and screamed at her.

I leaned over to the young girl from the back seat and whispered in her ear.

"They are going to put you in the dirt!"

When the young girl turned toward me, I saw the terror in her eyes, and then to my horror, I realized I was looking at my face from years before.

WATCH: Chapter 25: SEARCHING FOR ANSWERS
SAME QR Code

CHAPTER 26
THE PAST EXPLAINED

Months had gone by, I had become good friends with Lori, and we met more often for lunch and less for training Tala.

We walked into the Spanish-styled restaurant passing the giant chili peppers, big hats, and tiny details that seemed to be everywhere. We slid into our booth and ordered what had become our usual.

Sitting across from my friend, I considered myself blessed. I had finally made a friend in town.

"I know you said you couldn't do it, but I think you would enjoy the class. Just consider it?"

"Yeah, sorry, it's not the training class. I just do not want to commit to something I might not be able to show up to." I explained.

"What? You mean because of your back. Is that why you canceled our last few lunch plans?" Lori asked.

I looked at Lori and took a deep breath. How could I ever explain this? It sounded so crazy; how could I ever explain without sounding ridiculous. I had back pain all the time, some days were worse than other days, but that was not the whole problem. How do you tell someone you are re-living a time in your life you cannot remember? How can you explain this? You feel the event; you can hear it, but you don't remember it. Not all of it anyway, just bits and pieces. When this happens, I can feel the physical effects of being violently raped and with no memory of how I escaped

"Sometimes it's too…."

I looked at my friend across the restaurant table, her face filled with questions. I knew it was safe to tell her what had happened. Lori was kind and had no motives in our friendship, and she just wanted to be my friend. I had even mentioned this to Sandy. How uncomfortable it was to try to maintain a friendship and not be able to be honest. Sandy had advised me to tell Lori to stop hiding in fear and shame.

I took a long deep breath.

"When I was a pre-teen and teenager, I had a pretty hard time…" All I could think of was, *stop talking! Sandy is wrong, and I should not tell her or anyone else about this.*

I pushed the thoughts out of my head and just kept talking.

"I had already had a tough childhood. Then one night, right after my twelfth birthday, a man raped me. The next morning, I shot myself."

I did not tell her that doctors believed the man who attacked me *was my* father. Since my memory of that night was so confusing, I never admitted it may have been my father. It seems like such a horrible accusation if you are not sure. Time after time, therapists and doctors all came to the same conclusion; after so many years, I believed they had to be correct but still could not say it out loud.

"After I recovered and they released me from the hospital, I ran away again. I was a stupid kid, just 12 years old. I met an older man; he seemed nice, so long story short; he took me to New Mexico before I knew it. He was very crazy and hurt me a lot. I was with him, against my will, for a long time. No one knew where I was or was even looking for me. It messed me up. People have scared me ever since. I know it was a long time ago, and I should be over it, but sometimes I feel so scared it is hard to leave the house."

My mind went back to that time in my life.

I knew Michael Session was crazy after the first few moments I was alone with him. In the beginning, I was terrified, and then something changed; the fear subsided while I tried to understand what he wanted from me. Trying to predict his next thought or move, so I would not be hurt countermanded my terror. I remembered the threats he had made, knowing he would follow thru with them if he became angry. I quickly recalled my unsuccessful attempts to escape and the punishments that followed, and I remembered the drugs.

He had kept me high most of the time. Early on, I struggled every time he poked the needle in my arm, but soon, it became a sweet release from my reality.

I was unsure when it happened or why, but soon I felt love for the man who called himself only Session, and I had begun to relate to him in some ways. Later after years of therapy, I would discover the name for this, Stockholm Syndrome.

"Did you try to escape?" Lori asked.

"Yes, but he caught me; after a while, I stopped trying to get away. I just accepted it, and then it was not so bad. I gained his trust after a while. He started letting me have more freedom; he knew I started to believe the crazy things he told me. By then, he had successfully convinced me he could read my mind."

"Oh, I am so sorry. Did you try to leave again?" Lori asked.

"Yeah, I got out of the house and to the main street. I had met a woman weeks before who said she would help get a plane ticket for me. I knew where she lived one-night things were at their worst, and I ran away as soon as I could. I was hitchhiking to her house when a man in an old truck offered to give me a ride."

I could feel my heart start to beat faster, and I took another deep breath. My mind filled with my voice shouting to me to *Stop Talking! Do not say anything else. Do not tell her this!*

I looked down at the table and continued my story.

"I thought I was getting away, but the driver drove down about a block and then pulled over quickly. It all happened so fast. Another man opened the passenger door, and pushing me over, he got in and shut the door. I was so scared I did not even say anything. They drove me out to the desert."

"Oh my god, what happened?" She asked.

I looked into my friend's eyes, almost checking to see if she was still my friend, checking to see if she would be disgusted with me after hearing my story.

"I don't know. I do not remember much, just the two men talking."

But I *did* remember more of that night. I had been reliving the man's deep raspy voice for many months now. *"Why the fuck do they always cry?"* It terrified me, but the rest of their conversation was more frightening, and I could not bring myself to say it out loud.

"Afterwards, I don't remember anything; my next memory of that night is walking back to the house I was kept in," I said.

I held back the details. I recalled walking in the dark. How hard it was to see with one of my eyes swollen shut, the blood from the cuts and scratches all over me. The panic of what would happen when Session found out I had left.

Just recollecting that night, my heart beat faster, and it was hard to breathe. I never knew how I got away or most of what happened later that night. I knew they raped and beat me, but there was no real memory of it. I had no understanding of why I had blood and cuts all over me, no memory of how my face had swollen. All I could remember was the terror I felt and, recently, their conversation about where to put my body when they finished. How I ever got away from these men was always a mystery.

"Why do you think you went back?" Lori asked.

Unsure how to answer, I took a deep breath. I knew why I went back, but I also knew how it sounded; I reluctantly said the only thing I could.

"It seemed like other people were worse than he was. After he hurt me, he would be nice to me, but I wanted the drugs most of all. I just wanted to numb everything."

I looked at my friend's face, embarrassed I was describing this in such a matter-of-fact way. It had always seemed strange to me; I did not have much emotion attached to this time in my life. As if it happened to someone else. The only real feelings I had were recent and only about the men in the truck. I had never remembered crying about any of it, and I only cried over those memories when I experienced them again during a Reliving. Most of those tears were for the fear that I was going crazy.

"How did you finally get away?" Lori asked.

"He was arrested and just did not come back. So, it was finally okay to leave."

"What was he arrested for, what he did to you?" Lori asked.

"He was arrested for kidnapping and extortion involving another girl. One of his friends came to the house and told me he was in jail. He said he was going to come back and take me somewhere else. So, I left before he came back." I answered.

"What happened when you got away? Did you go home?"

"I did not have a home. I did stay with people who were like relatives, but I was never really part of their family. As soon as I could, I moved out on my own."

Thoughts raced inside my head. I had watched our three kids at all their different ages, how young and innocent they were at six, nine, and twelve. I could not imagine exposing children to the same lifestyle my parents subjected me to.

The many therapists I had seen felt I was what they called 'Set-Up' to meet someone like Session. I was doomed, in a way, by my own family, just as other survivors of childhood abuse have been.

"You're okay now; you seem so together." Lori proclaimed.

"Being in recovery has been amazing. When you go to A.A. for recovery, you're not recovering from the drugs and alcohol; that's detox. You work on the things that make you drink and do drugs.

Most of the time, it does not affect me, but from time to time, I still, I don't know, it seems worse since we moved here."

"So, when did you get sober?" Lori asked.

I didn't know what to say to her. When the waiter appeared with his arms full of plates, it gave me the time I needed to decide if I was even going to answer her question. The sizzling plates of fajitas were the perfect distraction; I had hoped she would forget her question and we could just eat our lunch.

I was embarrassed that I wasn't smart enough to reach out for help until thirty. For the first time, I felt loved, a love I had not ever experienced before from anyone. They wanted to help, truly liked me, and loved me into a healthy life. Until I was well enough to help others do the same.

I ignored her question and commented on our lunch.

Previously I had explored religion, read dozens of self-help books, and spent my adult life in some form of psychotherapy. For most types of psychotherapy, your therapist encourages you to talk about your thoughts and feelings and what's troubling you. It can be an impossible task when you have no memory of what happened.

"So when did you get sober?" she asked again

"Not until much later; I wish I could have been in recovery sooner but, God made it possible for me to go to treatment when I was ready, I guess."

"Is that what happened to your back?" Lori asked sheepishly.

I could not answer. Not out of fear, just pure uncertainty. There were so many reasons why my back and neck caused me pain. The morning I shot myself, the bullet passed through my body, carefully brushing my spinal cord. I endured many beatings from Session and, later, more physically abusive relationships. They all seemed to play a factor in why I had so much pain in my back. I recently found what might be an additional cause, something I had read while looking up information about "The Fight or Flight Response." The traumatic injuries I sustained were the leading cause, according to my doctors and MRIs, but some of the words I read remained ingrained in my mind:

The sympathetic nervous system originates in the spinal cord, and its primary function is to activate the physiological changes that occur during the fight or flight response. People who reported higher levels of psychological distress also reported higher levels of chronic back pain.

I was relieved when I saw Lori did not need her to answer. She reached across the table and set her hand on my fingers.

"Thank you for trusting me enough to tell me. Well, my friend, next time you are too scared to meet me, I will come to you."

I quickly changed the subject.

"I did some reading trying to understand what was happening in the house, and I found an article. It said people are more likely to experience paranormal events if they have severe post-traumatic stress. I guess that means it's all in my head?"

"Wait a minute; I saw your fan move; I can feel it, and Laurel heard and felt things, right?" Lori asked.

"I know, and we even recorded some voices, but there are possible explanations for the voices also. I need someone impartial to be there. Do you think you could come over and record with us?"

I explained how we had asked questions and recorded what seemed to be responses, the man talking, the little girl answering. It had only been myself and Laurel doing the recordings in the house until this point.

"I'll come over, and we can get to the bottom of this. I will be happy to help you do some recordings of the house. I am your friend, and if that's what you need help with, I am happy to do it."

I smiled at her, thinking of the last times I had shared this much of myself. Only with Jim, Serena, and Sandy had this been safe to do. My family was dismissive of everything about me, and past friends even attempted to compare situations. "Oh, if you think that's bad…."

I always felt accepted at meetings. But when I spoke at the meetings, I eased over my history. Especially if there were men in the room, I would never reveal too many details in that type of public setting. There were only a few people I ever trusted with this much information.

"Okay, so next Friday is good for me."

"Okay, next Friday it is, about six?" I asked.

"I'll be there!" Lori said.

CHAPTER: 27

CHAPTER 27
THE SéANCE

I set up the food in the kitchen, anxiously awaiting our guests. I felt torn by the contradicting feelings I was having. I was nervous to discover more about what was happening and experience more unexplained activity, and, concerned my guests would judge me- if I believed this, would they think I was stupid?

I thought back to the night I told Laurel about the plans with Lori. She told me she had made a friend at work and wanted to invite her, and I agreed with no hesitation. Now I was just hoping Laurel's new friend was as open-minded as I needed her to be. It was only recently I finally had enough experience in the house to take this seriously.

In the past recordings, I was still skeptical, sarcastic and had to keep myself from laughing.

Laurel spent days researching questions to ask at a Séance. The moment I heard the word séance, it made me cringe; in my mind, the phrase séance always seemed related to devil worship or charlatans taking advantage of desperate people. After doing some light research of my own, it was clear we were not having a séance. I searched the internet for words to describe what we were planning and found nothing. There seems to be no name for gathering people asking questions and waiting to record a disembodied response. Laurel jokingly said, "Let's call it "A Bodiless Anonymous Meeting" or "A Bodily Challenged Support Group" We both laughed and decided to call it a Séance.

Friday night finally came. The four of us ate the snacks I had set out on platters in the dining room. Once everyone had eaten, we walked down the wooden staircase in an almost military-like procession.

"I thought we would sit around the poker table if that's all right?" I said.

"Perfect," Lori said.

"Thanks for doing this, Lori; I know it's silly."

"Maybe not; who knows? Let's just see if anything happens." She answered.

"Mom, just be opened-minded okay? I think it's trying to communicate with you. Maybe we will find out something." Laurel said.

Lori took her seat to the right of me. Alison sat in the chair on my left, a soft-spoken, pleasant girl about Laurel's age who I instantly made everyone feel at ease. Laurel shut off the lights and lit a candle in the center of the table.

"We wrote a list of questions, but you can ask whatever you want. All I know about this process is we have to pause after each question. Oh, also, it takes twelve minutes before anything happens." I said as Laurel passed out the papers to each person.

"Twelve minutes before what happens?" Alison asked.

"We have never recorded anything before twelve minutes, so the first few things on the list are really just to pass the time," I explained.

"Who wants to go first?" Laurel whispered.

"I will," I said.

"My name is June; I live in this house. We are here tonight to attempt to talk with anyone who wishes to speak to us. We are not a threat to you, and we mean you no harm. Is there anyone who is willing to speak to us?"

I paused for a moment and then continued asking the questions on the list.

"Why are you here?"

Pause

"What is your name?"

Pause.

"Do you live here in the house?"

Pause.

"Did you die in this house?" I asked.

Immediately, Barkley and Briquette barked as if an intruder had come through the door. We waited, and the dogs calmed down. I asked the question again with the same result; the dogs instantly barked back, this time louder.

"This is silly. If you're talking through the dog, bark once for yes and twice for no." I laughed.

Bark!

"Did you die in this house?" I asked again.

Bark!

"That's weird!" said Alison.

"We have to stop; I will go put the dogs in my bathroom. I'll be right back."

I went upstairs and put Barkley and Briquette in my bathroom. I returned minutes later and sat at the table.

"Okay, we should be okay now; they are in the bathroom."

"I wonder why they were barking like that," Alison said.

"I don't know, but they can't hear us from the upstairs bathroom. Do you want to ask the question this time, Alison?"

"No, I'll wait," She answered, her eyes as big as saucers.

"Did you die in this house?" I asked in a much quieter voice.

We looked at each other in disbelief. As soon as I asked the question again, we could hear Briquette's distant one bark echo from the closed room upstairs.

"That's so weird. Let's stop asking that." Alison said.

Laurel looked over at her friend to signal it was her turn to ask.

"You go ahead," Alison said.

Seeing that, her friend looked worried. "Are you okay?" Laurel asked.

"Sure, I just don't want to ask that question."

"Oh, Just read the paper," Laurel said.

"Okay. Hello, my name is Alison. I am a friend of the owner of this house. I am here to communicate with the spirits in this house, and I wish you no harm. Can you make a sound noise, tap on the wall, move something, or speak directly to us? You may use one of the recording devices we have set up. Is there anyone here who wishes to speak to us?"

"Are you male or female?" Alison asked

Everyone looked at each other in amazement. The response sounded like metal clanging together.

"Maybe it's the dog's collars?" Alison said.

"Barkley and Briquette do not wear collars, and they are still in the bathroom," I answered.

"What was that?" Laurel asked.

The sound was as if someone was walking around upstairs. Alison and I got up and walked close to the staircase. Peering up in the dark, we both strained to see if anything was out of place upstairs; we saw nothing and sat back at the table.

"Maybe we can hear it better when we play the tape back," Lori said.

Alison asked the remainder of her questions. Then Laurel took her turn, and finally, Lori asked the items on her list and finished by asking a question of her own.

"I would like to ask a question of my own. Is there anything we can do to help you?"

We heard nothing but a few knocks and taps other than the occasional banging.

"I have more questions to ask," Laurel said.

"I'm going to have to go. I have to be at my daughters by ten." Lori said.

"Okay, I'll walk you out. Thank you for coming over, Lori. It really means a lot to me that you would be willing to do this" Walking Lori upstairs, I grabbed the recorder on the way.

"Sure, let me know if you get anything on tape."

I watched my friend's car disappear into the darkness as I heard Laurel and her friend come upstairs. They poured coffee, grabbed the plate of cookies, and sat in the dining room.

I loaded the file into the computer, fast-forwarded through the dogs barking, and pressed play. At first, we all sat in silence and listened.

'Okay. Hello, my name is Alison. I am a friend of the owner of this house. I am here to communicate with the spirits in this house, and I wish you no harm. Can you make a sound noise, tap on the wall, move something or speak directly to us'

-BARK

"That sounds like a big dog barking," Alison said.

"My Mom's big dogs are at the vet getting spayed, so that's not a dog," Laurel said.

"Weird, let's hear the rest," Alison said.

You may use one of the recording devices we have set up. Is there anyone here who wishes to speak to us?

-Hissing Sound

"What is your name?"

Whispering

"Are you male or female?"

-Metal clanking sound

"Sounds like a bracelet," Alison said.

"Maybe, then a female is the answer?" Laurel said.

"Do you wish to make yourself known?"

YES

"Are you keeping the owner up at night?"

___ ___ I COULD CARE LESS!

The remainder of the tape did not have any answers we could understand. Some sounds seemed to respond to the questions, but they were so quiet and unclear that we dismissed them and moved on to Lori's part. Nothing was recorded at all when Lori asked questions from her list. Then we heard Lori's last question.

"I have a question of my own. Is there anything that we can do to help you?"

The first few words were muffled and unclear; we could only hear the last few words.

___ ___ ___ care; I'm a master.

After an hour, Alison and Laurel went home. I slowly walked them to the door and hugged them both goodbye.

WATCH: Chapter 27: THE SéANCE
SCAN QR Code - KEEP OPEN

I nervously locked the front door and scanned the room.

Every corner of the house was now making sounds. Tapping, banging, clicking, and what sounded like a woman quietly moaning.

The loud noise of my bedroom door shaking almost made me run from the house.

As soon as the place was quiet, I grabbed my cigarettes and a can of soda and went to my room.

With the door locked and the gun beside me, I lay sleepless most of the night.

CHAPTER 28

CHAPTER 28
IT'S TIME TO WAKE UP

We had lived in the house for almost two years now. So many things have happened since we moved in, some good and some bad.

One afternoon, the most alarming thing happened when I was standing on the deck with the dogs—keeping them from what I thought was a moose in the overgrown secret garden. I just wanted to let the animal pass through with no incident. As I stood there talking to the dogs, I could hear the moose rustling the trees, and I called out.

"You better get outa here, Mr. Moose; these dogs will try to attack you."

As it came through the thick branches into the clearing, I was astonished. What I thought was an animal was a man. He sauntered along as if he were bored, shuffling his feet as he walked. There was no way he did not know we were standing there watching him. There was no way he did not hear me call out.

He was maybe six feet tall, wearing a brown baseball hat, dark jeans, and a brown jacket. The strangest part was he never looked back, and he never turned to acknowledge Pandora's fierce growling, so I never saw his face. He slowly walked across the secret garden, past the driveway, and disappeared into the trees.

I started to call out when I first saw him but stopped as soon as I saw how he carried himself. His hands stuffed in his pockets, head down, walking slow and cumbersome while dragging his feet in the dirt. I glanced around, making sure there was no one else with him.

It seems unnatural to not turn around and make sure the growling dog is not getting closer or, at the very least, make sure I was pointing my gun at his back.

At our house in California, there were a few times I had found someone in our yard. They always made a point of acknowledging me and saying, "Sorry, just getting our ball or Frisbee."

But this man's behavior seemed so eerie, as if he had every right to be here. It took almost five minutes for him to walk off into the trees at the slow pace he was walking. I did not want any interaction with this man, and the whole thing was exceptionally creepy.

It was not until months later I read a book where the author described something so similar it was disturbing. He told not of a shadowy figure or misty form but a solid person who behaved the same way as the man in the secret garden. He found an older woman sitting on his front stoop every day; she would not acknowledge him even as he stood right in front of her. She was never speaking or explaining why she was there. Bothered by her odd behavior, he wondered if this was a ghost. While I read this, I immediately thought of the man in the secret garden.

I crawled under the covers and sighed, looking at Jim's side of the bed. The first night was always the hardest. When he was home, we had so much fun just being together. Even a trip to the hardware store could be an entertaining event as long as we were together. It only took the first day and night, but it seemed that just as I had to acclimate to the cold weather in winter, I had to readjust to being alone again. I was not scared to be alone; I enjoyed alone time. I have always been okay by myself. But in this house, it's like you are never alone.

Once he was gone, the noises in the house increased. Many people will say it was because I was alone; I thought it too at first, but now it happened to my husband and the people who visited the house. Anyone who spends a good chunk of time alone in the house feels something or experiences something perplexing.

One night Jim was alone and went to relax in our bedroom. While watching television, he noticed the wooden plant stand in the corner of the room. Sitting on top, I had placed an angel statue. What drew his attention was the angel was the way it leaned forward. He went to investigate. The entire table was four inches off the ground, hanging from only a quarter-inch of molding on the wall behind. As he told me what happened, we tried to replicate it by slamming the door into the plant stand. Nothing we did would lift the table off the ground. It was impossible. A few nights later, the table crashed to the ground at 3:00 am, jolting us awake. The angel statue broke. It was startling at first and then unbelievably comforting for me to have this happen while Jim was home.

Strange things like this continued to happen in waves. One week it would be the bathroom noises; the next week, weird smells coming from nothing and disappearing just as fast.

The windows would tap as if someone was knocking on them, and then it would stop again.

Nothing ever came from the same place or reacted the same way.

One evening Jim had come home and noticed a candle warmer flashing. He wanted to disconnect the plug, throw it away, and buy me another one. After two days of the flashing lights, it stopped, never flashed again, and continued to work fine. Soon after the candle warmer, the flashing lights would start in another room. Eventually, Jim had decided we needed another electrical check of the house. Before I could get an electrician to call me back, it stopped.

Later, most of the flashing lights, or lights turning on without human intervention, were battery operated—candles. I had been purchasing these candles due to unexplainable power outages in the house. One of the candles we bought a year before had never worked, and then suddenly, one evening went on by itself. This particular candle only turned on when Jim came home. He switched the holders, placing the left sconce on the right and vice versa, but the same right side would turn on when he returned. Then one day, it just stopped happening. I took the candle out of the wall sconce and found the entire bottom had blown apart with the wires disconnected.

Both the downstairs and upstairs had fingerprints and smudge marks on the walls and windows. There was no explanation, and they would appear where it was impossible. Neither of us goes downstairs very often due to the extreme cold. I quit cleaning them out of frustration, and then it stopped happening.

It wasn't easy to sleep even when Jim was home. His sleep was also occasionally disturbed. One morning we both woke up as things left in our bed began pelting us in the head. We had fallen asleep with various objects between us, a roll of paper towels, cigarettes, a lighter, and two tv remotes. Maybe this sounds strange to some, but we have always gone to bed with the clutter of everyday items we use while watching T.V. in bed. When I awoke in the morning, the paper towels first hit me in the face. I thought at first Jim had pulled up the blanket, but as I pushed the paper towel roll away, it hit me again. When one of the remotes brushed my face, I jumped out of bed. It was as if something were throwing the objects at us but with no intent to hurt us.

I grabbed my camera one night to film the fish tank, as its lights went on and off like some type of Morse code, and then stopped. My husband was sure it was just another faulty product, and I thought he was probably right. I was still unclear how this fish tank lid could do this. The lighted cover had three settings, bright white, off, and blue moonlight. Every night I would turn it to the moonlight setting and watch the fish swim. To convert it to bright white, you first need to turn it off. It would immediately wake me up when it flashed the bright white light. We bought a new lid, but within six months, it started again. We gave the fish tank to Laurel, and it has never flashed at her house.

In the first few years living here, I was horrified at the thought of trying to explain these experiences to anyone. I feared people would assume I was crazy, but that all changed. My husband, my kids, a handful of supportive friends, and my new friends made it okay. So when unexplained things would happen in front of electricians, plumbers, or maintenance men, I would say the house has paranormal activity. Not one of them even seemed surprised. Most of the workers would make small talk about their church families and inevitably tell me *their* ghost stories. The religious people I had known in California did not accept anything out of the ordinary, let alone paranormal. People from our northern part of Spokane proclaimed God to be in charge and did not fear the unknown or feel it was the work of demons.

To this day, I have only met one person from our town who acted negatively about the house.

I met her at our small-town post office. She sold cosmetics, and more so than wanting the products for myself, I thought they would make fun gifts. Selfishly I wanted to ask her some questions about the town and its history. One afternoon she called me from the base of my driveway. "Your order came in early, so I thought I'd just drop it off for you. Can you come down?"

I drove down the driveway to the locked front gate. The makeup lady stepped out of the car's passenger side and waved.

"Hi there, I thought I would deliver this, and my daughter wants to see your house."

She looked over to the younger driver. "Would it be okay? she just wants to see it."

"You mean the outside?" I asked.

"Yeah, Yeah, she just wants to see it." As she rudely opened the lock and pulled the gates open, I felt for my gun on my hip, covered by my overshirt.

I was so concerned that this was some weird setup that I could only focus on watching their hands. The daughter pulled the car up just past the gate and stepped out of the vehicle.

She looked over at me and introduced herself. "Thanks for letting me see the house."

Still leaning on the car, the younger girl had her back to the house.

"Well, there it is, look at it; you wanted to see it," her mother yelled.

The daughter turned around, looking at the ground. Then placed her hands over her face and shouted, " I don't wanna look; I don't wanna look."

"Oh, for christ's sake, let's go then; thank you, June, let me know when you're ready to order anything else. Have a good day."

"Get in the car!" She shouted at her daughter.

The young girl hurriedly backed down the driveway, almost hitting our mailbox. I was relieved when I saw them drive away, and I locked the gate and went home.

It did not occur to me how weird this interaction was until about an hour later. All I could think of at the time was that these two women both seemed high to me, and I thought this was some weird way to rob us.

I was so frustrated with myself. W*hy didn't I think to ask any questions? What the hell was that all about? Why don't you want to look?*

I walked down to the office and looked up my address, expecting to find some newspaper article about the possible horrific event that the daughter was reacting to, but I found nothing.

I continued talking to my friends as often as possible, and as each week went on, I would hear the same comments. "You seem different, stronger somehow," Sandy was convinced the house was helping me, making me a braver and a more assertive person. It was changing me.

I came to a sad realization that some people in my life were extremely unhealthy. These relationships would not change, and I had been advised to close these connections years before. Family stuff can be challenging; you feel obligated to stay connected no matter how badly they treat you.

When I told Jim I had enough, he smiled and simply said. "Thank God, honey, I have been waiting for you to see what everyone else has seen for years. You deserve to be loved and respected."

I am not sure what changed inside me, but I am no longer willing to listen to the passive-aggressive and hostile statements just to sustain relationships; it turns out I did not need them at all. I discovered I have value.

Jim worked every weekday out of town and even some Saturdays, but we talked every night. Our marriage had always been great, but now I felt even closer to him than I thought possible.

Joshua called me every day when Jim was away. I knew Josh was noticing something in my voice. He was always asking me what was going on with the house. Many times, he could hear the happenings right over the phone.

Lori took a better job and moved to Seattle. Although she went out of her way to visit whenever possible, we rarely spoke because of her busy schedule.

The reliving experiences continued, but I found ways to lessen the effects, thanks to my husband. He brought me a dog-training tool to calm the dogs, intended for Tala. He told me how frustrated he was feeling one night on his way home, and he tried it. Jokingly he began sniffing the puff of lavender-scented air from the small tube. He said it worked and encouraged me to try it.

He was right; it does help. I purchased scented wax cubes with scents that made me feel a little more relaxed. I carry one in my pocket to help me recover during an episode, and it works.

While living here, one extremely distressing period was the change in our beautiful Sheppard, Pandora. Once full-grown, her behavior changed. The once loving, adorable dog who had bonded so tightly with Jim became dangerous, and the vet advised us to put her to sleep.

Pandora was so lovable and funny it made the change in her even more heartbreaking. She was undoubtedly Jim's dog, but I loved her so much, and the grief of losing Pandora was almost unbearable.

I would also miss the sense of peace with her in the room guarding the bedroom door. The loud sounds in the house sounding like someone was breaking in were easy to ignore if Pandora did not react.

I set the T.V. to a sitcom, and I began to laugh, closed my eyes, and went to sleep.

Nothing eventful had happened all day. The house was quiet and peaceful and had been for days; I even thought maybe it was over. I slept from midnight to almost six o'clock in the morning.

I woke up to Jim leaning on his side of the bed. I felt the sudden hard movement as if he had jumped on the bed. The startling jolt is what woke me up at first. I never opened my eyes; I just pulled the blanket closer.

Then he leaned over me and whispered in my ear. I could feel his breath on my neck and face.

"It's time to wake up." He said.

I lay there with my eyes still closed.

"Oh crap, what time is it? Is there coffee?" I said.

I sighed, then suddenly I leaped out of bed.

That's not Jim! Jim is not here!

I grabbed my gun and pointed it at his side of the room. My arms were shaking, my legs wobbling. I held the weapon out, moving from side to side, checking every corner of the room, wiping tears from my face with my arm. I slowly walked over to his side of the bed, expecting to see a crazy man hiding, lying on the floor. I scanned the room and then walked into the hallway to check the bathroom; I found nothing there, then the kitchen, and again nothing there.

Nothing.

Still holding the gun, I tried to catch my breath and flipped on the kitchen light. I saw something moving out of the corner of my eye. I looked towards the window giving me a direct line of sight to the top of our driveway. The vision was so fast had the man not been wearing blue; I would have assumed it was a deer. I only saw him from the back as he leisurely walked down the driveway and disappeared into the thick trees.

I set the gun on the counter, turned on the coffee pot, and opened the large bag from the hardware store. With my hands shaking, I opened and readied the contents. I armed every window and door in the house with the wireless alarm boxes as noises and muffled talking echoed from every room.

WATCH: Chapter 28: ITS TIME TO WAKE UP
SAME QR Code

Hours later, I heard banging noises from downstairs. There was no real fear like all the times before. I left my gun on the counter and started down the stairs. I am unsure if I made peace with this or the alarms that took away the fear. I leisurely walked down the steps running the morning over in my head.

If I had not woken up and turned on the light, was the man in blue going to break in?

If the light from the house startled him, why did he walk away and not run?

Who woke me up?

Who the hell whispered in my ear?

CHAPTER 29

CHAPTER 29
MORE VISITORS

I stood at the kitchen window, admiring the enormous amount of spring flowers scattered across the large yard. The vibrant flowers seemingly emerged from nowhere.

The seasons here are spectacular.

I was excited Sandy and Harold would arrive in just a few minutes. It seemed like an eternity since I had seen Sandy.

I heard the car and rushed outside to greet them.

Harold was the first to emerge from the car, a retired sheriff; he was a no-nonsense man with a kind spirit and a good sense of humor. The gentle sheriff was the only man besides Jim who made me feel safe.

"Hey, we made it," as he stretched his arms high into the air.

"Your driveway is not so bad; I was expecting much worse. Where's Jim?"

"He's on his way home; he'll be here soon," I said.

"Hey girl," Sandy yelled as she crawled out of the car, juggling packages and gift bags.

"Oh, Sandy, I can't believe you guys are here!"

"Of course we are. I knew we would be able to get here eventually." Sandy laughed

Packages and bags began to fall onto the ground. Sandy stood up, stepped over the bags, and hugged me hard. "I've missed you."

"Oh my god, I have missed you so much!" I said.

"Harold, can you get the box for June out of the car?" Sandy asked over my shoulder

"What box?" I asked.

"Well, when you left, you had to leave so much behind, so we saved some things for you that you could not take"

"You are so nice, thank you, Sandy," I said as I threw my arms around my friend again.

"This property is amazing; it's just beautiful here. Now let's see this house." She said as she grabbed the suitcase handle

We dragged suitcases over the dirt and pebble driveway to the front door. I held the storm door open, and Sandy stepped in first.

"Oh my, it's lovely in here!" she squealed

"Yeah, this is a nice house; you guys did good," said Harold.

"Sorry, you guys, the guest room is downstairs. I know it's a pain, but it's even harder to enter the downstairs from outside."

"No problem," Harold declared.

"We have only been here a few minutes, and you're already apologizing. Stop it now," Sandy stated in her most firm voice.

I laughed, guiding them through the foyer and to the guest room.

"I hope this will be okay, we...." As I opened the door

"It's beautiful!" Sandy sang out, reaching over and hugging my shoulder. "I'm so happy to see you; now show us the rest of this house!"

"Your bathroom is here," I said

I took them through some of the rooms downstairs, and Sandy asked about what each room-what it looked like before and what I had changed.

"What's this room?" Sandy asked.

A loud metal crashing sound came from upstairs as we approached the office.

"Oh, good, Jim's home," Harold said.

"No, he's not home yet," I said.

"I just heard him up there. It sounded like he threw his keys on the table." Sandy stated.

"No," I answered quietly.

"That must be Jim?" Harold said.

"No, Jim calls me before he comes home." I moved my shirt to display the holstered 22-caliber weapon on my hip.

"It sounded like keys being thrown on a table. What was that then?" Sandy asked.

"The house," I answered with trepidation.

"Great, it's welcoming us then!"

I laughed at Sandy's response. Sandy was always such an easygoing person; her approval and warm attitude made me feel accepted and loved.

"See, I'm not crazy. You two settle in, and I will make us some coffee. I'll be upstairs."

As I walked up the staircase, Sandy yelled, "We heard it! You are definitely not crazy! And coffee sounds great!" Sandy said.

At the top of the stairs, I heard our friends rustling about in the guest room as they unpacked their belongings.

"That was strange, and it sounded like keys hitting the counter or table," Sandy spoke softly.

"Yeah, I heard it too," Harold said quietly.

I put together a platter of cheese, crackers, and fruit and set them in the dining room.

"Harold is grabbing the other bag from the car, so we have a chance to catch up. So does that happen often? The sound of the keys, I mean." Sandy asked.

"This might sound strange, but the noises in the house sometimes seem as if they are mimicking us. One afternoon I was giving Tala a bath in the tub, and I had two empty gallon milk jugs to scoop water. When I finished, I threw the plastic containers into the bathtub, making a specific sound. A few days later, I heard the exact noise coming from the bathroom, but of course, the bottles were not there anymore. Sometimes at night, it sounds like someone is in the kitchen putting dishes away. Laurel woke up to the sounds of dishes being placed in cabinets all hours of the night when no one in the house was awake, much less doing dishes. So anyway, that key sound, I think that was just the house mimicking us again."

"Let's take this coffee outside and visit with Tala," Sandy said with a smile on her face.

"Sure"

We walked out, and I opened the gate, releasing Tala from the deck.

"Hi Tala, you are as pretty as your pictures." Sandy knelt to pet Tala's head.

As soon as we sat in the big wooden chairs, Sandy took a deep breath.

"I was only in the house for a few minutes, but coming outside, you can tell the difference," Sandy told me.

"What do you mean?"

"The house feels different, sort of a heavy feeling I can't quite explain."

"You're not the first to say that," I responded.

"It's very pretty, and you have done an amazing job on it," Sandy said.

"Thanks, Sandy"

Harold joined us, and they gave me an update on our friends in California.

Sandy helped me make dinner, and once Jim came home, both men disappeared into the target range.

After dinner, Sandy said she was feeling sick.

The following day Harold came upstairs and told us Sandy was feeling sicker. She was ill for three days. On day three, we needed to take her to Urgent Care in town. By evening, Sandy was already feeling better. I was relieved. She got so sick so fast. On the day we took her to the doctor, her fever was 102, and she looked weak and pale. Watching her health decline so fast terrified me. I even considered the possibility the house was making her sick, but I kept this potentially scary bit of information to myself.

Once Sandy felt better, we toured Spokane, fired guns in the target range, watched movies, and talked for hours on end. On the sixth day of their visit, I cooked breakfast as Jim packed for his next trip.

"Have fun. I will be back Thursday morning," Jim said.

"Jim, we sure enjoyed seeing you; we had a great time shooting guns with you. It's a lucky man who has his own target range." Harold said.

"I had a good time, too; I hope you guys can come back soon," Jim said.

"You bet," Harold said with a smile.

"Sandy, so happy to see you; thanks for coming."

"I love you, be safe" I turned and hugged my husband tight

"Love you too. I'll call you tonight like always. Have fun, honey," Jim smiled.

The entire day we drove to some of my favorite places in Spokane and surrounding areas. By evening, we were exhausted but unable to sleep. While we were relaxing on the couch, Sandy and Harold could hear the unexplainable noises in the house.

I asked if they wanted to try recording the house.

"Hell, yes!" Sandy proclaimed

I set up the table with cameras and lit a tall white candle.

"Well, what do we do? Do we ask questions?" Harold asked.

"Yes, I guess whatever comes into your head," I replied, turning off the lights.

"I want to go first!" Sandy said

I turned on the recorder, and Sandy began asking questions.

"Will you communicate with us?"

"Are you passing through?"

Harold asked a few questions as Sandy snapped her camera. Noises from every corner of the room, seemingly responding to Harold's questions.

After almost an hour, I turned the lights back on and retrieved my laptop from the office. I transferred the recorded session into my computer to increase the sound.

"The first twelve minutes, there is usually nothing on the recorder," I said.

"First twelve minutes, hmm?" Harold laughed.

I could hear the skepticism in his voice and started to play the downloaded file from my computer.

Sandy's voice rang out loudly from the computer.

'Will you communicate with us?'

Then a man's voice whispered in answer.

I looked at Sandy and saw her eyes get big.

"Oh my god, some guy is talking on there. Harold, did you hear that?"

"Yeah, I can hear him."

'Are you passing through?' The voice reverberated from the computer.

Then a whistling sound and whispering by several different muffled voices.

"Oh my god, it sounds like a group of people!" Sandy proclaimed.

We listened to the entire hour of the recording, and there was a distinct sound after every question. When the recording ended, we talked about how strange it all sounded; even though unclear, it seemed to be answering us. Exhausted, we all went to bed.

In the morning, Sandy told me they did not sleep well. She had heard knocking on the walls and kept getting up to take pictures. I asked her if she was afraid, and she answered with a resounding "No! There is nothing scary here at all; I think it is fascinating. I want to try it again tonight. This time I think we should speak much slower and write down some questions in advance." Sandy declared.

"Good idea," I said, smiling

After lunch, we wrote out our questions, taking serious consideration of each question.

"I recently had that dream again, about the two kids locked outside in the snow as punishment. Think I should ask about it?" I asked.

"Yes, I do," Sandy said.

My friend's relaxed attitude about it all made me smile. There was no judgment, no harsh words, just the occasional Hey, what if we ask this? It was extraordinary having a friend like this.

After dinner, Sandy set up the table and lit the candle. I set the recorder on the staircase and turned on some of the equipment Jim had bought me. Harold went to bed early, exhausted from the lack of sleep the night before.

We recorded for an hour, asking the questions from our list and taking pictures. When we finished, we were both shaking. The room was cold, and while sitting at the table asking our questions, we could hear sounds neither of us could explain. At about thirty minutes in, we could hear the muffled voices of people in the room with us.

I made coffee and snacks, and we sat and listened to the recording.

CAMERA

Unexplained whistling sounds

Hissing

ME: "What the hell was that?"

Whistling sounds

ME: "I don't know what that noise is, do you?"

SANDY: "Uh uh, that's why I wanted to put it right there."

ME: "Did you hear?"

SANDY: "Uh, huh."

Talking

Unexplained sounds

MALE VOICE "__ sit __ straight in your chair."

SANDY: "My name is Sandy. I am a friend of June's visiting from Southern California with my husband, Harold. We are not here to harm you; we are here to help June understand what's going on in this house."

Hey

FEMALE CHILD: "__ __ they can hear me."

WHISPER: "Soon"

Noises

SANDY: "Are you here with us?"

VOICE 1: "Yes"

VOICE 2: "Yes"

SANDY: "Are you passing thru?'

VOICE 2: "Shut up"

VOICE 1: "Yes"

WHISPERING: "No"

MALE VOICE: "Fuck off"

ME: "When we take pictures, we want to capture you in our pictures."

WHISPERING: "Yes"

WHISPERING: "Yes"

SANDY: "Or your energy."

VOICE 2: "Help"

Whispering

FEMALE VOICE: "One, two, three."

Whistling sound

DEEP MALE VOICE: "__ __ but you won't!"

SANDY: "Are you among strangers?"

FEMALE CHILD: "Yes"

WHISPERING: "__ __ strangers."

WHISPERING: "House"

VOICE 1: "Help"

VOICE 2: "Jesus"

SANDY: "Will you communicate with us?"

MALE VOICE: "Help"

VOICE 1: "Help me."

VOICE 2: "Help me."

VOICE 3: "Help me, Jesus."

VOICE 4: "Help me."

VOICE 1: "Help me."

WHISPERING: "Hey"

MALE VOICE: "Fuck you."

DEEP MALE VOICE: "HELP ME!"

WHISPERING: "Should help."

MALE VOICE: "Help"

MALE VOICE: "Help me."

ME: "Are there any children here?"

DEEP MALE VOICE: "Children No"

WHISPERING: "Children"

MALE VOICE: "Help us."

DEEP MALE VOICE: "HELP ME!"

MALE VOICE: "Help"

ME: "Are there any children that froze outside?"

WHISPERING: "Children"

MALE VOICE: "CHILDREN"

ME: "Is there anything I should…."

Noises

WHISPERING: "Children"

Whispering

Camera sound

MALE VOICE: "YES!"

Loud unexplained noises

DEEP MALE VOICE: "Test me NOW!"

ME: "Are you here now."

VOICE 1: "Yes"

VOICE 2: "yes."

VOICE 3: "Yes, I'm here."

WHISPERING: "Hey"

MALE VOICE: "Help us."

WHISPERING: "Help us."

SANDY: "Are you willing to communicate with us?"

Louder unexplained sounds

MALE VOICE: "Help us."

WHISPERING: "Help us."

MALE VOICE: "HELP US!"

Very loud unexplained sounds

Whispering

FEMALE VOICE: "Wait"

Loud eerie sounds then as if someone is yelling

MALE VOICE: "Jesus help."

SANDY: "Is there someone by name you wish to communicate with?"

MALE VOICE: "Help us."

Whispering

Slap or clapping sound

Talking and whispering

SANDY: "Is there one or more children here?"

Noises

SANDY: Is there a boy here?"

CHILDS VOICE: "Yes"

CAMERA SOUND

MALE VOICE: "Hey, you."

CAMERA SOUND

SANDY: "Is there a girl here?"

Loud sound and whispering

Whistle

SANDY: "If you're upstairs, can you come down the stairs?"

MALE VOICE: "YES"

Whistle

Unexplained noise

DEEP MALE VOICE: "YES"

SANDY: "Are one of you a woman here with us?"

MALE VOICE: "HE, Hey, Hey"

WHISPERING: Whispering child

2 or 3 people are talking, but we cannot understand

MALE VOICE: "Okay"

SANDY: "You may call me Sandy."

WHISPERING: "Sandy"

Whispering and talking, San-dy

ME: "Did anyone die in this house or on this land?"

WHISPERING: "Yes"

"YES"

Unintelligible, Strange unexplained noises

SANDY: "The man that June saw outside; are you with us now?"

Bang

SANDY: "The man who walks the Secret Garden, are you with us now?"

DEEP MALE VOICE: "SECRET!"

Sounds get louder

MALE VOICE: "Secret"

WHISPERING: "Secret"

MALE VOICE: "Secret Garden"

Deafening sounds

Clapping

SANDY: "If you're trying to communicate, we are trying to hear you."

WHISPERING: "Adam"

MALE VOICE: "Adam"

MALE VOICE: "That's what I came for."

MALE VOICE: "__ __ __ to pray for."

WHISPERING: "Show them now."

LOUD FEMALE VOICE: "ADAM!"

Sandy's eyes opened big; I replayed the last part.

The whispers became a muffled talking of several different voices as if a conversation was going on, then a quiet voice whispers,

"**Adam,**" another male voice says, **"Adam."** Then clearest EVP I had ever heard. **"ADAM!"** the women's voice, so much louder than the others, was completely clear.

WATCH: Chapter 29: MORE VISITORS
SAME QR Code

I paused the recording, and we just looked at it each. Sandy picked up her camera and started snapping pictures.

"That's the weirdest thing I have ever heard." Sandy declared.

"Me too, coffee?" I offered.

Sandy nodded, and I got up to go upstairs. At the base of the staircase, I heard a faint whistle and then a quiet moan right in front of me.

"Sandy, take a picture over here!"

Sandy snapped the camera in my direction, and I continued upstairs. We sat together for hours discussing the recording, eating all the remaining snacks, and drinking coffee and water. (Something happens after we do recordings successfully; everyone becomes ravenously hungry.)

"That's the loudest and clearest one for sure. Think the guy I saw was named Adam?" I asked Sandy.

"Seems possible. Have you had any success researching the house?"

"No, it's weird, but I cannot find anything about this house or this town. I tried to do a title search, but it is different every time I look it up. I cannot find anything about this house or even this town, and not on the internet or library."

"That is weird. Well, your house is beautiful, and we have had a wonderful time. It sure is nice to see you."

"I really miss you," I said.

"I'm exhausted; I hope you sleep well" Sandy hugged me hard.

"You too," I said

 "Goodnight, Adam!" Sandy yelled

The next morning Harold and Sandy quickly packed their bags and then came up for breakfast.

We played the last night's recording for Harold, and the three of us talked about it for hours. Then, Sandy and I went outside to spend our final moments together.

"When you first moved in, I know you were scared, but how is it now?" Sandy asked.

"After one of the episodes, I stopped being afraid of it. I'm still not sure what it is, but nothing here is hurting anyone. If anything, it helps. I know it sounds a little weird, but it's as if someone wants to get our attention, just wants to let us know they are here. I know *something* is here, and no one will be able to convince me differently now. Too much has happened."

"Lights, things moving around, and all the noises here, I'm not sure I would be able to live here," Sandy said.

"Hey, you ladies left me all alone!" Harold yelled as he came out of the front door.

"We thought you were sleeping," Sandy said.

"Well, I lay down for a bit, then went and sat at the poker table. I have to say you're a brave girl, June; I think it might be a different experience being in this house alone."

"What are you talking about?" Sandy asked.

"I was downstairs sitting at the table and playing solitaire. This whole time, I thought the two of you were upstairs; I could hear you! Then the room started to make noises. I thought maybe it was you two at first; then, I realized you were not even in the house. Having people in the house, when you hear a noise, you assume it is someone upstairs, but I bet this is a very different experience when you are alone, and you know no one else could be making the noise." Harold chuckled.

"Yeah, I don't know how you are here by yourself so much," Sandy said.

"Keep the guns loaded," Harold added.

"Well, just keep answering the phone when I call," I laughed.

"You know you have changed a lot since you moved here," Sandy stated.

"Yeah, maybe, I do know, things I never understood before making sense now," I replied.

A quizzical expression formed across her face as she asked, "Like?"

"I understand more every day about the people around me. As if I can see through them. Beyond the bullshit and lies, some people are good, and others are not."

"You mean like what you told me about people who visit the house?" Sandy asked.

"Yeah, you and I just got closer while others seem to develop almost a different personality as if they can no longer hide their true feelings," I said.

"Like a veil is lifted, and you can see them for who they really are?" Sandy feverishly asked.

"Yeah, exactly; once I see it, it does not hurt anymore. There are no more expectations of these people. I just know they are unhealthy, and I need to move forward with people who love me. They were never who I thought they were. It's the same with good people in my life; I can see how amazing they are." I responded

Harold stood back up, "I'm going to bring the bags out to the car. You ladies, just relax," Sandy smiled at her husband.

Once he was inside, she asked. "What about the episodes. You have not told me anything about them for a while now; can I ask if they are getting better?"

"When something triggers it, it is awful, but they are less frequent now. I don't think it's over, but I only stopped talking so much about it because it does not confuse me anymore. It is hard, though. I wish I had some tools to use to stop the physical pain. It sometimes takes hours for the awful feelings to go away. It's so weird, Sandy. Everything hurts all at once—like that feeling you have after you've been raped, and the adrenaline is gone. Then come the feeling of wanting to rip off your skin. I want that to go away."

I wiped the tear running down her face.

"Have you remembered anything else about the men in the truck?"

"I just remember walking in the dark very fast. I remember more about what I looked like." I took a deep breath before finishing. "They had hit me in the face so many times one of my eyes swelled shut, there were cuts on me, and red marks from their hands were all over my body. My arms and legs were swollen and bruised, clumps of my hair were missing, and my head was bleeding. My back and neck hurt so much I thought they had stabbed me in the back. I remember looking in the mirror that night before I cleaned myself up. For a second, I thought I was dead; I looked dead."

I laughed as I wiped the water from my face. "So, changing the subject, do you think our house is haunted?"

"Yes, yes, I do," Sandy answered.

"What do you think it is?"

"Energy, maybe even *your* energy, But it's not scary. I think it's protecting you." Sandy said.

I explained what happened before they arrived—days before I had walked into the bathroom to check on what was causing the strange noises. The washing machine's power lights were just going off as I walked in.

I stood still, trying to remember the last time I had used the washing machine. It had been at least two days. I turned from the room; the washer sounded off again. Ding ding-ding-ding. Turning back, I walked up to the machine and reached to press the power button. I held out my finger, but before I could touch it, the power button announced itself yet again. "Ding ding-ding-ding." With the machine off, I waited a moment and then started to walk out again. Upon entering the hallway, my skin began to crawl, and the hair on my neck rose, Ding ding-ding-ding.

"It happened over and over and then never happened again. I was on the phone, and the person I was talking to said maybe the machine was shorting out."

Sandy giggled, "Like everything in the house?"

"I know, to someone not there, it's a logical conclusion, but this was more like a game. Every time I started to touch the button, the power would go off on its own. Later, the dryer did the same thing the same night, and neither of them ever did that again. Like the fan, it does not move anymore, but now other things happen. If the same things happened all the time, I would come to a different conclusion. The cold spots are always in a different place too. One week its lights are flashing off and on, then items are moving all about the house for another week. The electrical problems only last for a few days or weeks, and then it stops, and then something else weird will happen."

Amused by the reported events, Sandy shared, "Sounds like it *is* trying to get your attention."

"Oh, it has my attention!" I shrieked.

Harold walked out of the house, dragging one of the big suitcases behind him. "We sure had a good time, but we better get on the road and check into the first hotel before the storm comes."

I stood up and hugged Harold and Sandy, trying to hide my tears. I said, "Thanks for coming. Thanks for believing in me."

"We love you."

"Your house is very nice, and we had a great time. Are you going to be okay here alone?" Harold asked.

"Yes, I'll be fine, and besides, Jim will be home soon. Thanks for coming."

Always with a silent sparkle in his voice and a comforting tone, Harold laughingly exclaimed, "Anytime."

I waved as they drove down the driveway and out of sight. I walked into the house, sat at the kitchen table, and called my husband.

"Hi, honey, when are you coming home?"

"I'll be home tomorrow afternoon. Did you have a good time?"

"Yes, I had a great time! I just wish you could have been here more."

"Me too; I'll be home tomorrow. I love you."

"Love you too."

I set down the phone next to a pad of paper Sandy had used the night before, and I turned it to read what she had written. In big blue letters, she had doodled SOMETHING IS HERE.

I picked up the pen and rewrote her words. One by one, I drew a line through each letter and rewrote it again, creating an anagram from the squiggly note.

SOMETHING IS HERE

SOMETHING HERE IS

SOTHG HERE IS IN ME

GOSTH HERE IS IN ME

GHOST HERE IS IN ME

I stayed up late and then collapsed into bed, and I fell into a sound sleep almost immediately. Lying in bed with the covers pulled closed to my face, I opened my eyes as soon as I heard the familiar sound of walking in the room. The wooden floor creaked as if someone were lightly stepping into the room. I sat up and looked around the room. The sound stopped. I assumed I had been dreaming and lay back in the bed, pulling the covers up to my neck. I closed my eyes and shivered in the cold room.

I am not sure how long I slept. The air in my ear was warm when I heard the young girl whisper, "They're coming back," I sat straight up in bed, turning to my left. I was sure I would see the girl standing there. I pressed my hand to my heart, trying to calm myself down. I slowly got out of bed, turned on the light, and wrapped my robe close.

Cautiously I opened the bedroom door and walked into the kitchen. I carefully scooped the coffee into the filter, watching my hands shaking violently. I poured the water and sighed as my trembling hands spilled most of it on the counter. I pressed the button, lit a cigarette, and sat at the kitchen table, reflecting on what had happened moments before.

For the second time, the feeling of the air on my ear is what woke me. I could visualize the girl who had leaned over me, and I could remember seeing her before she whispered into my ear.

Of course, it was only a dream. I know I was sleeping, but it all felt so real.

I sighed and looked down at the notebook on the table as my heart began to beat faster. I stared at the anagram I had created the night before as tears ran down my face.

I had seen the girl in my dream before. I had seen the bleeding and bruised young girl with tears in her eyes, the girl from the truck, the dead girl - the younger version of myself!

CHAPTER 30

CHAPTER 30
HALLOWEEN

Another year had passed. Visitors came to stay with us, and a few of them had no paranormal experiences. While others swore, they would never stay another night in the house. Interestingly, those people who have been scared here are no longer in our lives. As if the house itself knew these people were not healthy, something I knew but was not ready to accept until later.

Nothing happening in this house resembles any movies I have ever seen. Many people have visited the house waiting for something to start flying around the room or see our walls bleed. I have stopped inviting some friends over because of their expectations. Although they are good people, they seem to expect it to perform like a funhouse once they enter. The instant response only happens in the movies.

Since living here, I have watched numerous ghost shows where groups of people go into someone's house, and instantly, activity happens. Two minutes after turning on their recording devices, they successfully documented disembodied voices. Immediate reactions or EVP's on-demand have never occurred here, and I think people forget about editing. I am sure anyone investigating the paranormal will tell you it can take hours before you capture evidence. It is definitively a career that takes patience.

Halloween became a big deal at our house. New friends from Washington and old friends from California were always asking, "What are you doing for Halloween?" I guess it seems exciting to visit a haunted house this time of the year. So once again, I planned the annual party. Interestingly, the activity in the house thins out the closer we get to Halloween. We have documented many events before and after, but almost nothing takes place once the decorations come out.

I flew one of my oldest friends to the house from California to spend a long weekend and invited my new friends from Spokane. It felt incredible to have people drive so far to come to my party.

It seemed like it would take forever to set up the house and get everything ready. This year it was dinner and dessert for six and gift bags for each guest filled with every candy and trinket I could find related to ghosts.

We now had so many decorations and lights; it was hard to remember to turn them all on. The last thing to set up was the paranormal equipment. By this time, we had acquired a case full of documenting supplies: handheld video recorders, cameras, instant-read thermometers, E.M.F. detectors, and night-vision motion sensor cameras spread throughout the house.

After dinner, my friends would participate in an amateur ghost hunt before we sat down to do the annual recording.

As I heard the first car pull up, I turned on the last of the small cameras. Each guest came in, stopping first to admire the projected ghost image on the living room wall. After about an hour of introductions and stories about previous experiences in the house, we sat down for dinner.

Then I ushered all the ladies downstairs and explained how the equipment works. I instructed everyone to choose an item to carry.

Separated into two groups, each group would walk through all the rooms in the house in almost total darkness and record their feelings in each room.

Everything seemed uneventful until we sat down to record the house.

Suddenly the friend I flew in from California, the only woman who had never participated in EVP recordings, leaped from her chair and ran into the other room.

What we experienced that night was the definition of social conditioning. She proclaimed she could feel the evil and began to dry heave as if she would throw up.

One of my guests turned to her and stated harshly,

"Look here, if you're going to be sick, stop leaning towards me! Go lay down in the other room."

We spent the rest of the evening attempting to calm down or comfort her while she dramatically reenacted every horror movie with a haunted house scenario. Everyone frustratingly sighed as she circled back in from the guest room over and over, proclaiming that she could feel the evil.

The next day, I scanned the photos taken by the automatic cameras. The hair on the back of my neck stood up as soon as I saw the images the upstairs living room camera had taken. The first was a picture of two of my guests standing in the room talking. Next to one of my friends was an unmistakable small child. Except there were no children at the party.

Then I realized the camera had continued to take pictures even after we had gone downstairs. I sat at my computer, staring at the images, astonished by what I saw. Two of the photos looked like angels, but one picture made my stomach turn.

What the camera captured that night is unexplainable. Once I saw it, the previous night came back in a flash. I believe that what you focus on expands. The fears and statements she cried seemed mixed with mental illness and medieval ideas. If the declaration the woman described were to manifest, I think this might be what we would see.

WATCH: Chapter 30: HALLOWEEN
SAME QR Code

A day after the party, my friend from California started to act strange. Her behavior changed so dramatically it was frightening. I am not even sure she realized what terrible things she said.

As I stood there stunned by her strange words, I understood she harbored a secret hatred for me. Seemingly unable to stop herself, as if compelled, she verbally vomited her hidden feelings on me. After her ranting, insults, and odd behavior, she acted as if nothing had happened.

That night she complained of difficulty sleeping. She had told me it was hard to breathe in the room, and she explained that it was as if someone were sitting on the end of the bed, blowing tons of cigarette smoke in her face. I didn't think much of it since she was a smoker herself; I figured she smoked in the guest room, and this story would explain the smell of smoke. No smoking in the guest room was almost my only rule for overnight guests.

Of course, I did not know it at the time, but I would hear this exact description of overwhelming smoke from another hostile house guest in a few years.

Once she left, I chose not to speak to her again; I don't believe she remembers why, but I can't be sure. Although paranormal activity in the house seems to decrease during this time of year, its effect on people proved different.

We would experience this behavior with other people invited to the house. If someone with any form of mental issue spent more than an hour at Hill House, their condition would intensify.

Our daughter Laurel invited a girl she thought she knew well at another recording event. She was only in the house for approximately two hours before I had to get my gun to ensure the safety of my other guests.

None of these people seem to remember what happened.

In our home, when you Love, everything becomes more loving.

Fear becomes more Frightening

Hate, Hates more

Happiness is Happier

Sick gets Sicker

Peace is more Peaceful.

CHAPTER 31

CHAPTER 31
THE BOARD

My husband, Jim, was no longer a non-believer.

By now, he had encountered supernatural experiences for himself. The more open-minded he was, the more he experienced. I know he does not believe in the media portrayal of the paranormal, and neither do I. He is, however, fully open to the idea there is unusual energy here. I was no longer apprehensive about telling him what my encounters were.

During our nightly phone call, I told him how upset I was about something strange that transpired at the grocery store. I also told him about the level of creepy activity in the house. His response was simple:

"I'm not surprised the house seems to react to your energy. When you are very happy, sad, scared, or angry, the house becomes active. I think maybe it's responding to your emotions."

Jim was finally able to take some time off from work, and we took a quick vacation and drove to Montana. On the way home, we stopped at a few antique stores. In the last store we went into; we only stayed for a second. The lights were low, with a radio playing from a back room. Whoever was in the store was in the back. Jim suddenly rushed us out of the store.

"Something is wrong; we have to go right now!"

He quickly guided me out of the front door and straight to the car. Both of us were shaking. We talked about it most of the way home. The strange sensation he had something was wrong, very wrong. Some people would call it intuition, but they did not see his face. I had never seen him react like this before. I knew what he was talking about; I felt it too. The turning in your stomach when you know you are in danger. The difference was I did not speak up right away as he did. I was too worried about how it would sound. I know I would have walked out right away if I had been alone. It is hard to say this, but I was so concerned he would think I was senselessly dramatic; I was afraid to say anything. That experience taught me I could trust my feelings with my husband, no matter what.

Once at home, we decided to try the Ouija Board he bought a week before. The Ouija board Jim bought was a somewhat rare board from the 1920s, and the wood looked and felt like it possessed quite a history all on its own. The yellowing and dog-eared box was tattered from apparent frequent use. I was still on edge from our earlier experience in the antique store.

I was looking forward to changing our focus on anything else. Joining in the history of this sensationalized game sounded like the perfect activity.

"I read something online about a scientist who has been experimenting with EVPs. He said if you record two days straight, you would have better results. I want to try it." I said.

"We don't have two days, but I am willing to record twice in one day." He answered.

"Let's try it for a few minutes and then do what he said, make an appointment to come back," I said.

Jim agreed, and we went downstairs. I turned on the recorder and automatic cameras, and we set the board on the table. We asked a few questions and then said we would make an appointment and return when it got dark. We both went back upstairs, had dinner, and talked until it was dark outside.

We returned downstairs a few hours later; I turned the recorder on right away. Jim and I struggled to make some of the equipment work. The EMF detector and motion lights would not work even though I had just changed the batteries. We set up the equipment and extra cameras while we laughed about how many batteries we use every month while the recorder kept going.

Finally, we turned out the lights and sat at the table. We moved our chairs closer, put our hands on the planchette, and Jim made a joke.

"No one will be able to fit between us. All this trouble to come back from the dead, and we make it impossible, poor guy or girl" We both laughed and moved our chairs.

We asked questions for almost forty-five minutes.

"Do you still need help?"

"Please help us understand how we can help you."

"Can you help us to understand you better?"

"Show us how to help you."

"Is there a child here who needs help?"

We based all of our questions on the previously recorded messages asking for help. Jim asked about ten questions, and I asked about the same, all centered on the previous recordings I interpreted as people crying out for help.

While we were at the table, I could feel Blinky pawing at my leg, and I never moved him away or said anything. I knew the recorder would pick up any sounds I made, and I did not want to encourage the cat to make any sounds either.

We asked all of our questions and decided to end the session by being sure to say "Good-Bye." Neither of us believes in this. Of course, we were not surprised with no results from the Ouija Board. The planchette will have to move on its own before I would ever give this credibility.

Jim stood up and turned on the lights. I retrieved the recorder and found Blinky sleeping next to the bookcase.

"Blinky is here, but I could feel him next to me! He was just over there." I said.

"Did you hear the dogs?"

"No," I answered

"I was sure I could hear Briquette barking."

"Well, we can still listen to the recording; maybe we got something."

We shut everything off and went upstairs. While Jim made coffee, I transferred the recording to my computer. Jim set my cup next to me, and I pressed play. We listened as the room filled with our voices and conversations about batteries. Then Jim's joke

"Come back from the dead, and we make it impossible, poor guy or girl."

We could hear our laughter, and suddenly the laughing changed as if an entire room of people were laughing with us.

Then instantly, a voice. I was shocked as the voice echoed through the room.

It sounded like me, but it could not have been me.

I never said the words recorded on the device.

75-2

I Shepherd four people

Are you a real person or host of the Ouija Board?

Jim coughs

"That was Jim" (This is the only part from the recording I did say).

Talking to you make you stronger and make it easier to convey; you can make a very loud sound or bang on the wall if you want us to still, Adam, Not because our cat is making too much noise

DARE

I sat up in my chair and looked at Jim.

Suddenly the recorder played our voices again.

"Blinky is here, but I could feel him next to me! He was just over there."

"Did you hear the dogs?"

"No"

"I was sure I could hear Briquette…."

"Well, at first, I thought the batteries were dying, but now it's recording normally again," I said.

"Let me see the recorder," Jim took the small silver box and tested the settings. He tried to replicate what had happened and began re-recording us, and it recorded our voices normally.

Both of us sat there in shock. We had asked questions for over 40 minutes, and not one question was recorded.

Other than a cough, Jim's voice was never recorded at all. It had worked as expected while we were setting up the room.

That forty minutes on the recorder was reduced to 1.3 minutes; once we got up, it recorded as usual again.

It would have made some sense if it only recorded bits and pieces of what we said, but it did not. Neither of us ever said the words that were recorded.

I never said any of those words,

I never even said Ouija Board. It had occurred to me that perhaps the recorder malfunctioned and was adding words from previous recordings, but never in any recording would I have ever said the words Shepherd, 75-2, are you a real person. Nothing made any sense.

The voice sounded like me until the word **DARE**.

That voice sent chills through me.

WATCH: Chapter 31: THE BOARD
SAME QR Code

While my husband was examining the recorder, I listened to the tape again. I scribbled down the words.

We asked questions with the same theme: how can we help you?

I typed in some of the words into the computer search engine.

The word shepherd seemed odd, and I cannot remember saying the word since I was eight years old in vacation bible school.

When I typed in 75-2, the first search link I pulled up was Psalms 75:2.

I opened the link. Chills swept across me as I read it

PSALMS 75:2

"I choose the appointed time; it is I who judge with equity."

I read it to Jim, and we both sat quietly, looking at each other.

It could have all been a coincidence. Earlier, we asked to schedule an appointment, and now I am looking at a scripture telling me we do not get to schedule the appointed time?

Then there were the photos; I opened the program displaying the automatic pictures taken from the day. The first time we had recorded, we were only there for a short time, but the cameras captured things I would never have expected. One camera had snapped photos of a blue mist seemingly coming down the stairs. I would have ignored it and assumed it was an illusion from the light coming into the window, but then I saw another camera from upstairs capture the same thing. The following picture shows one of the arch-shaped windows downstairs next to the staircase. (A window that would scare Laurel when she had to walk by it)

Our standard arched-shaped window in the photo had an ornate decorative, wood-like frame around it?

Then I opened the file for the photos from later the same night. Some were strange, but two of them were astonishing. One of the cameras had been right on the table, so it photographed our hands on the planchette. These are motion sensor cameras, so if you are moving, they will be blurry.

Both hands were clearly visible since we had stopped moving and just rested the planchette on the board. There was another hand on top of Jim's hand.

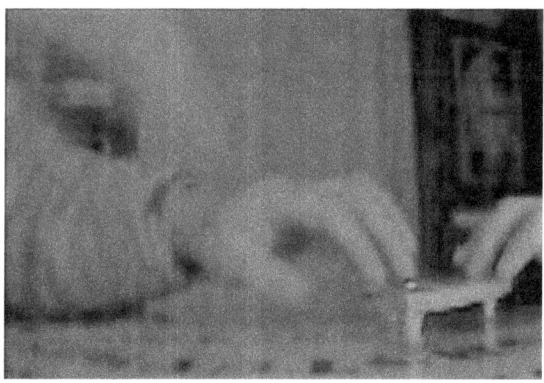

Many people may think it is just some accidental lighting issue, but I am very familiar with how these cameras work. This picture is unexplained. The most shocking was a picture of Jim standing in front of the table while we were putting things away. He was moving around, so of course, the image was a bit blurry. There was still no way the camera could have captured what I saw—a child-size black shadow standing directly in front of him. The picture surprised me, but the fact that it appears to be a child did not. My husband has had many experiences with children.

On the SLS camera, we filmed him interacting with children many times.

He has heard a child singing and a child running past the fireplace.

We have no explanation for what happened.

I have struggled to understand if there was some message in these words. The only part of this that made sense….

We do not have control over when we can communicate.

That is solely up to them.

CHAPTER 32

CHAPTER 32
EMBRACED FROM BEYOND

As the months went by, the strange things in the house continued. I realized we had many things happening I had never heard of before. Mimicking was the most bizarre. Every day sounds like Jim getting water from the refrigerator dispenser or toilets flushing would replay in the house. At first, it happened when I was alone, but now it has happened many times while other people were in the house.

I filmed many different events in the house, and I no longer questioned myself or my sanity. I was still trying desperately to understand why this was happening. There seemed to be no pattern to anything.

All the notes and documentation I had done never explained anything at all. If lights flashed off and on, there was never any pattern.

The theory Jim had; the house was responding to my emotions

only seemed possible occasionally, and there was no consistent pattern. The lack of motive for the paranormal events bothered me more than the events themselves.

The morning our lights went out, they had come back on within ten minutes, and I went to reset the flashing digital clock on the oven. Before I could even push the settings for the clock, the lights went out again.

After a few more times, I left and went outside to play with the dog. I saw the lights had come on inside the house and returned inside. As I walked in, I expected to see all the digital displays on the ovens flashing, but the clock I had previously attempted to set now displayed the time.

This type of oven clock does not reset itself

I called Sandy and told her how frustrating this was for me. At first, she did not seem to understand why I was so upset.

Then I said, "If they can reset the clock, write me a fucking note and tell me what you want!"

Whatever was frightening me, in the beginning was now gone.

Unless it was the shocking sounds of banging and crashing that sounded like an intruder in the house. Those sounds remain to be the only scary thing about living here.

The re-livings continued; most were not as severe and quickly passed.

One afternoon, home alone, I had one excruciating episode. I have no idea what might have triggered this. Sometimes I can tell right away. Television episodes depicting rape or even music are easy to recognize. This time I can only guess it may have been a smell. I know it has triggered it before.

Sitting in my kitchen, I was overwhelmed with the pain and awful feeling again. I cried for what felt like an hour. It took longer this time to shake the man's voice as it repeated in my head. I grabbed my jacket and walked outside, hoping the cold air would help me feel better. I walked across our backyard, following Tala as she ran to the end of our property. She stood on top of a large rock and stared intently into the vacant property next door. It was something she had done hundreds of times before.

As I stood there watching her, I could hear the hushed voice of a woman. First, I looked around, trying to ascertain where the sound was coming from, looking for someone in the abandoned acreage over the fence. It was winter, and now it was easy to see through the trees, and there was no one there.

I clenched my jacket around me tighter, not because I was cold because I was still feeling my skin crawling from earlier. I choked back my tears as they started again.

Tala jumped from the rock and ran to me as a large mass of mist formed close to where she was standing. It was over six feet tall and maybe two feet wide. It appeared as a thick mist or steam. It was usual to see the fog in these temperatures. Over the river, a fog would form every morning. The temperature of the water and the contradicting temperature of the air forms mist. What was unusual was it was only in this one spot and nowhere else. There was nothing in the area capable of causing this, and there was no explanation.

I watched in absolute awe as it then began to move. I could hear the woman talking again. My entire body started to tingle and become warm. The previous feelings I had vanished as the warm, comforting sensation covered me. Tears, now from relief, streamed down my face.

Regardless of how this may sound or what you believe, at the very moment, I knew I was not alone. I am not sure where this comes from exactly, but I knew in front of me was a woman who was there to console me and identify with everything inside me; she understood how I felt and why.

Talking to people about what was happening and what I was remembering was very difficult. Trying to explain you can hear the voice of a man who attacked you years ago makes people automatically believe you have some mental illness. At least, that is what I feared. I think this woman was there due to my fears and inability to explain what was happening.

I do not know her name- if she is a ghost, angel, or spirit, and I only know what I felt.

She let me know I was not alone and that I mattered.

The mist started to change shape, and I reached into my pocket for my camera. I turned it on, set it to video, and tried to capture what I had been seeing, but now it was no longer the same. It extended from two feet wide to maybe twelve feet wide. It grew taller and shrank smaller and moved down the hill until it vanished. What I have on video is not as spectacular as what I had seen, but I am grateful I could record it at all. Whenever I look at the video, I cannot stop my tears. I never captured what she said on tape, and I could never hear what she said. I guess I did not need to. The love and compassion I felt at the moment was the most miraculous thing I have ever encountered.

There are far fewer times I experience a re-living, and they are much less intense when I do, and I recover quickly. That was my last severe re-living experience.

WATCH: Chapter 32: EMBRACED FROM BEYOND
SAME QR Code

CHAPTER 33

CHAPTER 33
THEIR MEETING PLACE

We were both exhausted, but Jim and I wanted to try recording again before bed. We only recorded questions for about thirty minutes, and I asked my last question, and after waiting for a few moments, we turned off the recorder.

The following day I kissed my husband goodbye as he went on another trip. Laurel came over to the house to spend a few days with me. We each made a cup of coffee and sat at the kitchen table as I loaded the file into the computer. It did not take long to load the short recording from the night before.

We heard strange noises and knocking responding to our questions.

When the last question played, we both stared at each other.

We replayed it over and over and smiled at each other every time the voice responded.

"Is this house a meeting place?" I asked

"YES"

"YES"

WATCH: Chapter 33: THEIR MEETING PLACE

SAME QR Code

We may never know why a paranormal experience happens to one person and not the other, and I am no expert and still have no clear understanding of why it happens here. I don't believe our house is the only one, and I have met a few people from this town who say *their house is haunted.* One lady I met at the town post office said she thought it was the entire town.

I have no idea if the previous residents ever experienced anything here themselves.

I believe that some places may be more active than others, but once I accepted the reality of this house, I remembered things that happened all through my life, Events I dismissed as coincidence, but now I feel were also paranormal.

Post-Traumatic Stress likely played a substantial role in my experiences. PTSD keeps you in a higher *state of awareness* of the world around you. I can often hear sounds or notice changes inside the house before others. Those with PTSD precisely understand what I mean; we can walk into a room and almost instantly notice if something is out of place or even if someone has been in our home.

Since 2016 when the 1st edition of this book was published, numerous people with PTSD have contacted me, explaining their paranormal experiences. There does seem to be a connection, but many people will experience phenomena they cannot explain, and Post-Traumatic Stress does not apply to everyone.

There have been paranormal events reported in every culture, religion, and society. In many countries, the idea of spirits is commonplace, not the taboo subject it seems to be in the United States. One of my closest friends comes from a culture that believes the souls of the dead are always present and are respected and honored. As a child, she was *not* programmed to fear them but to appreciate that they come to guide the living.

When I tell people I am writing books about the paranormal, I am stunned by the number of people who openly tell me about their own experiences.

One hundred percent of the people I have talked to say they believe in the paranormal. The catch was they would not speak about it when others could hear. People tend to keep their stories secret out of fear. I was afraid to write this book because I know how narrow-minded many people can be; I thought it was this country; I was wrong. Now I understand; I just surrounded myself with the wrong people.

Past family members were the only people who have ever given me negative responses to our house or anything paranormal. If this is something you have familiarity with, I suggest going to www.TheirRules.com. It is one of my books, but it is also a community of members who have exposure to the paranormal and has been a help to others. (you do not have to buy the book if you need support- it's free)

An experience with the after-life requires your dignity and respect.

Those who tell me about their encounters with the other side always say, *This experience has changed me.* I can only speak about my encounters, but the more I ignored what was happening, the more I dismissed it, the crazier I felt, and the more intense it became. As if *they* were insisting, I recognized them.

There are many different voices and impressions of more than just a few people inside our home. I believe at least one is here who had similar experiences to mine, and we can heal together.

Your acknowledgment of them requires an open mind. What follows will become a spiritual experience beyond all of your understanding.

In an attempt to understand what was happening to me, I reconnected with Serena. I apprehensively told her about the house and even explained I was trying to write a book about it, and I assumed she would decide I was crazy and hang up on me. After only a few moments on the phone, I was totally at ease. It was great talking to her again; now a doctor, she and I spent hours discussing how the academic world immediately discards paranormal experiences with the rolling of their eyes and sarcastic statements. We became close friends and now talk almost every day.

Something new seems to happen every few weeks but does not always coincide with a re-living episode.

I occasionally speak with women on the phone, usually requested by their counselor, to discuss the effects of rape, incest, or physical/emotional abuse. Some emotions can be embarrassing to talk about; I can put people at ease when talking about subjects like these, enabling women to tell the secrets that made them sick. Many of them have also spoken about unexplainable things happening around them. I found this shocking, but the women I spoke with were even more terrified to talk about paranormal events as they were the causes of their C-PTSD.

Many will not believe these are paranormal experiences, although Paranormal simply means *out of the realm of ordinary occurrences*. What happens in this house or in the life of a PTSD survivor is *out of the realm of ordinary occurrences*.

I can understand better than anyone why so many people refuse to open their minds to the possibility that there is life after death.

It is hard to accept that what you believe could be wrong. As hard as it was for me to accept, it is easier for me and others in recovery. To maintain sobriety, we must open our minds and admit that we don't know the answers. I needed to replace the church god I felt hated me with *a God of my own understanding*. Now God loves me and everyone else.

The entities we have communicated with in our home are frightened of the unknown. Afraid of their church god sending them to hell. It seems they fear their mistakes in life are some hell-bound train.

I am not an expert (no one is); all we can do is ask them if we can pray for them and then ask God to give them peace, guidance, and understanding of the love God has for them. We share our higher power with them, and some leave our house—some stay.

Many we speak with ask to stay here; most tell us they are children and feel safe here.

No one knows what is or is not possible in the amazing world we live in, only God knows for sure, and there is no direct mouthpiece for God. No one knows what might be right where the supernatural is concerned. I know some people who have had frightening experiences, but it is not always negative. Waiting for the terrifying event makes you miss the fantastic one. We will miss the miracle if we cannot be open-minded to what we do not understand.

I firmly believe *Intention Matters;* if you come into our house and expect to be scared, you will be afraid. If you come here with an open mind, you will leave amazed.

It has to be my ego, forcing me to think I should have the ability to figure this all out and understand why this is happening.

In response to some of my readers, I feel your frustration.

On TV, the paranormal programs all show the homeowner doing a little research and quickly and easily finding the answers, and poof, it all makes sense. The homeowners always discover the reason for the Haunting. At times, I have been so frustrated I felt like screaming. This town must have records somewhere, but no one knows anything.

We have been unable to find any accurate records regarding the house. Newspaper articles and crimes here never mention the town's name.

What happens here- Stays Here.

In 2020 I finished another book, THEIR RULES. *Effective Methods for Documenting the Paranormal, if you follow Their RULES*

Publishing was delayed due to my health and the 2020-2021 virus;

Our daughter Laurel moved back home to wait out the quarantine.

The activity inside our home increased by unimaginable levels at this time. Laurel and I documented and communicated with them almost daily. We discovered that what we once believed were their rules had changed, and we re-wrote the book together.

We still do not know who ADAM is, but his name continues in EVPs.

One afternoon Sandy and I were talking about what I call "Chaos" in the house, how nothing makes sense or has any pattern. Her idea was the house might be some sort of entry point. Unlike a haunted house (in the movies) where spirits may connect to the home or land, her theory was our home was like an AA meeting. Where personalities of all types would enter, some would return, and some would not; some stay for years and others never return at all. We both agreed that it would explain a lot. Her scenario was the only one to make the chaos make sense.

If we could all stop rushing around and sit quietly, we all might *feel* answers to questions and consolation from the pain within our lives. No human beings set foot on this planet and get away free and clear. We are all broken, and some more than others, but we all carry scars. If we can become still and open-minded, we might all feel the unseen comforting hand on our shoulders, telling us we are not alone.

WE ARE SPIRITUAL BEINGS, HAVING A HUMAN EXPERIENCE

CHAPTER 34
TESTIMONIALS

The following pages are testimonials from some people who have experienced paranormal activity in our home.
I was happy to add their experiences told from their perspective. I am so grateful to the people in my life who have stayed open-minded and loving enough to help me understand and learn with me.

JIM MATTHEWS

My wife is not only the love of my life, but she is also my best friend, most trusted advisor, and a beautiful trusting spirit who helps me remember everyone and everything has good in it. She placed all of her trust in me when this job opportunity came to fruition, and I whisked her away from everyone and everything she knew and loved. She found herself living in this remote, albeit beautiful new location to start our next journey in life together. My new employer had not given me much time to settle in, as they were very anxious to get me up and running. Unfortunately, this left my wife alone on a hillside where trees and deer outnumber people by a million to one.

On my long drives home, we would often chat about the events of her week and all the weird noises and "happenings" occurring in and around the house. I would typically try to be the level-headed and practical husband explaining away these noises and occurrences. Little did I know I was frustrating her to no end. I thought it would be comforting to describe a "rational" reason for these things, but she did not hear them that way. I was so worried about her I would mention 'just selling the house and moving back to California". She seemed so scared initially, and I am sure some of this still was based on the fact she was alone and lonely.

Our daughter soon came to move in with us. I thought we would kill two birds with one stone. Give our daughter a chance to adjust to her surroundings, save money to have a good start on her new life, and have companionship for my wife since I was gone so much.

As the months rolled into years, my wife stopped talking to me about these strange things, and if she did, I would try to be analytical about the reasons, or so I thought.

I have heard many things, and I see some weird things like this one candle that will go on by itself for no reason. It is a battery-powered candle and has a matching sibling next to it. At first, I blamed it on the source of the items manufacturing country; but I have switched the two around. Low and behold, the exact location will inadvertently turn on; it is not the particular candle but where the candle is.

I have no explanation for this. I have also woken up to severe crashing sounds, and a couple of times, I said maybe it was an animal (deer or moose) trying to get out of the cold. Ha, no way, my friend, I was simply scared. I have jumped up and walked our house and property with my handgun and knife on several occasions with no visible proof to drive this action.

My wife and I are pretty much on the same page now. I do believe she still holds back what she sees and hears, but it is my fault. We have had conversations about "things" that have happened to me in my past; I can only describe them as supernatural. I love my wife, and I hope she knows how much I support her in this book or series of books.

I do not know which are natural vs. supernatural occurrences engulfing our new home, and I do not know how much has to do with our past life traumas or even if those traumas simply have opened 'doors. You will have to decide for yourself what you believe, what you don't, and what is real and what is not. Good luck.

Jim Matthews

LAUREL COOPER

This is my short account of my experiences at my parents' house. It is also what I have witnessed at my parent's house. The house now referred to as THE RELIVING HOUSE (aka Hill House Estate)

I first heard about the odd occurrences of my parents house while I was still in California. My Mom would tell me things that would happen that did not seem possible and could even be considered far-fetched. My Mom is an honest woman who never says crazy things, so when I heard about what she was experiencing in different areas of the house, I took her seriously. I started to look up any info on the house as well as what these "happenings" could possibly be. Once I had moved to Spokane, Washington. I was leery that these things would even happen, but after a few nights, I knew that this was NOT an ordinary house.

The first time walking into the house, it felt cold. Now I do not mean temperature. The atmosphere felt cold, which is odd because I had never felt like that in any of our houses. She has always decorated to create a warm and loving environment, and yet something else made it feel uninviting.

I assumed that it was moving to a new state and would just take some getting used to, but after the third night, I started feeling like I was being watched, especially when I was trying to go to sleep. In the first month, I heard odd noises and would smell things (smoke and other things I could not identify) but could never find the source.

My brother came to visit for Christmas, and I let him stay in the guest room and moved into my Dad's office. The entire time I stayed in his office, I felt even more uneasy; the closet and office door would move by itself, the windows appeared to have a shadowy figure looking at me, and I would hear banging noises. The room was unbearably cold and made it very difficult to get any sleep.

After a few months, my Mom and I decided to do some recordings. Once we played back the tape, we heard a man swearing and what sounded like a little girl. For months after, we continued to record the house as well as taking pictures and EVPs (audio recordings.) When we heard noises, we started taking pictures, and the results were astonishing. Whenever possible, if we heard a noise that was unidentifiable, we took a picture. Every time we did this, our pictures would contain strange bright orbs or smoky like figures. The recordings usually had talking that seemed to be responding to our questions. One day we were ending our recording and walking back upstairs. My Mom still had the recorder on and said, "Okay, say something before we turn off the recorder" On playback, a man said, "Hello."

As time went on, I began to hear some of the voices in the house without the assistance of the recorder but with my own ears. In the guest room, I heard someone whisper right into my ear! On the staircase, my Mom and I both heard a man talking.

During one of our recording sessions, we decided to split up. I was downstairs, and my Mom was upstairs with the recorder in the center of the house. That night was the first time we heard a scream or cry; I thought it was my mom, and she thought it was me, but it was neither of us.

We started bringing people over to see if they would experience the same things. We did a recording with a new friend I had made at work. While we asked questions, there was a flashing bulb from the chandelier, but the lights were all out. There was no electricity to the lamp. My friend was spooked after that. When we played back the recording, we heard that the "ghosts or spirits "responded to my friend.

I personally have heard, seen, felt, and even smelled odd things in my Mom and Dad's house. I am interested in finding out more about what it is. My parents may be skeptical about the afterlife, but I am a believer that once we die, we may sometimes not "cross-over." I do not feel that the entities at the house are evil, but in my opinion, the do exist, and they are desperately trying to make themselves known. My parents are the most honest, upstanding, and level-headed people I would ever know. That they hear and see these things daily just makes these occurrences even more remarkable.

Laurel.

JOSHUA

I visited my Mom and Dad at the house many times in the last few years. Each time I have been there, something unexplainable happened.

My first visit was Christmas. I was so happy to see Mom, Dad, and my sister, who had already moved to Washington. My Mom had told me about some of the things that happened in the house when she was alone, so I did not expect anything to happen with a house full of people.

My sister told me about her experiences; still, I did not believe I would see anything.

On the second night, I was proven wrong. In the family room, we could hear noises coming from the guest room. We went to check it out only to find the closet door opened on its own. I was still thinking; maybe I had not closed the sliding doors at all. We closed it and went back to finish the movie. We heard it again, went to check, and it was open!

The house would become very cold, and we all had the feeling there was someone else in the rooms with us. There were many strange noises, banging, tapping, and knocking sounds having no explanation.

I came with my brother on the next visit, and we saw, heard, and felt things. My Mom had told me how the house seemed to mimic everyday sounds. If she dropped a dish, a few days later, she could hear what sounded like a dish breaking. She would check, and there would be nothing broken or no reason for the sound. My brother and I experienced this very thing. My Mom, brother, and I were all sitting downstairs talking; my Dad had gone to bed. Then we heard him walk across the kitchen floor upstairs, get water, and walk back. Not surprising, except that my Mom went upstairs seconds later, and he was actually sound asleep. Whoever was walking around it was not my Dad. The house scared me at first, but not anymore. Nothing terrible happens; it does not feel like there is really anything to fear. Nevertheless, when you hear the noises or see something move on its own, it is understandable when the hair on the back of your neck stands up, and it can feel creepy.

My Mom has never believed in ghosts or anything paranormal, and I have spent hours talking to her about the house and reassuring her that she is not crazy. For a long time, she would not accept it was even possible for a home to be haunted. I was worried about her since she is alone in the house for days at a time, and I am not sure I would be able to stay there alone in that house.

My Mom has had a very hard life, and in some way (I do not totally understand), I think the house is helping her. Since moving into this new house, she has removed negative people from her life, seems stronger and happier.

My parents always had a great marriage, but since moving into this house, they seem even closer and more caring of each other. My parents are honest people; they are both clean and sober and very logical. I know they both believe now, Although my Mom calls it energy, and my Dad jokes around about it.

We all agree that whatever this is, it is trying to communicate. The house is not scary, but yeah, it is haunted.

JOSHUA

LORI McCALLISTER

My name is Lori McCallister; I became friends with June in 2011. She had hired me to help her train her Husky puppy named Tala Dakota. I met June at her home. The moment I took the first few steps into the house, I could feel something different. I prefer to train dogs in their homes, so I have been in many houses. This house had a different feeling.

June and I hit it off right away, and on our first meeting to train the puppy, I asked her if she had ever had any trouble in the house. She confided in me that some weird things had happened, and we talked for hours. After that, we would plan to meet for coffee or lunch as often as we could or as often as June felt safe. We have been good friends ever since.

I once told June that I loved her house. "It has everything I love in a house the rock wall, wood floors and fireplace but I would be afraid to stay here alone. It feels creepy"

During one visit to her house, as I walked in, I saw the ceiling fan spinning very fast. June simply said, "It just goes on and off by itself" down the stairs, I could feel the sudden change in temperature, and the hair on the back of my neck stood up as if I was intruding in someone else's house, not the home of my friend. The cold downstairs does not make any sense. The temperature drops what feels to be 20 degrees colder than the staircase.

On another visit to the house, I came to attend a sort of Halloween Party. I met her daughter Laurel and one of her friends. The four of us sat downstairs in the family room. Laurel set the recorder on the stairs. We began to ask questions. June and Laurel had told me about previous recordings they had made where someone answered or seemed to respond to the questions they asked. I started first, reading from a list June had made. I asked the questions. A few times, there were banging sounds, which seemed to be in response to my questions. Later, when the tape played back, a man was talking.

I asked,

"Is there anything that we can do to help you?"

The entire answer we could not make out. Only the last part of the sentence could we decipher.

"___ ___ ___ I am a Master"

June asked, "Did someone die in this house?"

Every time she asked that question, the smaller dogs would bark so loud, she had put them in the upstairs bathroom. She asked again this time, the dog began to bark again. I remembered this because the dogs only barked when she asked that question.

Now due to my work schedule, I am only able to visit a few times a year. I can say without hesitation that there is absolutely energy in her house. It is not evil or scary but seems to want to communicate; perhaps it is even angels.

Lori McCallister

SANDY AND HAROLD HORSLEY

My name is Sandy, and my husband's name is Harold. We have been friends with Jim & Junes for several years now and could not wait to visit them in the north woods

June and Jim moved to Washington a few years ago, and as we had become such great friends, I missed her terribly. We communicate by phone a lot, but it is just not the same. June has told me about the strange happenings in her home. I never knew June to be interested or involved in any way with the paranormal. This was new, and I know her to be honest and not makeup stories, so I had no reason to believe anything different from what she was saying to me. She made us this cute Halloween video trying to keep humor in the things that were scaring her. The pictures and videos of the orbs were amazing enough, but then the footage of the bowl in the kitchen really stunned my husband and me. I had heard many things from June as we talked on the phone. In the beginning, I knew she was terrified. Jim travels so much for his job; all I could do was be a good listener and try to reassure her that she would be ok.

We planned our trip to their house, and on June 5, we left the San Gabriel Valley and headed north. Our journey through Nevada, Oregon, and Idaho into Washington were beautiful and pleasant. I had started having some headaches, which I am not prone to, so I assumed it was all sinus-related. By the time we reached June's home on the seventh, I was not feeling myself. Still, I was excited to be there and see the "house."

While my dutiful husband brought in the bags, June and I talked like two excited teens in the kitchen. I took in all the lovely work and decorating that June had been so busy doing for the past two years. Her home was gorgeous. I could not imagine this house being anything but a typical woodsy-style home with a fantastic view of the valley of massive evergreen trees.

On Harold's last trip in with our luggage, we both followed him downstairs to see the lower part of the house. Her husband Jim was still away on business and not expected in until much later. As I was in awe of all the beauty of her home, we were talking while she took us on the tour to the guest room and then the office. We walked around and approached the staircase; we heard a sound I can only describe as someone throwing keys on the counter in the kitchen. I recognized the sound immediately because, as a child, my Father always threw his keys on the counter of our home when he returned from work. We were all downstairs, standing next to each other, so there was no way that this sound could have come from us. I looked at June and then Harold and said, "Did you hear that"? Harold turned to me and said yes, and June had a look of knowing on her face and said, "It's the house." I asked Harold what it sounded like to him, and he said it sounded like someone throwing keys on the counter, which was exactly what it sounded like. Now I have to tell you, my husband is slightly hard of hearing and had no problem hearing that sound. June and I decided the house was saying hello, and she explained that many of the sounds she would hear in the house were sounds normally heard in the house at a given moment, but the house seemed to be mimicking the sounds. She would hear these different sounds but was alone most of the time while Jim was working. The look on her face was vindication as she said, "See, I'm not crazy"! Well, we settled down from our trip and got to catch up, visiting with "Tala," her beautiful dog, and just relaxing. Unfortunately, I started to feel very ill and was unaware that I had started running a fever.

By Saturday morning, I was feeling sick. Poor June felt so bad, and it was not her fault, and I reassured her it wasn't the house. Just two days later, I was feeling 100% better. Now the visit got more fun. Back at the house, we had forgotten all about the "keys" incident and would eat like kings and watch movies.

One night June asked me if I felt up to doing some paranormal investigation, and I was very excited by it. Nothing eventful had happened the past few days, so why not?

The first night we had tape recorders on the stairs and cameras on the table by us with some heat sensors that June had purchased a while back. Harold was a bit pessimistic but found it fun to play along.

We got it all set up and then started asking questions that would pop into our heads and wait. We could not hear anything other than some strange sounds upstairs in the kitchen area that didn't resemble anything household. We took intermittent pictures, and I involved the little digital camera that I had brought along for the trip. We asked questions and took pictures for about an hour, then turned off all the equipment.

June started replaying the recorder, and I started looking at pictures on my camera. Right away, I saw them! The room was lit up with orbs. Large, small, and even colored. I got excited, to say the least. It wasn't just June's camera, it was mine as well, and I can honestly say I had never had orbs show up on any photos and, it wasn't just orbs! In a couple of pictures, there were strange grayish shapes that appeared to be like an apparition near the staircase.

When June played the recording, we heard whispering sounds almost as if someone was talking through a bubble. That is the only way I can describe it. However, there is no doubt in my mind they were the voices we had recorded. We heard the whispering voices several times in answer to some of the questions we had asked. We had not prepared questions. We just said whatever popped into our heads.

We kept trying to reassure them that we were in no way there to harm them but only wanted to communicate with them. The orbs were enough to excite Harold and me along with the whispering and muffled voices, so when June asked us if we wanted to do it again the next night, mine was an immediate yes.

The next day June and I discussed what we could do to make the sessions more productive. We decided to compile a list of questions that we felt were important to us, and maybe to whoever was coming through.

We had our list of questions ready and started to begin. Harold was tired, so he went into the guest room. Understand that while we are asking the questions, the record is on the upper staircase, where most of the activity seems to be the most notable, so we don't hear answers until the playback of the recorder.

It would take too long to write out and discuss all the questions, so I am going to go through the specific questions that we found had a relevant response. June and I would take turns asking questions from our list. The room was dark other than a small-lit candle in the middle of our table, the heater was off, and no appliances were on during this other than the recorder and the use of the heat sensors and electrical sensor.

We began by reassuring them that we wanted to communicate with whoever felt comfortable communicating with us. We also repeated specific questions we thought relevant.

After we listened back to the recordings, this is what we heard.

1. Will you communicate with us? (Second time asked). A man's

voice whispering sounds were audible.

2. Are you passing through? Whistling then whispering by several different muffled voices.

3. Are you amongst strangers? Whispering and then a clear young voice replied, "Yes," and we could hear bumping noises coming from the upstairs. (Mind you, Harold, June, and I are all downstairs). Hearing the yes reply startled me but did not scare me, it just reaffirmed we were getting somewhere.

4. The man who walks the secret garden, are you with us now? Whispering of several different voices as if a conversation was going on. A whisper "Adam," a different voice was whispering "Adam" and then clear as a bell, a woman's voice says, "ADAM!" I have to say, this raised my excitement level immensely as well as the hairs on my arms, and I have no doubt of what I heard on that recording!

5. Please don't fear the flashes from our cameras—garbled voices in the conversation.

6. If you are willing to communicate with us, we are willing to listen. Whispering and then, "oh, ok."

7. Do you like this house? (Slight pause) then, garbled sounding voices like several people having a conversation amongst themselves.

These are what I recall as the most significant questions and answers. I have to say, I was amazed and excited by what I was hearing, and I know it was further validation for June of what she had already been witnessing the past few years. Several times, while listening to the playback of the recordings, I would hear what sounded to me like a male voice, strong but muffled, and what I thought was the word "fuck." I did comment to June that someone had a potty mouth, but on reflection, even though I associate that word with anger, I do know people who use that word descriptively in everyday conversation. I have to assume that even when we leave this life, as we know it, our verbal skills do not necessarily improve.

Harold listened to the recordings the next morning. His reaction was much like mine. My only regret was we were leaving, and I would not have a chance to do this again for some time.

I have watched a few paranormal ghost series on TV off and on, and I have never seen or heard the validation that we got right there in June's home. I actually became bored with the shows and gave up watching them. But, now, I have no doubt there are other spirits or beings trying to communicate to us from a different world, and it seems to me the challenge is like trying to talk through a wall of jelly (best I can explain it). Why, on some questions, the answers were so clear, I can only surmise that their energy is stronger and able to come through where other's energy may not be as strong.

Sandy and Harold Horsley

CHAPTER 35
ABOUT C-PTSD

COMPLEX POST-TRAUMATIC STRESS DISORDER

Complex post-traumatic stress disorder (C-PTSD), also known as multiple interrelated post-traumatic stress disorder, is a psychological injury that results from protracted exposure to prolonged social and/or interpersonal trauma in the context of either captivity or entrapment, a situation lacking a viable escape route for the victim.

The symptoms of PTSD apply well to people who have experienced a discrete or short-lived traumatic event, such as a motor vehicle accident, natural disaster, or rape. However, the symptoms of PTSD do not always completely map onto the experiences of people who have experienced chronic, repeated, or long-lasting traumatic events, such as childhood sexual and/or physical abuse, repeated violence, or captivity (such as being in a prisoner of war camp).

The traumatic events connected to Complex PTSD are long-lasting and generally involve some form of physical or emotional captivity, such as childhood sexual and/or physical abuse. In these types of events, a victim is under the control of another person, usually in captivity, and does not have the ability to escape.

Ford, J.D. (1999). Disorders of extreme stress following a war-zone military trauma: Associated features of posttraumatic stress disorder or comorbid but distinct syndromes? Journal of Consulting and Clinical Psychology, 67, 3-12.

Herman, J. (1997). Trauma and Recovery: The Aftermath of Violence from Domestic Abuse to Political Terror. Basic Books.

Roth, S., Newman, E., Pelcovitz, D., van der Kolk, B., & Mandel, F.S. (1997). Complex PTSD in victims exposed to sexual and physical abuse: Results from the DSM-IV field trial for posttraumatic stress disorder. Journal of Traumatic Stress, 10, 539-555.

Whealin, J.M. & Slone, L. Complex PTSD. URL: http://www.ncptsd.va.gov/ncmain/ncdocs/fact_shts/fs_complex_ptsd.html. Accessed on 7/22/2009

CHAPTER 36
C-PTSD & THE PARANORMAL

CPTSD & PARANORMAL BELIEFS

Cognitive and Psychological Mediators of Anxiety: Evidence from a Study of Paranormal Belief and Perceived -Childhood Control- koestlerunit.files.wordpress.com And the development of anxiety, Chorpita, and Barlow (1998)

A relatively large body of research has examined the functions and origins of such beliefs. One line of work has examined the notion that people tend to hold paranormal beliefs because they possess psychological attributes that make them more likely to misattribute paranormal causation to normal experiences. People who perceive themselves as having little control over their lives may come to develop paranormal beliefs, in part, because such beliefs help provide an enhanced sense of control some individuals who experience anxiety through childhood trauma and childhood experiences of diminished control may develop fantasy proneness and paranormal beliefs as a form of coping. However, the large number of seemingly well-adjusted individuals holding paranormal beliefs suggests that for many people, the etiology of their beliefs remains, yet, a mystery.

The second line of investigation, conducted independently of the first, have shown that reports of an abusive and traumatic childhood are positively correlated to the paranormal.

CHILDHOOD ABUSE

DSM-IV diagnostic criteria for Post Traumatic Stress Disorder (PTSD)

Childhood sexual abuse is considered one of the worst forms of trauma, and its effects, long term signs and symptoms are now found to span a large range of conditions documented in the psychiatric reference manual known as the Diagnostic and Statistical Manual of Psychiatric Disorders, (DSM-IV). Sexual abuse is considered "soul murder" as it literally robs the child victim of their innocence, severely disrupts their developing ego structure and sense of Self, and will later distort the then adult's ability to function and to form healthy relationships with themselves and others.

Given a child is entirely dependent on adults for their safety, guidance, and appropriate gestures of love and nurturance, it is easy to see how this vulnerable group can be targeted and abused.

Childhood sexual abuse appears to cut across all of society's demographics and socio-economic and religious groups, as well as geographic indicators. Still, some vocations such as clergy, doctors, teachers, daycare workers, volunteer, youth group orders are over-represented as areas from which abusive environments and scenarios are acted out.

An adult survivor of child sexual abuse cannot be categorized in any way; such is the complex dynamics and deep trauma at work in this situation. Generally speaking, adults will normally have one of two postures towards life after such abuse, they will either collapse, or they will attempt to rise above the abuse. The collapsed outcome is an adult who often has easily recognizable symptoms and problems that stop them from being functional in one or more areas of their life, often with depressive, or addictive, or victim status personas, or require ongoing medical assistance to cope with life.

The second outcome where one "rises above the abuse and its shame" are nominally those who dissociate from the abuse trauma, soldier on and maintain for some time an intact functional life in work and social settings, but who often withdraw or have impairment issues in relationships.

David Kinchin, Author, Post Traumatic Stress Disorder EXCERPTS from the research paper

CHAPTER 37
TRAUMA & THE PARANORMAL

THE RELATIONSHIP BETWEEN TRAUMA AND PARANORMAL EXPERIENCES

Traumatic experiences have frequently been connected with reports of the development of psychic ability or having a subsequent paranormal experience (Kelley, 2010).

These experiences could be a visit from a loved one who has passed; to visions of an 'angel' during a traumatic experience, a visit from a spirit guide during a time of struggle, or even a demon (Reiner, 2004).

It is vital for the therapeutic community to be prepared to assist individuals who have had these experiences and have nowhere else to turn; and to visit the notion that the experience of trauma could be related to a paranormal experience (Wright, 2006).

It can be assumed that many people before having a paranormal experience may have never expected anything such as that would occur in their life, expressing doubt until one claims to have a paranormal experience. Some people don't find comfort in the thought that a dimension could exist near them yet remain unseen and potentially impact their lives.

Several types of paranormal experiences have been reported throughout recorded history. Traumatic experiences have frequently been connected with reports of the development of psychic ability or having a subsequent paranormal experience (Kelley, 2010).

The fields of quantum physics and particle physics bring a curiosity that has led to the discovery of the law of superposition. A particle can appear in two places simultaneously without the physicist to witness the movement (Zukav, 1980). Science has yet to explain how the particle has moved, yet they know it is the same particle relocating.

The Degree of Masters of Arts in Adlerian Counseling and Psychotherapy

G M. LeMoine September 2013

CHAPTER 38
ABOUT THE AUTHOR

Born into an abusive and violent home, June was moved from parent to parent until the age of 12. A runaway for years, she experienced horrific violence and abuse, followed by a lifetime of dysfunction and sadness until she entered an Alcohol and Drug treatment center. The treatment center changed her life.
She remained clean and sober while still struggling with memories from her past.

Life and career changes led June and her husband to pack up their life in California and move into their dream house in an idyllic small town in Eastern Washington. Alone in their new home, while he traveled for work, peculiar events unfolded, and her life was changed forever. A lifelong skeptic, June would never have imagined she'd become a paranormal researcher and author. What happened in the house forever changed her views on spirituality, the paranormal, and what it means to heal.

She wanted to share her unique story with the desire that it would help others on their journey toward recovery and renewal.

Today she remains a private person, markedly restricted physically from injuries but no longer chained to her past. June and her husband Jim still live in the house, where she is hard at work on her next book, a sequel to THE RELIVING. She continues her paranormal research and working on another book to share her techniques on Electronic Voice Phenomena. She loves entertaining guests in her home, taking pictures, creating jewelry with her daughter, crafting, decorating her house, and target shooting with her husband.

She is a proponent of The 12 Steps of Alcoholics Anonymous.

I visit her at the house frequently as it is hard for her to get out due to physical limitations; many times, I am able to help her with whatever current home improvements she is working on. (installing wood floors, tile ....)

I am also present for one of June's favorite things, the yearly Halloween Party.

Written by,
Carolyn Martell

CONNECT WITH THE AUTHOR

AUTHOR WEBSITE:
www.AuthorJuneMatthews.com

THE RELIVING WEBSITE:
www.TheReliving.com

ALL FACEBOOK:
Author JUNE MATTHEWS
facebook.com/AuthorJuneMatthews

THE RELIVING
Facebook.com/TheReliving

FACEBOOK GROUP:
Friends Who Like THE RELIVING

FACEBOOK GROUP:
Inside THE RELIVING HOUSE

INSTAGRAM:
Author June Matthews

YOUTUBE
THE RELIVING

TWITTER:
Author June Matthews

LINKED IN:
Author June Matthews

PINTEREST:
Author June Matthews

TUMBLR:
The RELIVING

TIKTOK:
THE PARANORMAL IS REAL

MORE BOOKS

THE PARANORMAL IS REAL,
An Interactive Book Series

Each book in the series can be found on the AMAZON Just scan the QR Code to open the series.

THE PARANORMAL IS REAL QR CODE

THE RELIVING 1st Edition 2016
PTSD and The Paranormal-

Why are things moving, lights flashing, doors opening and closing? Some therapists believe people who suffer from C.P.T.S.D. are prone to paranormal experiences. While others say, the opposite is true. The "Paranormal World" is attracted to people who live with the disorder. Drawn to people who are themselves haunted, literally invited in by.... THE RELIVING

This 1st Edition is still available for purchase until May 2022

THEIR RULES

www.TheirRules.com

Effective Methods for Documenting the Paranormal, if you follow Their RULES.

In our home, we discovered that to capture paranormal activity; there were specific guidelines that needed to be followed; we call those guidelines THEIR RULES.
This book will change the way you view The Paranormal
written by June Matthews & Laurel Cooper

SCAN THE QR CODE TO open THE PARANORMAL IS REAL SERIES on AMAZON

THE PARANORMAL IS REAL QR CODE

THEIR MEETING PLACE A True Story written by June Matthews; www.TheirMeetingPlace.com

The Sequel to THE RELIVING COMING October 2022

Over the years, we have recorded many people in our home, men, women, and children- lots of children! These experiences with so many children inspired me to write the sequel to

After years of paranormal research, these homeowners now understand more about the unexplained activity they have lived with for ten years. With hundreds of recorded cries for help, children's voices, intelligent responses, and recorded videos, they discovered their home plays an essential role in the spiritual world. They are not just living in a haunted house. This family lives inside THEIR MEETING PLACE

DREAM HOUSE

The RELIVING JOURNALS, written by June Matthews

There is more than just haunted activity inside this house; there are also THE DREAMS!

Currently DREAM HOUSE is on KINDLE VELLA and can be accessed from The PARANORMAL IS REAL QR Code.

Read the chapters for free for a limited time.

By The 7th Chapter the book will be removed from KINDLE VELLA and added as a hardcover or paperback book in the book series.

.

THE PARANORMAL IS REAL QR CODE

CHAPTER 40
GLOSSARY

ADDLEPATED: adj. Confused or befuddled

ANOMALOUS: or Anomalous Activity-Deviating from what is standard, normal, or expected or inconsistent with the common order

AUDITORY PAREIDOLIA: this is a situation created when the brain incorrectly interprets random patterns as being familiar patterns in the case of EVP. It could result in an observer interpreting random noise on an audio recording as the familiar sound of a human voice.

BODILESS: Lacking a body

COMPLEX POST TRAUMATIC STRESS DISORDER-(C-PTSD): also known as developmental trauma disorder (DTD or complex trauma, is a proposed diagnostic term for a set of symptoms resulting from prolonged stress of a social and/or interpersonal nature, especially in the context of interpersonal dependence. Subjects displaying traits associated with C-PTSD include victims of chronic maltreatment by caregivers and hostages, prisoners of war, concentration camp survivors, and survivors of some religious cults. Situations causing traumatic stress that can lead to C-PTSD-like symptoms include captivity or entrapment (a situation lacking a viable escape route for the victim.)

COUNTERMANDED: To cancel or reverse

DENIALISM: an essentially irrational action that withholds the validation of a historical experience or event when a person refuses to accept an empirically verifiable reality.

DR. CARL JUNG: A well-respected pioneer of psychotherapeutic theory and practice, spent a great deal of his life and career researching the effects of the paranormal on humanity and defining it as phenomena that have no rational explanation. It also appears his maternal family lineage is chock full of personal paranormal experiences. Jung began to experience his unexplainable occurrences at the age of seven. It is to these experiences that Jung contributes his decision to enter the field of psychiatry (Main,

1997). Jung had a strong desire to investigate, understand, and rule out frauds and 'snake oil salesmen, as well as a rule in those who were honest and open authentic. To this end, Jung attended multiple séances for several decades, investigating multiple mediums throughout that time (Main, 1997). Jung, having worked closely with Freud and Adler for some time, shared his theories of the paranormal with Freud

(Ansbacher & Ansbacher, 1956 & Main, 1997).
The Degree of Masters of Arts in
Adlerian Counseling and Psychotherapy
Gypsi M. LeMoine

ELECTRONIC VOICE PHENOMENA (E.V.P's):

Sounds found on electronic recordings are interpreted as spirit voices that have been either unintentionally recorded or intentionally requested and recorded. Parapsychologist Konstantīns Raudive, who popularized the idea in the 1970s, described EVP as typically brief, usually the length of a word or short phrase. Wikipedia

ENMESHED: Involve (someone) in a difficult situation from which it is hard to escape. A word that frequently comes up in family therapy is enmeshment- it's a therapeutic term that is sometimes misused and often misunderstood.

EXPLICATING: an explication can not be accurate or false, just more or less suitable for its purpose. A rationalization, a defense mechanism in which an attempt to justify controversial behaviors or feelings and explain seemingly rationally or logically without an actual explanation, is made consciously tolerable.

FIGHT OR FLIGHT SYNDROME: Defense physiology is a term used to refer to the symphony of body function (physiology) changes that occur in response to stress or threat. When the body executes the "fight-or-flight" reaction or stress response, the nervous system initiates, coordinates, and directs specific changes in how the body is functioning (physiology), preparing the body to deal with the threat

HAUNTING PHENOMENA: Reports of haunting phenomena are often characterized by two types of ostensibly anomalous phenomena that may repeatedly occur over long periods of time in a given location. There are subjective phenomena that tend to be experienced by our senses, such as seeing apparitions or ghosts, sensing an unseen presence (sometimes accompanied by feelings of apprehension or fear), and hearing various kinds of sounds that may either be suggestive of physical disruptions (e.g., crashes and banging noises) or be representative of a presence (e.g., voices, footsteps, doors opening and shutting). Then some phenomena may have some degree of physical objectivity, such as floating lights ("orbs"), temperature variations ("cold spots," which can be measured with a thermometer), electrical disturbances, and the occasional instance of apparent object movement.

HYPNAGOGIC: Or hypnopompic hallucinations are visual, tactile, auditory, or other sensory events, usually brief but occasionally prolonged, that occur during the transition from wakefulness to sleep (hypnagogic) or from sleep to wakefulness (hypnopompic).

PARANORMAL: Out the realm of normal occurrences or relating to the claimed occurrence of an event or perception without scientific explanation, as miracles, psychokinesis, extrasensory perception, or other purportedly supernatural phenomena such as angels, demons....

PAREIDOLIA: "The Pareidolia Effect"

Perception of a pattern or meaning where it does not exist, as in considering the moon to have human features.

"Auditory Pareidolia" is a situation created when the brain incorrectly interprets random patterns as being familiar patterns in the case of EVP. It could result in an observer interpreting random noise on an audio recording as the familiar sound of a human voice.

POST-TRAUMATIC STRESS DISORDER- (PTSD)

Once called shell shock or battle fatigue syndrome, it is a serious condition that can develop after a person has experienced or witnessed a traumatic or terrifying event in which serious physical harm occurred or was threatened. PTSD is a lasting consequence of traumatic ordeals that cause intense fear, helplessness, or horrors, such as a sexual or physical assault, the unexpected death of a loved one, an accident, war, or natural disaster. Families of victims can also develop PTSD, as can emergency personnel and rescue workers. WebMD

PREDILECTION: A preference or particular liking for something; a bias in favor of something.

PRETERNATURAL: Beyond what is normal or natural. Out the realm of normal occurrences-Paranormal

PSYCHOTHERAPY: Types of psychotherapy; Psychotherapy is offered in different formats, including individual, couple, family, or group therapy sessions, and it can be effective for all age groups.

RATIONALIZATION: Made consciously tolerable.

RE-LIVING-"A RELIVING": The recurrence of a prior experience. To undergo or experience again. A psychological phenomenon in which a person repeats a traumatic event or its circumstances over and over again. Some people with PTSD relive the memories of their traumatic experiences in great detail during waking hours; the accepted term for this waking intrusion of memory is a "flashback." Other people relive their traumatic experiences in the form of nightmares. This "re-living" can also take the form of dreams in which memories and feelings of what happened are repeated

REPUDIATION: The rejection of a proposal or idea. Denial of the truth or validity of something.

STOCKHOLM SYNDROME: feelings of trust or affection felt in many cases of kidnapping or hostage-taking by a victim toward a captor.

SOUND REFRACTION: Refraction of sound waves is most evident in situations in which the sound wave passes through a medium with gradually varying properties. For example, sound waves are known to refract when traveling over water

SYMPATHETIC NERVOUS SYSTEM: While the sympathetic system is also important at rest, it is essential for preparing us for emergencies, in other words, for "fight-or-flight" responses. If you have ever been scared or anxious, attacked or threatened, you have basically experienced activation of your sympathetic system. To prepare yourself for an emergency is a "fight-or-flight" response, the sympathetic system activates numerous complex pathways and components to achieve faster breathing, increased heart rate, and blood pressure, dilation of pupils, changes in blood flow, so blood leaves the skin, stomach, and intestines and goes to the brain, heart, and muscles where it's needed, increased sweating and "goose-bumps" as the hair on your skin stand on end; all those things you feel during a fight-or-flight response.

TIMOROUSLY: Showing or suffering from nervousness, fear, or a lack of confidence.

TINKLING: Make or cause to make a light, clear ringing sound

PHYSIOLOGICAL: relating to the branch of biology that deals with the normal functions of living organisms and their parts.

PSYCHOKINETIC: Psychokinesis can be defined as the ability of using mind over matter without any physical intervention

www.ingramcontent.com/pod-product-compliance
Lightning Source LLC
Chambersburg PA
CBHW071958150426
43194CB00008B/921